# Gender and Sexuality in Online Game Cultures

## Routledge Advances in Feminist Studies and Intersectionality



Routledge Advances in Feminist Studies and Intersectionality is committed to the development of new feminist and profeminist perspectives on changing gender relations, with special attention to:

- Intersections between gender and power differentials based on age, class, dis/abilities, ethnicity, nationality, racialisation, sexuality, violence, and other social divisions.
- Intersections of societal dimensions and processes of continuity and change: culture, economy, generativity, polity, sexuality, science and technology;
- Embodiment: Intersections of discourse and materiality, and of sex and gender.
- Transdisciplinarity: intersections of humanities, social sciences, medical, technical and natural sciences.
- Intersections of different branches of feminist theorizing, including: historical materialist feminisms, postcolonial and anti-racist feminisms, radical feminisms, sexual difference feminisms, queerfeminisms, cyberfeminisms, posthuman feminisms, critical studies on men and masculinities.
- A critical analysis of the travelling of ideas, theories and concepts.
- A politics of location, reflexivity and transnational contextualizing that reflects the basis of the Series framed within European diversity and transnational power relations.

1 **Feminist Studies**
A Guide to Intersectional Theory, Methodology and Writing
*Nina Lykke*

2 **Women, Civil Society and the Geopolitics of Democratization**
*Denise M. Horn*

3 **Sexuality, Gender and Power**
Intersectional and Transnational Perspectives
*Edited by Anna G. Jónasdóttir, Valerie Bryson and Kathleen B. Jones*

4 **The Limits of Gendered Citizenship**
Contexts and Complexities
*Edited by Elżbieta H. Oleksy, Jeff Hearn and Dorota Golańska*

5 **Theories and Methodologies in Postgraduate Feminist Research**
Researching Differently
*Edited by Rosemarie Buikema, Gabriele Griffin and Nina Lykke*

6 **Making Gender, Making War**
Violence, Military and Peacekeeping Practices
*Edited by Annica Kronsell and Erika Svedberg*

7 **Emergent Writing Methodologies in Feminist Studies**
*Edited by Mona Livholts*

8 **Gender and Sexuality in Online Game Cultures**
Passionate Play
*Jenny Sundén and Malin Sveningsson*

# Gender and Sexuality in Online Game Cultures

## Passionate Play

**Jenny Sundén and Malin Sveningsson**

Routledge
Taylor & Francis Group
NEW YORK LONDON

First published 2012
by Routledge
711 Third Avenue, New York, NY 10017

Simultaneously published in the UK
by Routledge
2 Park Square, Milton Park, Abingdon, Oxon OX14 4RN

*Routledge is an imprint of the Taylor & Francis Group, an informa business*



Typeset in Sabon by IBT Global.

First issued in paperback 2013



*Library of Congress Cataloging-in-Publication Data*

Sundén, Jenny, 1973–
Gender and sexuality in online game cultures : passionate play / Jenny Sundén, Malin Sveningsson.
p. cm. — (Routledge advances in feminist studies and intersectionality ; 8)
Includes bibliographical references and index.
1. Internet games—Social aspects. 2. Internet and women.
I. Sveningsson, Malin. II. Title.
GV1469.15.S86 2011
793.93'2—dc23
2011027170

ISBN: 978-0-415-71970-4 (pbk)
ISBN: 978-0-415-89766-2 (hbk)
ISBN: 978-0-203-14314-8 (ebk)

**To all the IMBA players of *Mercenaries* and *The Others***

# Contents

# Preface

It was early 2005, and we were sitting at a sports bar in Karlstad, Sweden (the glamour of academic life). The conversation followed a winding path, and came to circle around the topic of computer games. Having done research in online worlds and communities for about a decade, the world of gaming had never been far off. However, even if we had known each other for many years, it was not until that night that we realized we both had an interest in games, and above all, that we enjoyed playing them (action, adventure, strategy, role-playing games (RPG) . . . ). Two closeted female gamers, so to speak, which is not an unusual position to inhabit for women with an appetite for games. This disclosure, then, did not only lead to our 'coming out' as gamers, but also came to form the point of departure for a research project on affective encounters between female players and online games. This book is one of the results.

Writing a book is always an effort that draws on many diverse contributions and inspirations, and there are many people to whom we are indebted. First and foremost, we would like to thank the many fabulous players who populate the pages of this book—our interviewees, informants and co-players within and beyond the guilds of *The Others*, *Mercenaries*, and *Eternal Sun*. Without your openness, curiosity, and generosity, this book would never have been written.

Our work has also greatly benefited from participation in partly overlapping networks of colleagues and friends, most importantly within the contexts of Association of Internet Researchers (AoIR) and Digital Games Research Association (DiGRA). We have multiple points of entry, connections, and relations within these circles, and we would like to mention, in particular, Nancy Baym, Ann Beaulieu, Annika Olofsdotter Bergström, Janne Bromseth, Elizabeth Buchanan, Mia Consalvo, Hilde Corneliussen, Mirjam Palosaari Eladhari, Jessica Enevold, Charles Ess, Mary Flanagan, Radhika Gajjala, Charlotte Hagström, Ken Hillis, Sal Humphreys, Ylva Hård af Segerstad, Kylie Jarrett, Lori Kendall, Helen Kennedy, Lisbeth Klastrup, Nalini Kotamraju, Ben Light, Jonas Linderoth, Mia Lövheim, Nora Madison, Annette Markham, Torill Elvira Mortensen, Lisa Nakamura, Kate O'Riordan, Susanna Paasonen, Celia Pearce, Åsa Rosenberg,

Terri Senft, Nick Taylor, T.L. Taylor, Ragnhild Tronstad, Jill Walker Rettberg, and Michele White.

Moreover, there are a number of other brilliant people without whom this text would have been far less consistent and intriguing. Among these, we want to express our gratitude to Bodil Axelsson, Stina Bengtsson, Tom Boellstorff, Göran Bolin, Katarina Bonnevier, Eve Bowen, Ulrika Dahl, Leif Dahlberg, Elza Dunkels, Mary Ebeling, Michael Joyce, Rosemary Joyce, Marianne Liljeström, Cecilia Duijts Lindahl, Ellen Mortensen, Elisabet M. Nilsson, Ulrika Nilsson, Annakarin Nyberg, Tim Portlock, Ingrid Ryberg, Eva Svedmark, Anne Scott Sørensen, Jami Weinstein, Ann Werner, Liz Wood, and Eva Åhrén.

We are also most grateful to Nina Lykke and Jeff Hearn for their generous offer to include this book in their series Routledge Advances in Feminist Studies and Intersectionality. It has been a true pleasure working with Max Novick and his colleagues at Routledge, New York. An important part of this collaboration was our textual encounters with three anonymous reviewers, whose sensible readings and insightful suggestions have been indispensable for the writing process.

Last, but not least, we acknowledge our lasting gratitude to the Swedish Research Council (Vetenskapsrådet), which has made this book possible by providing funding for the research project "Gender Play: Intersectionality in Computer Game Culture".

Jenny Sundén and Malin Sveningsson
Stockholm and Gothenburg in June, 2011

# Introduction
## Into the Game

*Jenny Sundén and Malin Sveningsson*

It was one of those light Swedish spring evenings, and we were sitting at Malin's large kitchen table. The door to the garden was half-open, suggestive of the comings and goings in the world out there. Living in different cities, one in Stockholm, the other in Gothenburg, our research collaboration was usually mediated by phone calls and emails. But once in a while we traveled from one coast to the other to write together and discuss each other's texts. This was one of those encounters, which took place at a fairly early stage of our research project on online game cultures.

During the day, we had compared notes and experiences from our initial ethnographic studies in the online game *World of Warcraft*. Well after Malin's two children had been put to bed, we filled up our wine glasses with Zinfandel and placed our computers right next to each other. We belonged to opposing factions in the game, as well as to different servers, so co-play was not an option. Nevertheless, we showed each other our researcher characters and provided guided tours in parallel worlds to places difficult to visit if you belong to the 'enemy'. Next, we created a new character for Malin that she needed for an upcoming LAN-party with guild mates. They had decided to all create dwarf characters with whisky names for this gathering, level them up to nineteen and do battlegrounds together. No later said than done, Blackvelvet took her first stubby steps through the snow, two lousy blades at her sides. Jenny was the rogue coach, since her main character at the time belonged to this class of sneaky, soft-footed, up close and quite brutal assassins. We had a hard time to stop laughing at the first clumsy attempts of the dwarf girl as she had a go at the wolves of Coldridge Valley, not to mention the amorous and quite persistent male character who tried to make a pass at her. Black Velvet did not make it far into the game, but some of our other characters certainly did, in particular those we used explicitly for our research. It has been a long and winding journey in an intriguing borderland between work and play. This book is one of the results.

*Gender and Sexuality in Online Game Cultures: Passionate Play* consists of what we have chosen to call a 'twin ethnography' that develops two parallel stories. Both ethnographies use participant observation in the online game *World of Warcraft*, combined with qualitative interviews with female players, to explore intersections of gender and sexuality in online game cultures. We have followed two trajectories to gain insights into the different conditions of play for female players. Sveningsson studies 'straight' game culture, and makes explicit that which is the norm by exploring the experiences of female gamers in a heavily male-dominated gaming context. Sundén investigates 'queer' game culture through queer potentials of mainstream *World of Warcraft* culture, as well as through the case of a guild explicitly defined as LGBT (lesbian, gay, bisexual, transgender/transsexual). In our ethnographies, the focus on female players does not exclude discussions of male players, as they are part of the gaming communities, nor does gender in this context simply equal femininity. We work along a range of femininities and masculinities, mixing them up along the way through readings of, for example, 'female masculinity' (Halberstam 1998), male femininity, and queer femininity, or 'femme' (Dahl 2008). The concepts of gender and sexuality are understood less in terms of identity or position, and more as forms of actions and desires that shape and orient players in the game (cf. Ahmed 2006). From this follows that our distinction between 'straight' and 'queer' cultures in *World of Warcraft* is not that clear-cut. Even if this distinction does important rhetorical work in pointing at differences in player cultures and expectations, it has less to do with self-identification, and more with ways of moving, sensing, and making sense of particular norms and contexts of play. Put differently, straight versus queer is not taken to neatly organize the discussion along the lines of normative versus anti-normative, obedient play versus disobedient play, etc. To think queer as disorderly and transgressive *per se* provides little insight into how queer communities of play are, indeed, normative too. Conversely, to conflate heterosexuality with heteronormativity does not take into account the differences between various orientations and desires within heterosexuality, nor does it speak to how the seemingly 'straight' and obedient may trouble the game as norm too.

This book is one about female players and their passionate encounters with game technologies. It takes seriously women's passions in games, and as such it draws attention to questions of pleasure in and desire for technology. None of the women appearing in the ethnographic stories that span the pages of this book take their interest in games lightly, and an emphasis on their passion in play may work as a way of expanding the space in which femininities (and masculinities) are done and perhaps may become un-done in games. The book ties together female players, passion, and game technologies in ways that forcefully confront the idea of women as somehow lacking, not only in tech skills, but also in passion for technologies.

If passion about machines is closely associated with men, and more importantly to masculinity, then to claim close links between femininity, passion and games works by necessity to *queer* femininity. It is a queering of femininity in the sense of bending it and making it more elastic, in order to accommodate alternative types of relations, feelings, and meanings, of 'inappropriate' relations between women and technologies as it were (cf. Kennedy 2006). This may be a queering in literal terms, as in the case of those queer women populating parts of this book—the tomboys, the machine vamp femmes, the tech-butches and others. But it should also be understood in terms of a more general pushing up against the limits of the hetero-normative and the 'normal', to make room for a multiplicity of connections between femininity, masculinity, sexuality, and technology.

## GAMES, FEMINISM, AND INTERSECTIONALITY

The research area of 'gender and games' (which more often than not translates as 'women and games') appears to be expanding steadily, and yet critical feminist game studies scholars are still relatively few and far between. Important work has been done by, for example, Diane Carr (2002; 2005) and Helen Kennedy (2002; 2006) on preferences and pleasure, Jennifer Jenson and Suzanne de Castell (2005; 2008), Jenson, de Castell and Fisher (2007) and Jenson, Fischer and de Castell (2011) on gender and learning, Mary Flanagan (2005; 2009) on critical play and alternative game design, Lisa Nakamura (2008; 2009) on race and ethnicity, Diane Carr (2010) on disability, Nick Taylor (2011) and Taylor, Jenson and de Castell (2009) on gender and gaming cultures, and T.L. Taylor on gender and embodiment in online games (2003a; 2003b; 2006b). As concerns critical accounts of sexuality, work has been done in virtual worlds such as *Second Life* (see, for example, Brookey and Cannon 2009). However, when it comes to sexuality and computer games, such studies are still something in the making. For work in this direction, see for example Mia Consalvo's investigations of sexuality in games in general (2003a) and of queer potentials in the Sims in particular (2003b), Zek Valkyrie's (2011) work on sexuality in MMORPGs,[1] Ben Light's (2009) research on representations and experiences of LGBT gamers, and Adrienne Shaw's (2009) exploration of LGBT representation in games from a production perspective.[2] One challenge that the continuous investigation of sexuality in games faces is a critical discussion of *hetero*sexuality in games, of that which is of the norm in game communities in terms of gender and sexuality. Sexuality in games tends to be a taken-for-granted category in ways that neither acknowledges that the sexuality in question is most often of the straight variety, nor that it depends on a heterosexual framework to operate.

Previous research on women and games points in several directions. For the most part, researchers have painted a fairly gloomy picture of the ways in which women are positioned by the game industry, and the kind of spaces they may create for themselves. It has been made evident that women's participation in game cultures is relatively low (Bryce and Rutter 2002; 2003a;

2003b; 2007). Then again, when looking at statistics, it appears to be the case that the gap between men and women who play computer games is not considerable. For example, according to the ESA (2010), in 2010, 40% of the US game players were female. Even though these figures give the impression that women make up a substantial part of the gaming community, it is important to consider what kinds of games are included. For example, the computer games most often played by women are solitaire or casual games (Kafai et al. 2008; Nielsen 2008), which are often not seen as 'real' computer games either by the industry or in the field of game studies (Fron et al. 2007). When it comes to what counts as 'real' games—or games with high status among game producers and game scholars alike—these have usually belonged to supposedly 'masculine' genres and styles of play, such as action games and hardcore or competitive gaming.[3] On the other hand, the picture gets more complex if we take into account the success of Nintendo's Wii, as well as the mainstreaming of online games such as *World of Warcraft* during the last few years. *World of Warcraft*, especially, is listed as the most popular non-card computer game among male and female players alike. With these developments, it is getting increasingly difficult to ascribe certain groups of players or playing styles to certain games or game genres. Notably, the variety of possible playing styles and in-game goals that *World of Warcraft* as well as many other MMOs provide both blurs such distinctions, but also serves as a powerful way to open up new possibilities for players, and make them try new ways of playing that they might not otherwise have considered. As Yee (2008, 92) states, "MMOs have the potential to broaden game playing for both men and women".[4]

One strand in the research field of gender and games relates to women's (supposedly different) gaming preferences. Studies have, for example, found that girls generally prefer other types of game content than boys (see, for example, Greenberg et al. 2010; Hartmann and Klimmt 2006). There are those who believe that the best way to get girls to play computer games is to adapt to what market research declares that 'girls want', and thus design what is commonly referred to as 'pink games' with fairly gender stereotypical content, focusing for example on appearance and clothing. In a second phase of the girl game movement, 'purple games' emerged: games that could be seen as a counterpoint to the pink games (Kafai et al. 2008), but which still reflected "the social realities of most girls' lives" (Laurel 2008, 24). The purple games typically dealt with 'real-life' issues that are assumed to be of interest to girls and women, for example relationships (Kafai et al. 2008). Others have argued that the content of both pink and purple games will eventually cement old gender hierarchies, that the girls' present gaming preferences only reflect social expectations tied to gender roles (Jenson and de Castell 2007; Pelletier 2008), and that if the girls had had the chance to try the 'boys' games', they might actually like them too (de Castell and Bryson 1998a). To this it seems sensible to add that there are plenty of female players out there who are already enjoying these 'boys' games', and have been enjoying them all along (Jenkins 1998; Taylor 2008b). Studies have also shown that gaming preferences and playing styles may be more connected to the game culture (Yee 2008), and to the players' experience of gaming than to their gender: "what often looks like a 'women gamers' problem is very regularly a 'newbie' issue" (Taylor 2008b, 63). This claim finds support in for example Jenson, Fischer, and de Castell (2011), who found that once the girls had been given the chance to train, their playing styles were no longer different from those of the boys. In a similar way, Yee (2008) points at age as another crucial factor to consider. Players are less likely to be achievement driven as they get older. Female MMO players are generally older than male players, thus, this can be one explanation to the differences in their stated motivations and gaming preferences. Thus, as Jenson and de Castell (2011) argue, previous studies about gendered gaming preferences and styles of play may suffer from serious sources of error due to the research practices and methodologies that were used.

It has been argued that gendered differences in terms of game preferences may not be so huge after all: "the overwhelming majority of men and women like to do the same things in online games" (Yee 2008, 91). The game industry's segmentation of the market according to gender stereotypical tastes and interests has also been seen as detrimental to the development of the business altogether: "designing games based on extreme stereotypical preferences leaves out most of what boys, and girls, find fun" (Lazzaro 2008, 203). This last standpoint is also clearly present in Diane Carr's (2005) way of forcefully taking apart the argument of gendered preferences, contending that there is a logical fallacy in the question of "which games women want", since it presumes that there *are* meaningful differences in play preferences in terms of gender. She notes how women's patterns of gaming around the world are complex to the point where gender as a sole denominator is less than reliable. She emphasizes how preferences in play are not merely about what the player enjoys doing in a game, but that preferences need to be understood in terms of a range of social and cultural contexts. As T.L. Taylor (2008b) also points out, social networks is a crucial ingredient in play, for both male and female players. It is through family members, friends, or co-workers that players get access to games. Whether play is enjoyable or not, then, has everything to do with factors such as what facilitates or impedes one's access to games, how one is introduced to them, who one is playing together with, and what it feels like to play. Stressing that content is but one component together with other ones, such as local social context, marketing, and technical competency, Taylor also points to the game industry's part in the construction of games as a male space. She argues that a crucial factor for what leisure activities people take part in is whether they perceive them to be "something that you can do, that is not at odds with your sense of self or your social world" (Taylor 2008b, 55). The game industry, says Taylor, knows this and works along these lines when they provide male players with information about new games, ultimately signaling that "this is your and your friends' play space". However, if the same is ever done for female players it is generally constrained to a very small slice of 'girl games'.

Finally, in a much needed review of gender and games research over the past three decades, Jennifer Jenson and Suzanne de Castell (2010) show how gender in this field has actually been neglected. They identify a refusal to consider gender at all in the sense that gender has been conflated with sex in ways that result in relatively essentialist understanding of *women*, games, and preferences, and thus preventing alternative storylines to surface (cf. Jenson and de Castell 2008). If gender equals woman, and women are, somehow, fundamentally different from men, the discussion of 'gender' and games appears to be stuck at a dead end. A logical next step would be to un-stick this line of thought and make it more open to continuous critical interrogations.

Along with issues of gendered gaming preferences, another important strand in previous research on gender and games is how game characters are shaped. The representations of gender, race and age in games tend to be biased along the lines of masculinity, whiteness and youth (Williams, Martins et al. 2009). Moreover, the critique of femininity in games often engages with how female characters tend to be designed according to a sexist, 'hyped-up' sexuality (Dickey 2006; Dovey and Kennedy 2006, Grimes 2003; Ivory 2006; Jansz and Martis 2003; Miller and Summers 2007; Taylor 2006b). This argument often presumes that excessive female sexuality is a problem, since it turns women's bodies into objects of a (straight) male gaze. For example, it has been argued that games that objectify women increase male players' tendency to behave inappropriately to women in social situations (Yao, Mahood, and Linz 2010). The view on excessive female sexuality as problematic also presumes an understanding of play primarily based on identification, at least in those studies where hyper-sexualized female bodies in games are assumed to alienate female players, or negatively affect their self-concept (Behm-Morawitz and Mastro 2009). There have been alternative readings of how, for example, the body of Lara Croft in *Tomb Raider* is not merely a visual object, but also a powerful and pleasurable subject, a vehicle, and a piece of finely tuned machinery of game play (Carr 2002; Flanagan 1999; Kennedy 2002; Schleiner 2001). To this it would be interesting to add that there is not necessarily anything wrong with the female body as object and visual spectacle. There are other pleasures to be had than those directed by the straight male gaze, but this understanding would need a different point of view—which could be termed queer.

As this overview has shown, gender and computer games is not an under-studied subject, but there is work left to be done. As Kafai et al. (2008, xviii) note:

> The fact that girls and women now play games in increasing numbers is not an indication that the conversation about gender should end.

> Instead more information is needed on the games they play, why, and with whom they play them, and whether they take advantage of in-game opportunities to generate, not just consume, game experiences. We need more information on how girls and women are entering the gaming and why they are not. And we need to take note of the ways in which gender is both performed and constrained.

What we see as particularly urgent is to look at games from a feminist, intersectional perspective. This book seeks to expand the domain of research into gender and games by developing intersectional, queer, feminist studies of online gaming. The theoretical framework spans feminist notions of performance, performativity, and positionality as well as the recent turn to affect and phenomenology within cultural theory. In the essay "On Cyberfeminist Intersectionality", Sundén (2007) argues for the need to bring together feminist studies of media technologies with one of the more recent feminist discussions of differences, namely 'intersectionality'. Intersectionality, in brief, is concerned with the ways in which various power relations—such as gender, sexuality, ethnicity, class, age, and ability—co-construct one another in multiple ways. Surprisingly, discussions of intersectionality rarely engage with technology. And yet, feminists theorizing technology have made obvious how technologies are (all the more) entwined with our bodies, embedded in our everyday experiences to the degree that it becomes pointless to think embodiment and difference as phenomena that can be intelligible 'before' or 'beyond' technology (cf. Barad 2007; Haraway 1991; Smelik and Lykke 2008; Suchman 2007). It becomes imperative, then, to rethink intersectionality and embodiment along the lines of technology, to emphasize technology as yet another important principle of differentiation.

In this book we take on the challenge that the discussion of intersectionality poses by exploring how bodies collide and intersect with digital technologies. One useful concept here is 'technicity'. To Dovey and Kennedy (2006, 16), "technicity comes to stand for identities that are formed around and through [ . . . ] *technological differentiation*" (italics in original). Technicity is about the privileging of certain technological skills, the ability to quickly adopt and to be at ease with new technologies. At the same time, technicity is about the ways in which (other) identities and differences—such as gender, sexuality, ethnicity, and age—are increasingly mediated by technologies. In games, technicity is about the political implications of certain tech skills, as well as of how players and their abilities, practices, and relations come into being through game technologies. This book takes shape, most evidently, in the very intersection of gender, sexuality, and game technologies.

We had an initial interest in looking at intersections of gender, sexuality, and ethnicity. However, the material that we gathered throughout our studies turned out to not easily lend itself to such an investigation. While discourses on gender and sexuality were a major ingredient in both our research contexts, we rarely saw any references to ethnicity. Just as we found the implied player to be 'male' and 'straight', similar assumptions appeared to be made about 'whiteness', if yet in a more hidden manner. Stating that ethnicity did not emerge as a salient category from our material is not to say that it is irrelevant. However, it does suggest that ethnicity as a principle of differentiation is not made explicit in the coming together of the particular gaming communities that we came into contact with. It may very well be made evident in other gaming communities and/or for other observers. What you see depends on how you are looking, and from which position. We could of course have set out to investigate the silences and absences to reveal the norms and regulations of the unspoken, to read ethnicity between the lines as it were. Or we could have made something of the few occasions that we did see, such as when the one player in Malin's guild who was known to origin from a non-Scandinavian country, and a Muslim at that, was once jokingly referred to as 'the Taliban' by one of his friends. On the other hand, at least in the parts of the game world that we met, something that seemed to be of greater importance than ethnicity was nationality and locality. In a realm of play where the only common denominator is 'Europe', the nationality of players may be what ties them together. Furthermore, the local connections between players who know each other offline have important repercussions on their interactions online (as is evident when they gather at LAN parties in each other's homes, to play together). In this way, nationality and locality may conflate the differences that ethnicity makes evident. To be Swedish, for example, or to live in Gothenburg, or Stockholm, is clearly not the same as being white, even if whiteness operates as the norm of the taken-for-granted.

## A WAY INTO GAME STUDIES

The study of digital games is an emerging, shifting, and inter-disciplinary domain of research. Initially, this field was constructed primarily through a polarization between narratologists, who understand 'games as stories' (Murray 1997; Ryan 2001; 2004), and ludologists, who approach 'games as games' (Aarseth 1999; 2004; Eskelinen and Koskimaa 2001; Juul 2001). A focus on digital games as story media with certain narrative potential explores games as aesthetic objects—or, more broadly, as media texts with affinities to other media and genres—open to critical readings. The study of games as medium-specific rather aligns digital games with the history of (other) games and forms of play, with a critical eye on how rules, goals and incentives enable and structure play.[5]

The relation between readers or viewers and the story worlds of literature or cinema is different from the relation between players and games (Juul 2001). Games are played, not merely read or watched. They perform a simultaneous splitting of the subject, as well as perhaps a re-joining of her parts. In most games you perform in and through a different body, a screen-based representation which becomes your vehicle for gameplay. Gameplay consists of consecutive actions and re-actions, of endless cybernetic feedback loops in which you and the game are entwined and altered. You are not only playing the game, the game is also, most concretely, playing you. And perhaps more than literature and cinema, gameplay is an embodied activity (Lahti 2003). Story worlds, in general, may certainly give rise to shifts and changes in reading, viewing bodies. The difference with games is the ways in which the body is activated, involved in, and propelled into the unfolding of events, both physically and symbolically.

Questions of what makes games different from other media forms are still of central importance in game studies, but the initial tension between narratologists and ludologists no longer fuels much debate. The current split within game studies is rather disciplinary and methodological in nature. Aarseth (2007b) notes a tension within game studies that has to do with different ways of understanding 'the player'. On the one hand, humanist approaches to games are united through an interest in game aesthetics and player positioning, where the player is an implied player, and the emphasis is on concrete games and their content. The preferred method in this camp is 'close playing'. On the other hand, social science-oriented perspectives focus on either gamers or the activity of gaming, and thus concentrate on other, 'actual' players. The player is 'real', situated, and the emphasis is on the social and cultural dimensions of play. This approach to games and gaming as social practice tends to employ an eclectic set of ethnographic methods, including observations, interviews, self-play and social play (see also Williams and Heide Smith 2007).

The specific area of interest is yet another factor that sometimes makes researchers collide in their views of what game studies is and should be. Aarseth (2007a) lists three areas of interests: gameplay (including the players' actions, strategies, and motivations), the game structure (including rules) and the game world (including the fictive content, topology, textures, etc.). However, the surrounding context and player cultures are also vital for the understanding of games (cf. Taylor 2008b). A different, less antagonistic, and more interdisciplinary way of thinking of the formation of the field of game studies is to emphasize how issues of game aesthetics and game mechanics have become part of a growing body of research which holds a wider interest in *game cultures* and in gaming as situated everyday practices (Carr 2005; Crogan and Kennedy 2009; Dovey and Kennedy 2006; Mäyrä 2008; Pearce and Artemesia 2009; Rutter and Bryce 2006; Taylor 2006b).

One strand of research that holds a lot of potential for feminist studies of games is the growing interest in digital games as a decidedly embodied medium that aim at and involve the bodies of players in fairly intense ways. Game scholars have begun to theorize the embodied nature of play in terms of, for example, affect (Carr 2006c; Colman 2008), pleasure (Kennedy 2006; Mortensen 2004; Taylor 2003a; 2006b), and the phenomenology of play (Bogost 2008; Crick 2010). This book is yet another step in this direction.

## DOING ETHNOGRAPHY

One vital development within game studies that this book aims to push further is the growing body of ethnographic research on online games (see also Boellstorff 2006; Nardi 2010; Nardi and Harris 2006; Pearce and Artemesia 2009; Taylor 2006b). During the last decades, ethnographic method has grown in popularity and has come to be applied in diverse disciplines outside of the 'mother' discipline of anthropology. It has been used in different ways, depending on the specific demands of the discipline the researcher belongs to, and the baggage that the discipline carries in the form of ontological and epistemological assumptions. This has resulted in an increased fuzziness of the word 'ethnography', which has come to carry slightly different meanings in diverse settings. Sometimes, 'ethnography' is even treated more or less as a synonym for 'qualitative methods'. In other words, to do ethnography seems to mean different things depending on where the researcher comes from. This concerns what specific methods for data gathering and analysis that are being used, and how, but above all what perspectives guide the research. Because of the uncertainties surrounding the concept of ethnography in interdisciplinary research fields, we find it important to spell out our way of thinking and doing ethnography.

To start with, we see ethnography not as *one* method, but rather as an approach including a collection of methods. The most commonly used is of course participant observation, which has sometimes even come to be treated as synonymous with the word 'ethnography' (Emerson, Fretz, and Shaw 1995). Participant observation means that researchers study an environment and the people within it through intense involvement. However, while some researchers use participant observation merely as a way to observe and describe what is going on, our aim was always to go further. As other ethnographers have done before us, we see as the point of participant observation to *participate* in the culture and to experience it from within. By interacting with people and participating in the activities that are central for the phenomenon that we attempt to understand, we have sought to become part of the local world with its traditions and value systems. We have aimed to come close to people and attain an insider's perspective, while recognizing that the borders between insiders and outsiders in the field are always in motion (for the researcher as well as for those she studies). Through these ethnographic practices, our aim is to come to understand the situation in much the same way as those who found themselves there before our arrival (cf. Van Maanen 1995).

Participant observation has its limitations. For example, it does not say much about how people within the studied group think or feel, or how they understand or describe what they do. Therefore, participant observations are often combined with other methods, such as interviews. As Sveningsson, Lövheim, and Bergquist (2003) discuss, in its most characteristic form, ethnography means that researchers participate, openly or candidly, in people's everyday life during an extended period of time. They observe what goes on, listen to what is said, and ask a lot of questions. But they also use other material that can help them understand and get a feel for the culture in question. As a matter of fact, they gather and analyze any material that can help to shed light on the research questions: photographs, maps, diaries or other items (Hammersley and Atkinson 1995; Silvén 1999). Thus, ethnography can be seen as an umbrella term that reveals something about the researchers' perspectives, rather than what specific research methods they use.

What, then, are these perspectives that ethnography takes as its point of departure? Within ethnographic research, the issue of culture is central—the cultural perspective has even been identified as *the* aspect that distinguishes ethnography from other qualitative research traditions (Patton 1990). Culture can be defined in many ways (see for example Storey 1993), but in ethnography, and is commonly understood from a holistic point of view, as 'a whole way of life', regardless of whether the ethnographer studies a group, a subculture or an organization. The assumption that guides ethnographic research is that people who spend time together will eventually come to create ways to organize and understand the world around them. Culture then denotes the shared patterns of behaviors and values that structure the lives of the group's members. In other words, ethnographic research means to investigate people's world views, norms, thoughts and values, and the practices that are tied to them (Patton 1990).

Within participant observation, there are different modes of participation. Building on critical feminist and queer ethnography, we have worked with ethnographic methods along an ethics of participation, closeness, and involvement, acknowledging that ethnographies are based on affective investments and embodied practices. Feminist and queer ethnographies are ethnographies that commonly research the lives of women and queers, but they also hold the potential of critiquing the normative logics of ethnographic research itself, such as the idea of there being clear distinctions between here and there, self and Other, insiders and outsiders, closeness and distance (we will return to and develop this point in the closing chapter). In our specific case, to be close has meant that we have played together with the participants and become members of the groups we are studying. Our position as insiders (no matter how unstable a category) included letting ourselves get involved in the guilds we studied, contributing to them in terms of being active players, but also in terms of creating relationships to other members and making ourselves a place within the groups. We experienced and explored at depth the cultures at hand, and also allowed for player participation in our analysis. Having as a goal to study the culture from within, and to start to understand the world in the same way as the informants do, means that we (as researchers and participants) have to get close to the (other) participants. Closeness—to the field and its inhabitants—is seen as one of the most important strengths of ethnographic research, but at the same time one that has caused ethnographers trouble due to an understanding of 'science' and 'the scientific' as something in need of certain amount of distance. We, too, have struggled with questions of closeness and analytical distance, but have arrived at an understanding of closeness as not in opposition to, but as something in close conjuncture with critical, analytical thought. We have also experienced that closeness evokes questions about research ethics. These questions will be further discussed in relation to our specific case studies in Chapters 1 and 5 of this book.

If closeness is one crucial aspect of ethnography, so is reflexivity. Reflexivity is commonly understood as a researcher's self-awareness in the field, and more broadly as a problematization of the production of ethnographic texts. The 'reflexive turn' in anthropology was initially an answer to a set of disciplinary crises. One of these was recognition of the colonial heritage of anthropology, which gave rise to a call for reflective analyses of ethnographic practices as sites of colonial power (Asad 1973). Another strand of critical voices was concerned with the seemingly transparent relationship between fieldwork and field writing. This heightened attention to writing strategies served to highlight the ways in which ethnographic writing co-creates (rather than merely reflects) cultures (Clifford and Marcus 1986; Marcus and Fischer 1986). Yet another critique came from feminist scholars and was aimed at 'the ethnographer' as a seemingly neutral (yet distinctively masculine), objective observer. Part of this critique was an emphasis on situatedness—the fact that knowers are always somewhere in particular, and that acts of knowing are always partial (cf. Haraway 1991). In her seminal essay "Situated Knowledges", Donna Haraway (1991) speaks of the production of knowledge as always situated, partial, and collective. If scientific ideals turn the scientific gaze into a universal perspective from nowhere, Haraway insists on how ways of seeing are always located somewhere in particular, always embodied, and hence always incomplete. To Haraway, it is the split, paradoxical subject who can be accountable:

> The topography of subjectivity is multi-dimensional; so, therefore, is vision. The knowing self is partial in all its guises, never finished, whole, simply there and original; it is always constructed and stitched together imperfectly, and *therefore* able to join with another, to see together without claiming to be another. (p. 193, italics in original)

From this follows that to see, or to bear witness, is never a neutral act, but always a matter of being accountable for what one sees.

There is a burgeoning methodological discussion within game ethnographies of, for example, self-reflexivity and the need for closeness, and we sense that the time is ripe to bring out even more clearly a discussion of the roles we play as researchers in the field as co-players and co-producers of knowledge. We believe that there may be important, untapped potentials within more general discussions of feminist and queer ethnography that could vitalize ethnographic work on games. Researcher subjectivity and embodiment, the constructed nature of ethnographic accounts, and the fact that ethnographies are always partial, implying the choice of telling one story among many other possible stories, is at times treated as something problematic within game studies. In this book we attempt to make a different move by exploring the critical potentials of being up-close and personal. Here, personal experiences, emotion, desire, and embodied ways of knowing games are treated as something with the potential to create important knowledge (see also Campbell 2009; Kendall 2009a; Sundén 2009a, as well as Sundén, Chapter 5 in this book).

## PASSIONATE SCHOLARSHIP

As much as this book is one about women's passionate relations to computer games, it is also one about passionate scholarship, about working with and through one's passions as a researcher, and of allowing for such passions to guide and shape ways of thinking and writing scholarly texts. As such, we set out to think and write embodied ways of knowing games. The academic discussion on embodiment, more generally, has grown rapidly during the past decades. In an attempt to reclaim what was lost in the wake of academic traditions that consistently paired critical thought with reason (in relation to which the feeling body was a danger in ways that has everything to do with gender), the focus on embodiment in cultural theory and feminist theory was an attempt to put the body (back) into the picture, as well as making embodiment a fundamental part of intellectual work (see, for example, Braidotti 1994; Conboy, Medina, and Stanbury 1997; Price and Shildrick 1999; Weiss and Haber 1999). Feminist thinkers have been imperative in this discussion through their insistence on embodiment as something always materially specific and situated, in terms of, for example, gender, sexuality, ethnicity, and nationality.

The more recent interest in, or 'turn' to affect and emotion needs to be understood against the background of this longer discussion of questions of embodiment in cultural theory. At the same time, the interest in affect formulates a critique of how cultural theory has been pre-occupied with 'text', discourse and meaning in ways that leave limited space for movement, change, sensation, and that which somehow escapes language, or is difficult to put into words (see, for example, Ahmed 2004; Berlant 2004; Clough and Halley 2007; Liljeström and Paasonen 2010; Massumi 2002; Ngai 2005; Probyn 2005; Sedgwick 2003). In this book, we work with affect and with emotion conceptually to think games as an embodied medium. Notably, we also work with and through affect and emotion in methodological terms. The academic discussion of affect is usually ontological rather than epistemological and only rarely spells out the methodological consequences of making sense through sensation.[6] For what does it mean to work in an *analytical* register of embodiment and emotion? What do we, as researchers, make of our own 'gut feelings' and desires in research? In what ways may bodily remembering, relating, and belonging be used as sources of knowledge? In this book we set off from such queries to explore a range of sensorial ways of knowing online game cultures.

In sum, this book seeks to develop an affective, embodied, situated ethnographic approach to games. In particular, the book renders problematic the idea of participation in ethnographic work on online games by examining ways of coming to, and *coming out*—as a researcher—in the field. We also discuss ways of playing together over time, of simultaneously being a co-player and a researcher in ways that always need to be situated, embodied and ethically responsible.

## INTRODUCING *WORLD OF WARCRAFT*

*World of Warcraft* is a MMOG (Massively Multiplayer Online Game) created by Blizzard Entertainment.[7] The game went online in 2004, and in 2011 it had 12 million players world-wide, distributed over servers in Europe, North-America, and Asia (MMOData.net 2011) This enormous player base makes it the largest MMOG in the world, and also the most popular non-card game title as measured by number of players (Nielsen 2008). The game offers a Tolkienesque fantasy world in which players come together to solve quests, defeat monsters, and loot treasures. Players create and gradually develop player characters by completing quests and slaying monsters, in order to take on all the more complex missions. In the beginning, the character is gently guided through a protected corner of the game world, to learn the ropes and obtain some basic skills. But soon enough s/he is sent out on more dangerous roads, lined with threats more difficult to master. By performing quests, the character gains experience points to 'level up', as well as cash (in-game gold) to be able to purchase better armor and weapons from vendors and auction houses. By leveling, the character grows stronger and gets access to all the more powerful and refined skills and strategies in battle. The starting level is 1, and the highest level is, at the time of writing, set to 85. But far from being the end point, many players experience the max level as when the game begins anew in terms of endgame content, such as raids and instances,[8] which hold the most valuable rewards in the game.

To move through and interact with the game world is a physical, multisensorial experience. Action-packed battle scenes that require focus, velocity, coordination, habit, and collaboration, are mixed with routine visits to banks, auction houses, inns and weaponry workshops. Modes of transportation vary: from moving on foot to riding and flying mounts, from subway rides between main cities to inter-continental boats and zeppelins. Players move between cities and villages, over green hills, burnt soil, dramatically snow-covered mountain chains, through deserts, oases, deep woods, lakes, and underwater landscapes. Each area has its own musicality (which sometimes is doubled onto other places, but which nonetheless gives a particular atmosphere and feel to the game landscape). The individual experience of playing *World of Warcraft* depends on a range of factors, such as type of realm (Player versus Player, Player versus Environment or Role-Play) and war faction (Horde or Alliance). PvP-realms allow open combat between players; PvE-realms focus on the game world itself, on quests and monster slaying; and RP-realms have an emphasis on role-play and character development (cf. MacCallum-Stewart and Parsler 2008; Tronstad 2008; for a discussion of the implications of one's server choices, see the closing chapter of this book).

The game builds on a bi-polar gender division (male or female), but opens for a range of profiles and player positions through the choice of race, class, and profession. The races of the Alliance are human, night elf, dwarf, gnome, draenei, and worgen, and for Horde the choice is between orc, troll, undead, tauren, blood elf, and goblin. Jessica Langer (2008) shows in her postcolonial analysis of the construction of race in *World of Warcraft* how the Alliance is constructed as the familiar and the well known (from a white, Western perspective), whereas the Horde is consistently positioned as the Other—the wild, the savage, the foreign. The Alliance as the empire tends to build in solid materials such as stone and marble, while the Horde, with obvious allusions to, for example, the Caribbean (the trolls) and Africa (the orcs), uses wood and leather for their Native American-like tepees and other huts (McGregor 2006).[9] The construction of femininities and masculinities follows the same route. Male and female characters of the Alliance are almost all human-like, strikingly light-skinned and heteronormal featuring muscular men and slender yet voluptuous women—with the exception of dwarfs and gnomes who are short and chubby. Horde characters span a broader spectrum by more clearly including the non-human, such as animal components (the tauren) and a zombie race (the undead).[10] Horde intersections of gender and sexuality also open up more readily for queer readings in offering options for female masculinity (the female orc), male femininity (the male blood elf), bears (the tauren) as well as perhaps a tomboy position incarnated by the androgynous, slouching female undead. Interestingly, players seem to largely conform to Western norms of whiteness and heterosexuality in their choices of, for example, factions and races. According to Ducheneaut et al. (2006), players belonging to the Alliance outnumber Horde players 2 to 1, Humans and Night Elves are by far the most popular races (25% and 23%) and orcs the least popular (only 7%), which suggests a reluctance to take the positions of 'the Other' and the 'ugly'.

The player class determines the player's position in battle, and is as such significant for the type of experience the player wants to engage in. The classes on offer are death knight, druid, hunter, mage, paladin, priest, rouge, shaman, warlock, and warrior, distributed over the roles of tanks, damage dealers, and healers. Tanks need a sturdy build and the most solid type of armor to be able to head first draw in the monsters as well as taking a lot of damage without dying. Tanks are backed up by damage dealers, either with sharp bladed weapons up-close, or using ranged weapons or spells from a distance. Last but not least, the whole group in battle depends for their survival on the capacities of healers. Players also decide on two primary professions for their characters (the choices on offer being alchemy, blacksmithing, enchanting, engineering, herbalism, jewelcrafting, leatherworking, mining, skinning, and tailoring). These skills are gradually developed and refined in order to make money in auctions, or to outfit friends and allies with good equipment.

No matter which war faction, race and class the character belongs to, the player has relatively large freedom to decide how to play the game. This relative freedom of ways of moving through and playing the game is often held out as one of the key reasons behind the mass appeal of *World of Warcraft*. Richard Bartle (1996) delineates different motivations or player types in online games, making distinctions between what he terms achievers, explorers, socializers, and killers.[11] For achievers, the major draw is in-game goals and accomplishments, such as scoring, leveling, and accumulation of in-game currency. Explorers are primarily interested in exploring and uncovering the game world. Initially, this usually means traveling carefully through the game landscape and mapping the game's topology, whereas later on, the focus may rather be on experimenting with game mechanics and the ways in which the game functions as machinery of play. For socializers, the game world is first and foremost treated as a meeting place, emphasizing the communicative and social dimensions of play, including role-play. Killers, finally, are mostly intrigued by the possibilities of defeating other players provided by the game, of being trouble-makers and causing distress to others. In reality, players usually belong to several of these types at the same time, and the style of or motivation in play may shift over time. Nevertheless, this rough sketch may still indicate important differences in ways of coming to and of playing the game.

The variety of styles of play—the fact that there are several 'games within the game'—has also been used as an exploratory factor for the relatively large population of female players in *World of Warcraft* (compared to many other computer games). According to Nielsen statistics (Nielsen 2008) women make up for about a third of the players in the game. The game facilitates solo play as well as social play, and holds a variety of goals and ambitions (Corneliussen and Walker Rettberg 2008a). *World of Warcraft* is a game that is easy to learn, but difficult to master, which makes for an inviting environment for casual gamers, while providing plenty of challenges for more experienced, or hardcore gamers. These elements, combined with the continuous updates and expansions, are most likely important reasons for why the game manages to not only attract, but also keep such a large and devoted player base.

Even if it is possible to solo-play in *World of Warcraft* all the way to level 85,[12] the backbone of the game is its social dimensions and possibilities of co-play. Many in-game activities, such as group quests, instances and raids are made for groups of players. These groups may be created ad hoc, by a more or less random coming together of players to complete a particular mission (a so-called 'pick-up group', or 'PUG'). However, it is more common for players to organize through guilds in the game, which are more stable groups of people who get to know each other and play the game together. Guilds may differ significantly in terms of goals, ambitions and ambience, one important distinction being between 'casual' and 'hardcore' gaming. According to Williams et al. (2006), these different styles of play are usually related to the size of guilds. Big guilds are often instrumental and aim for raid progress and achievements, the ambiance reminiscent of that in 'military barracks'. Small guilds, on the other hand, tend to consist of friends playing together, with an atmosphere closer to that of 'tree house play spaces', putting playfulness and socialization first. Then again, guilds may certainly also be a mix of the two, for example combining high end raiding with heartfelt socializing.

## A TWIN ETHNOGRAPHY

This book consists of what we have chosen to call a 'twin ethnography' that develops two parallel stories. The two trajectories of the book are relatively independent, and can be read separately. Then again, there are multiple conversational points of both convergence and divergence between the two storylines, some of which will be made explicit in the collaboratively written closing chapter. In this sense, the chapters can also be read in tandem, guided by our cross-references between chapters as a going back and forth between the 'straight' and the 'bent', which provides a different reading experience.

The first section of the book consists of the ethnography performed by Sveningsson on 'straight' game cultures, and opens with the chapter "Go with Your Passion!". This chapter serves as an introduction to Sveningsson's section of the book. At the same time, the author takes a closer look at some core methodological questions that ethnographic games researchers need to confront. For example, how do we gain access to the groups we wish to study? How much involvement or immersion in the game is productive? How close is too close, and why? And, perhaps most importantly, how do we negotiate our relationships to the people that we meet during our fieldwork?

Computer game culture is often described as a homosocial, masculine sphere, where female gamers are actively or symbolically excluded. But there are other stories to be told. The point of departure of the chapter entitled "The More the Merrier" is the type of positive discrimination that female players sometimes experience, and the fact that many male gamers seem to strongly welcome women into the gaming communities. Positioning theory (Harré and Langenhove 1999) is used to illuminate how female gamers are positioned, and how these positions in turns may be accepted, negotiated or contested. Also, Robert Connell's (1995; 2005) theory on hegemonic masculinity is used to illuminate how male gamers relate to each other in a complex structure of hierarchies, and how female gamers are sometimes used as resource in their masculinity work. Female gamers may serve as a contrast to technical expertise, or as counterparts in manifestations of heterosexuality (as is developed in the following chapter). On the other hand, because male gamers feel that they are expected to play 'nice' when women are playing, the presence of female gamers is also seen as a way to escape the norms and ideals of hegemonic masculinity.

"The Straight Game" explores the ubiquitous heterosexual tension of male-dominated game spaces. This tension is constructed in diverse situations and behaviors, in 'innocent' flirtatious jargon, which may be used as 'a game within the game'. But the flirts sometimes go too far and turn female gamers into subjects of unwelcome sexual advancements or even harassment. In this chapter, Sveningsson looks at how gender and sexuality in various ways permeate the female players' interaction with other players, primarily male ones, how sexuality can be used as a communicative resource and as yet another dimension of play within the game. Romantic and sexual encounters and relationships often have a great importance for the players' gaming experiences as a whole. Moreover, they also fill an important function in the players' gender work, the regulating of norms of gender and sexuality, and ultimately in upholding gender hierarchies in the game.

If previous chapters have discussed how female players are often seen as strangers, and as lacking of technological skills and interests, the chapter "Playing Along" looks into how female players experience and handle this situation. In this chapter Sveningsson also discusses some of the available coping strategies for female gamers within a male-dominated context, and draws parallels to research on women in other male-dominated areas, such as the armed forces, the music industry and journalism. This is the closing chapter of the first section of the book.

The second section of the book consists of Sundén's ethnographic work on queer cultures of play. It opens with the chapter "Desires at Play", which serves as an introduction to this section of the book, as well as providing the story of a particular and affectionate introduction to the game. The chapter discusses knowledge production in game studies by exploring notions of emotion, closeness and (queer) desire in new media ethnography. Drawing on the body of ethnographic work interrogating erotic subjectivity and desire in the field, the discussion makes use of personal experiences as potentially valuable sources of knowledge. In making visible how desire and emotion may circulate through game spaces, Sundén argues for an articulation of desire as something intimately related to technology.

The next chapter is titled "A Feel of Play", which offers a theoretical take on 'close playing' as a critical strategy in understanding and analyzing *World of Warcraft*. By investigating affective investments and experiences within game spaces, Sundén develops queer feminist studies of online gaming, as well as argues for an expansion of game studies along the lines of 'the affective turn' in feminist and cultural theory. Digital games as media genre tend to aim at and involve the bodies of players in intense ways, which calls for an affective, experiential, passionate approach, theoretically as well as methodologically. Ultimately, the chapter asks what an online game like *World of Warcraft* puts in motion, and what consequences such stirring may have for ways of thinking—and feeling—games critically, yet sensitively.

The following two chapters are based on the phase in Sundén's ethnographic work where she played with and studied a guild explicitly defined as LGBT. "Coming Home and Coming Out" takes shape in the borderland between ethnography and play and explores the notion of participation in ethnographic work on online games. The chapter tells the story of how players who orient themselves as non-straight have made themselves 'at home' in the game, as well as discusses multiple acts of coming out—as a researcher of games and as a non-straight player. Building on a series of performances and playful turn-taking between the roles of researcher, researched, players, and queers, the discussion covers ways of playing together, as well as ways of doing and playing research together. In addition, the chapter is an attempt to investigate the meaning of 'queer' for ethnographic work. Queer ethnography usually marks research of queer cultures, but also holds an important potential of critiquing the normative logics of ethnographic research itself.

In the chapter "A Queer Eye on Transgressive Play", Sundén continues the discussion of how sexuality is 'at play' in the game for players who orients themselves as non-straight, in particular by exploring acts of 'transgressive play' in the intersections of queer culture and *World of Warcraft* culture. The notion of transgressive play is usually taken to mean play against the 'ideal' or 'implied' player of the game, of playing the game in ways not anticipated by game design. For queer gamers, sexuality comes into play in ways that make visible the cultural norms of the ideal player—*a player who is at least symbolically male and straight*. Sexuality is performed as a playful point of connection as well as a community border practice. The chapter discusses the transgressive potentials, but also the limitations of playfulness. No matter how LGBT-inclusive, this place is not without its own norms, regulations, and expectations.

Finally, the chapter entitled "Closing Chapter: Writing a Twin Ethnography" is the collaboratively written closing chapter of the book. In this chapter, we discuss experiences in writing twin ethnographies and make explicit what a combination or entwinement of our parallel trajectories may teach us about intersections of gender and sexuality in feminist ethnographic research on online game cultures. The chapter starts out with a discussion of 'the specificity of play' by a comparison between the two case studies. Then, we complicate the structure of the book and its division in a 'straight' versus a 'queer' ethnography by looking at the results of both studies in relation to Sedgwick's (1985) notion of 'homosociality'. Finally, our aim is to clarify what the study of games may bring to feminist theory and feminist studies.

## NOTES

1. MMO and MMOG are acronyms for Massively Multiplayer Online Game, whereas MMORPG aims at the specific genre Role Playing Game.
2. For an overview of queer studies of new media more generally, see O'Riordan and Phillips (2007).
3. Casual games are usually described as fun and accessible games that are easy to understand and learn. They address a mass market, also people that do not think of themselves as gamers. Casual gamers play as a form of relaxation, and to have fun alone or with friends. Hardcore games and hardcore gamers put more emphasis on skills and competition. The games have a longer learning curve and are more complicated to handle than casual games. Hardcore gamers play often and for many hours: from 20 hours a week and more. They are oriented towards competition and achievement and seek to master the games' most difficult content. The distinction between casual and hardcore gaming and its implied difference in status has everything to do with gender, but also with age, as hardcore players tend to be male rather than female, and young rather than old (Rice 2009; Yee 2007a).
4. Mizuko Ito (2008) makes similar claims about the Japanese game culture, which by its mixing of various media outlets opens up many ways into the games, both for male and female players.
5. Some of the paragraphs in this section have been used before in Sundén (2010a).
6. For important exceptions, see for example Armstrong (2000); Liljeström and Paasonen (2010); Pearce (1997); Sobchack (2004).
7. For a good introduction to humanist- and social sciences oriented approaches to *World of Warcraft*, see Corneliussen and Walker Rettberg (eds.) (2008b). For a nice overview of the social dynamics of the game, see Nardi and Harris (2006).

8. Raids and instances are tasks that are solved in groups, often in maze-like caves or ruins. The mission is to, by concerted efforts, proceed through the instance, kill the monsters (mobs and bosses) that are there and gather the loot that they carry. Instances refer to missions that are done in five-man-groups while raids can be done in groups of ten, twenty-five or forty persons. They all require a large amount of teamwork and coordination between the players.
9. This postcolonial reading is slightly complicated by *The Burning Crusade* expansion of 2007, which introduced animal components for the Alliance embodied in the draenai, which is a centaur-like race with a human upper body and an animal lower body complete with tail and hooves. News for the Horde side were the addition of the blood elf, which gave the Horde a more conventionally 'pretty' option to the more menacing appearances of orcs, undeads, and trolls. The distinction between the Alliance and the Horde as a divide between the familiar and the Other is further complicated by the expansion *Cataclysm* in December 2010, and the two new playable races: worgen and goblin. These give a wolf-like race to the Alliance and a human-like race to the Horde.
10. However, the most recent additions of races go against this pattern: draenei and most notably worgen on the Alliance side appear to deviate from the human-like, whereas the blood elves and goblins on the Horde side approach it.
11. The model has been further developed by Bartle (2004) and other categorizations of players have been made by Yee (2007b), but for our purpose, the first model of player motivations is enough.
12. An important distinction is that it is perfectly doable to 'level up' a character to 85 without ever speaking to another player, but if one is interested in proceeding and continuing to develop one's level 85 character, one is dependent upon groups.

# 1 Go with Your Passion!

*Malin Sveningsson*

In the very beginning of the project that forms the basis for this book, I was hesitant about what aspect of gender and gaming to focus on. I was faced with various possible angles and perspectives that I found very hard to choose between. The turning point occurred when a scholar friend told me: "Why don't you use yourself and your own gameplay as a resource?" and "Go with your passion!" I took her advice, letting my curiosity, enthusiasm, and excitement take the lead in an ethnographic journey into the world of gaming, where my own experiences of gaming and the gaming worlds were allowed to guide me to certain essential aspects of gaming as related to gender.

My overarching focus eventually turned out to be on how female gamers experience the games, gaming activities and gaming cultures, from their perspective as female gamers.[1] Important questions were how they become included (or not) in male dominated gaming cultures—how they position themselves and how they are positioned by the male players, what the group dynamics look like, and, generally, how they as female gamers 'play along' and on what conditions they are given (or claim) a space. In my work I used several kinds of research material: discussion fora of online gaming communities, qualitative offline interviews with female gamers, and ethnographic fieldwork in the online game *World of Warcraft*, including participant observations and informal in-game interviews with players—both male and female. The context in which the data was gathered was European, white and heterosexual. In a way, this choice reflects my own position as I am all of these things. But it also reflects my gaming experiences and what and whom I actually got into contact with during my fieldwork. Although I did meet players from several European countries, a majority of the people I got to know during my fieldwork was Swedish. Their gaming community had strong local connections, which influenced the interaction in certain ways. The gaming contexts I encountered also generally considered being heterosexual as a norm that was mostly taken for granted. In addition to studying female gamers' experiences, I also wanted to look more closely at the norms of heterosexuality, making visible that which permeated much of the in-game interaction.

As my first task, I set out to get an insight into the state of computer games and female gamers. I browsed in and read through the contents of three online gaming communities.[2] These were all Swedish, they had a general scope, and were not aimed at particular games or target groups. They all included discussion fora as well as other content such as game reviews. They were governed in three different ways: as a grass-root initiative, by a media company, and by a non-profit organization. The forum discussions allowed me to see how (predominantly male) gamers talked about female participation in gaming cultures and how they positioned female gamers (Sveningsson Elm forthcoming). But above all, they functioned as a way for me to get a first insight into the subject, which led me into wanting to take a closer look at how female gamers themselves experience the games they play and the gaming cultures.

In order to know something about this, semi-structured interviews were made with eight Swedish adult female gamers, chosen to mirror a variety of gaming experiences, preferences and styles. The interviewees were 23 to 50 years old, they played different kinds of games and platforms, and had different life situations, the common denominator being that they were all deeply involved in their gaming activity. The sample was strategic, meaning that the informants were chosen to cover a variety of diverse perspectives, rather than to give a representative picture. The interviewees were not representative for Swedish women, or even for Swedish women who play computer games. They were chosen because of their deep involvement with the gaming activity, despite being engaged in different games and having different playing styles—some of them played in a more casual way while others were hardcore gamers or even semi-professional. Thus, the results cannot be generalized into a larger population but, like qualitative studies in general, they show one of many simultaneously existing pictures.

In order to understand what my interviewees talked about, I set out early on to try their favorite games and play them at least once. When trying *World of Warcraft*, I was caught by the immensely social and interactive character of the game, and I was deeply fascinated by the player cultures that I saw there. Needless to say, perhaps, I was also caught by the appeal of the game. After a few weeks of playing, I realized that much of what my informants had brought up in the interviews I could observe in the game too—I even experienced some of it myself, which prompted the idea of complementing the interviews with participant observations. The process through which this fieldwork was initiated and performed will be described more thoroughly in the following sections.

The three separate methods taken together allowed me to grasp different aspects of the situation: how male gamers talk about female participation, how women feel they are met in the gaming environments, and finally, what it is really like being a woman in a male dominated gaming context, and what kind of situations one may encounter.

## GETTING ACCESS

One of the first challenges that an ethnographer confronts is how to get access to the field. Access can here be understood in several senses. First, it concerns finding the place where to perform the fieldwork, but it can also be understood as creating oneself a space within the studied environment.

The point of ethnography is often described as trying to come close to people in the studied culture and to attain an insider's perspective of it.[3] Through this perspective, the researcher comes to understand the situation in much the same way as those who normally find themselves there experience it (Van Maanen 1995). In order to share the group's experiences, the ethnographic researcher must, then, in a sense become a member. The first task is thus to become accepted by the group. So, in what kind of environment did I do my fieldwork and how did I get access to it? As is true for most female players (Bryce and Rutter 2003a; Jenson and de Castell 2005; Schott and Horrell 2000), I too was introduced into the gaming culture by a male acquaintance, in the following text referred to as Erik.[4]

> We are having a party for my husband's colleagues. I am talking with Erik, who is the husband of Anna whom I've met before. Erik asks if I play computer games, in a way that makes me understand that he already knows that I do—either Anna or my husband has told him. I am not sure whether I can really call myself a gamer so I answer him hesitatingly: "Yeah . . ." The reaction from him and the other guys around us is direct and positive: "Cool!" Erik asks if I play online games and stumbles on the words "massively multiplayer online role-playing games". I fill in with the word "mmorpgs". The guys seem impressed that I can pronounce it, or is it that I know what it is at all? Anyway, Erik invites me to join him and his friends in the game—they'll help me level up my character, he says. I've wanted to start to play WoW for a long time now, but I guess I've been afraid that I wouldn't be good enough. But it feels kind of safe to have someone you know there. So I've made up my mind. Tomorrow, I'll go and buy the game. (Field Diary, 09/13/08)

Already this very first note from my field diary has a lot to say about the way women are met and positioned within gaming communities, which will be discussed more thoroughly in the following chapters. For now, let us just note the passages where I, being a female, feel uncomfortable with classifying myself as a gamer and feel insecure about my entering the gaming community; the guys' astonished yet positive reaction to the fact that I do play computer games; and finally Erik's offer to 'help' me.

Even if I was new to *World of Warcraft*, I was no stranger to computer games in general. I had been playing other games before, on various platforms—console and PC—and from various genres: mostly strategy, adventure and RPGs (role-playing games). However, all of them had been single player, and I had never been part of a gaming community. Even if I had wanted to, I had not yet summoned the courage to try a MMO. It is true that I had decided to try WoW as part of my research, since it was one of the favorite games mentioned by my informants, but it was not until Erik asked me if I would want to join him and his friends that I actually got on with it. So I bought the game, created a character at the server where Erik and his friends played, and I started to level up and learn. I had been playing mostly alone for about three weeks, had accepted an invitation from another guild just to see what it was like, and reached level 24, when I got the invitation from *Mercenaries*, the guild that Erik was a member of.

As Taylor (2008c) notes, guilds have different group cultures. In the case of *Mercenaries*, it is likely that its RL demographics played an important role for the way it was run. *Mercenaries* was what Williams et al. (2006) would describe as a 'huge' guild—at that time containing 152 characters (and at the time of writing, over 250). However, out of these, many were alts, i.e., alternative characters of members with several characters. Counting only one character per member, the actual number of active members was about fifty-seven, so in that sense *Mercenaries* instead would classify as a 'large' guild. The guild was wholly Swedish, most of its members lived in western Sweden, or even Gothenburg, and it consisted of an extended network of friends and friends-of-friends.[5] Most of the members were between 25 and 40 years old, with an emergent player base in the members' sons and nephews and their friends. Most of the members lived in long-term relationships and many of them had children.

Guilds have different goals and levels of ambition. In its web site, *Mercenaries* described itself as a "casual hardcore guild", which very accurately describes the ambiance and the general attitude of the members. Research papers otherwise abound with accounts of high end raiding guilds with strict (not to say militaristic) rules concerning participation, and sanctions for those who do not obey the strict rules (Yee 2006c). This image is often contrasted with the image of casual gaming activities as being sporadic, uncommitted and detached. However, as Williams et al. (2006) point out, guilds often resist simple categorizations and may combine several goals, for example socializing and raiding. *Mercenaries* combined the casual and the hardcore in what I find a quite interesting way. There was a widely shared understanding of (at least certain) RL activities as being superior to guild activities, especially family commitments, such as caring for children. There was seldom any pressure on members to participate, and should an important RL occurrence interfere with the raiding (even during a raid) no one would object, at least not openly. Williams et al. (2006) state that huge and large guilds are often likely to be militaristic, with strict rules for participation, while smaller guilds tend to be more focused on socializing and having fun together, described metaphorically as 'military barracks' respectively 'tree house play spaces'. Here, Williams et al. may be pointing to the wrong factor to explain the ambiances of guilds; I believe that small guilds are more oriented towards sociality and casual play not because of their size, but primarily because they typically consist of circles of friends who know each other offline and use the game as a way to spend time together. Large guilds, on the other hand, more often consist of people who do not know each other offline and whose only connection is their shared interest in playing instances and raids, hence the more goal-oriented focus on raid progress rather than on sociality.

Despite being a 'large' (or even 'huge') guild, the ambiance in *Mercenaries* was more reminiscent of a 'tree house' than a 'barrack', with a liberal attitude towards members' commitment and choice of playing styles. I believe this was because of its composition, being put together by networks of people who knew each other offline. The relaxed attitude of players was something that I appreciated, which I reflected on during my first months in the guild:

> One thing that I have noticed is that this guild is very tolerant as to the ways people choose to play. For example, when you ask people what spec to choose,[6] several of them just reply, "Play the way you think is fun". (Field Diary, 11/03/08)

> I have noticed how different guilds can be—comparing Mercenaries with my first guild, where people seemed to be quite young and the tone quite crude. For example when they invited people to raids it was with the words "those who are above 56 can come. Plz no low levels". It is self evident that you can't come if your character's level is too low, but there are different ways of phrasing it. When Thad invited me into Mercenaries, I said to him "tell me if there's something I can do or if I can help with something". He answered: "level up to 70 so you can come raiding with us". In one way, the meaning is the same: you cannot join until you're on a higher level. But the way you phrase it has something to say about your attitude to other people. In Mercenaries, I felt welcome, as if they really wanted me to be there. (Field Diary, 10/07/08)

However, despite its laid-back and relaxed attitude, the guild still ended up being quite successful in its raiding activities. During its most intensive periods, the guild organized 25-man raids four nights a week and spontaneous 10-man raids occurred every now and then, albeit with decreased activity during the summer vacations. The guild also held quite a high ranking—during my time as a member, it oscillated between 10 and 24 on its server.[7]

In order to become a true member of a guild one has to play, preferably on the same conditions and in the same manner as the other members. As Constance Steinkuhler notes in an interview, one has to spend what is considered for the community a standard amount of time in the game to be able to write about it, and one also has to master the game in order to be taken seriously by the other players (McKee and Porter 2009). For that reason, I have been playing quite a lot—as much as any of the other guild members, and more than many of them. For *World of Warcraft*, Steinkuhler says, at least 20 hours a week has to be put on standard maintenance and a hardcore gamer would have to play about 40 hours a week. I am not sure I agree with Steinkuhler's numbers here, because I believe that guilds do differ a great deal in what standards they set up for play time and members' participation. In *Mercenaries*, some of the members spent 50 hours a week or more, but there were also others, especially those with families and children, who played considerably less, some of them only one night a week or even less. However, I find that my own playtime basically coincides with Steinkuhler's standards. Over my time as a participant observer, I have had an average playtime of between 15 and 60 hours a week. I spent more time during the first year, when I leveled up my main character and got to know the guild members. As time went by, my playtime decreased. From the second year onwards, I settled for joining guild raids and playing instances with my max level characters, or playing my low-level characters in a more casual style. I would then play 4–7 nights, with an average playtime of about 15–35 hours a week. I guess this fits Steinkuhler's description of what it takes to do 'standard maintenance'—both as regards upholding my main character's gear, my own performance, and my relations with the guild members.

One reason why I spent all this time playing was of course to gather research material and to get acquainted with and understand the environment and the informants. Another reason was that I came to enjoy the game, which eventually turned out to be my preferred leisure activity. In that sense I did become a true member, acquiring the perspective of a casual hardcore gamer. But playing extensively is not only a way to learn the culture and get to know informants—it also works as a way to gain credibility with the studied group (McKee and Porter 2009). Thus, for me, playing extensively also was a way to signal that even if I had not been playing for as long as most of the other guild members, and even if my initial motivations for entering the game were different from theirs, we were still birds of a feather—we shared an interest and a passion.

## BEING A RESEARCHER AND A PARTICIPANT

One important aspect of the fieldwork concerns the researcher's role in the studied group, and to how large an extent to position oneself as a researcher. One may, for example, frame oneself mainly or exclusively in the researcher role. Sometimes, this is the only possible alternative, as in cases where the studied culture revolves around an activity that the researcher cannot or does not want to participate in, or holds values and world views that the researcher does not wish to share—for instance, criminal subcultures (see, for example, Ferrell and Hamm 1998). This emphasis on the researcher role may coincide with a decreased participation in the group's activities, so that the researcher may be participant, partly participant or only an observer (Patton 1990). In the two latter cases, the group will likely not come to look upon the researcher as a true member of the group, and may therefore not share all aspects of their everyday life with him or her.

In order to get an insider's perspective, the researcher must participate in the group's activities under much the same premises as the regular members, so that s/he learns the culture to the extent that s/he becomes a member of it. But then, how does one balance the role of member with that of researcher? Here, a number of ethical considerations must be taken into account. One consideration to make concerns when to speak as a fellow gamer and when to speak as a researcher (for a discussion on the urgency and potential delicacy of this question, see Campbell 2009). In the role of fellow gamer the researcher may enter into personal relationships with participants, meaning that s/he comes close to them and the researcher and the informants may share confidences with each other. There is indeed a possibility that people would tell a fellow gamer or a friend certain things that they would not tell a researcher. Here, careful decisions must be made about what to include and what to not include in one's writing, but also, as Campbell notes, about being open towards informants and explicitly telling them when one is speaking as a group member and when one is speaking as a researcher.

In my work I made the decision to ask each particular informant before I mention him/her or anything s/he has said or done in my writings. This decision, of course, has consequences producing other dilemmas—for example, I will be restricted as to what perspectives I can mirror. Like so many other ethnographies, my work will have a bias and tend to show mostly the nice sides of the studied culture while downplaying the darker sides of it (Ehn 1996). However, this is a risk I decided to take to not abuse the confidence of my informants.

In my oscillating between the role of a fellow gamer and a researcher, a certain confusion of roles may cause feelings of awkwardness for the people involved. For example, in my role as a gamer, I was long seen as a newbie, holding a relatively low position in the implicit hierarchy of the guild (even though it greatly improved after I reached max level and could take a more active part in guild raids and also contribute more with my crafting skills). Belonging to a guild that included some really experienced players, I often positioned myself (and was also positioned) as someone in need of advice, and I was careful to respect other guild members, as well as guild rules and standards of conduct. The times when I was talking from the point of view of a researcher, however, my position was different. Being a Ph.D. and associate professor, my educational level was higher than that of any of the other members. My role as a researcher, who observed and would write about the guild, was yet another thing that placed me in a potentially superior, or at least a very different, position.

Being an ethnographic participant observer, one should try to reduce the distance between oneself and the group under study, and one way of doing this is to try to appear to be as similar as possible to the informants, through manner, behavior, and language style. This does not mean that I pretended to be someone or something that I was not, only that I sometimes would emphasize similarities (such as gaming interest, music and movie taste, and my role as a parent). This was facilitated by the fact that the guild seemed to be diverse with respect to class and educational level (although less so with respect to ethnicity and gender). However, I noticed that as time went by, and I took an active part in the guild's activities and became acquainted or even friends with more of the guild members, I gradually came to let more and more of my personality shine through. For example, where I initially would have kept a low profile, adapting my language style to not scare people away or make them think I was an academic snob, I have come to express myself in a way more consistent with how I would do with friends, blending game argot with nicely phrased sentences, and mixing philosophical reflections with lavatory humor. My language and interaction style is quite different from that of most other members, but I no longer see this as an obstacle. Getting to know the members made a difference for my way of relating to and interacting with them, which, I believe, in turn made me come even closer to them.

In all ethnographic studies, some individuals and thus some perspectives are given more attention than others. I have had a number of key informants in the guild, people who I would ask questions about the social dynamics in the game and about the way they looked upon certain issues (above all issues that related to gender).

Renee was an officer in the guild. I never conducted an offline interview with her, but she was the source of much knowledge about the game and the guild, its social dynamics and its standards of conduct. I would ask her questions in the game, and she also read three of my first texts and commented upon them in a series of long e-mails between us.

Erik was the person who introduced me to the game, and I also had real life connections to him and his partner. Through Erik, I got to know Mats, David, and Miles, who I would meet at LAN parties and who became one of my circles of close guild mates. When I first joined the guild, Miles was one of the officers.

Another circle of key informants consisted of General, Sergey, and Dragon, who were also friends offline. I got to know these players during the spring of 2009. I talked quite a lot in-game with General and Sergey for a few months, until they quit playing during the spring and summer of 2009 (although General eventually came back). Dragon continued to be one of my closest guild mates.

Lisa joined the guild during the fall of 2009. I interviewed her offline in January 2010, and also asked her questions in-game and through chatting on Facebook. As with Dragon, the relationship between us developed so that in the end she would turn out to be more of a friend than an informant. Nevertheless, she continued to serve as a valuable source of information.

## COMING OUT AS A RESEARCHER

In Chapter 7 of this book, Sundén discusses the 'coming out process' as a researcher. She describes her feelings of anxiety when asking for permission to study the group she had found her way into. The obvious question that meets a researcher in this situation concerns whether the group will agree to being studied. But even more important questions that troubled us both in our respective case studies were whether our respective groups would look at us in a different way after we had 'come out', and if they would still accept us as members. Maybe our coming out as researchers would make people shy away from us, or it might even get us kicked from the guilds. Thus, as Sundén points out, the coming out process as a researcher has several similarities with the act coming out as non-straight.

One important ethical consideration concerns when to present oneself as a researcher to the group. If this is done when one first approaches the group, it may be hard to be assigned the role of a member afterwards, and one will in a sense always remain the observing outsider. Or, one might not even get entrance into the group in the first place. If, on the other hand, one joins the group, and then after having been accepted as a member reveals oneself to be a researcher, one risks losing the other members' trust.

In my case, these ethical decisions were facilitated by the fact that when entering the guild I did not know that I would want to write about it (although already from the start, I did write field notes to document my own gameplay). When the thought of using the material as data came to my mind, I first discussed it with Erik. I also brought the issue up with Dark, who was the guild leader at that time. He allowed me to write about him, and said that he did not mind me writing about the guild either, but that I might want to post a message to the discussion forum at the guild's web page, which I did.

As has been discussed elsewhere (Sveningsson 2001; 2003; Sveningsson, Lövheim, and Bergquist 2003), attaining informed consent may be very difficult in various Internet settings. Who do we really reach with our questions? Is it enough to get the consent of some members or do we need to reach them all? In my case, all guild members did not visit the guild forum and read the posts. Thus I knew that a post to the guild forum would not find all members, and that I would not be able to get the informed consent from everyone. Still, I felt that I had 'come out' as a researcher; I had informed publicly about my intentions, and asked for consent to include the guild in my writings, of course without naming guild, server, members or characters. In my accounts and excerpts from the guild, I have changed the names of guild, users and characters. When doing so, I have tried to keep as close to the original name as possible without making it possible for an outsider to identify the person. My way of doing this has been to use the nicknames and abbreviations of characters' names that were used within the guild, and then change them slightly. Thus, the members of the guild will know whom it is I am referring to, but it will not be possible for others to identify characters. Including Erik and the guild leader, a total of twelve members answered my post and explicitly consented. No one objected, although four members expressed an interest in reading the resulting texts. Thus I concluded that I had sufficient permission to write about the guild in general terms, but in addition, I promised to address them individually and ask for consent from each separate guild member who would appear in my writings.

In retrospect, I understand that the introduction of my identity as a researcher came by degrees, as I got to know people and they got to know me. We interacted with each other, played together and gabbed together on the guild chat, and on voice chat. It seems like most of the members came to accept me as a fellow gamer and a familiar 'face'. When I took part in guild activities, I also tended to see myself more as a guild member than a researcher.[8] Yet, despite being positioned mainly as a fellow gamer, there are other aspects that influence how one is met, such as gender, age and class. *Mercenaries* is heavily male dominated: during my first year and a half as a member, when the main part of the data was collected, the active members included only four female members, of which only three (including myself) played during the same period.[9]

Being female in a male dominated guild holds both advantages and drawbacks. Despite the common view of female gamers facing difficulties when trying to enter into gaming communities (see, for example, Carr 2006a; Delamere and Shaw 2008), I have rather experienced the opposite. For example, after I had joined, Erik told me that the guild is generally quite fastidious when it comes to accepting new members. Being a newbie I would not have stood a chance, had I competed on equal terms. Of course it made a difference that I was introduced by someone who was already a member, but as Erik said: "At first, the guild officer that I asked sounded hesitant, but when he heard you were a girl, he said: 'It's a girl? No problem, she can join'". As will be shown in the next chapter, belonging to an under-represented gender in gaming contexts sometimes brings advantages to the player (see also Sveningsson Elm forthcoming).

But there are also drawbacks. For example, a female researcher in a male dominated culture can never merge into the group in the same way as a male researcher could. In a way, she will always be a foreigner—a welcome visitor, maybe, but still a foreigner. If this is good or bad for the research is hard to tell. On the one hand, my difference made a true sharing of the group's perspective impossible. Due to both the treatment of me as a female player, and my baggage from previous RL experiences as a female, I will never come to experience the gaming activities and culture in the same way as a male player would. On the other hand, my difference from the majority of the group was what allowed me to see the things that I was interested in studying. My research questions dealt with the difference that gender can make: how one as a woman can merge (or not merge) into the male dominated gaming cultures, and what issues, problems and opportunities one is confronted with. Here, it was my difference from the majority of the studied group that made it possible to experience such aspects. It is also important to stress that a group cannot be seen as homogenous; all members have their individual perspectives and points of view.

## SPENDING TIME IN THE FIELD

When ethnologists or anthropologists go on fieldwork to study a cultural field, no one considers it strange that they spend much time there, together with the 'ordinary' inhabitants. Nor would anyone be surprised that the researcher shares the activities of the group or tries to become accepted by its members. These things only increase the researcher's credibility, since it gives the closeness required to understand and portray the culture from within. However, spending much time in the field is considerably more problematic when the researched field is in the popular cultural sphere. It is seen as suspect that a researcher spends his/her working time doing something that other people do in their leisure time, as recreation. I want to stress that I do agree with previous authors that in order to gain an insider's perspective into gaming cultures, one has to play and be immersed,[10] both in the games and in the gaming cultures (see for example Aarseth 2007a). In order to be able to participate in the activities of a raiding guild, the researcher's character needs to be the same level as the others', and so must the researcher's skills as a player—s/he must have the knowledge to play his or her characters to be able to join the group in its activities (Steinkuhler, in McKee and Porter 2009). Much of the culture in MMORPGs also revolves around the process of leveling—the long and winding road through which a character successively climbs up and acquires the skills necessary to join the endgame goals and activities of the game.

Even if I do agree that ethnographic games researchers should spend much time in the gaming environments, there are reasons to discuss how long they should have been playing before they enter the gaming contexts as researchers. Many ethnographers see the point of ethnography as getting an insider's perspective on an 'initially unfamiliar social world' (Emerson, Fretz, and Shaw 1995; Taylor 2008a). This unfamiliarity is supposed to facilitate the researcher's noticing and questioning all the things that are taken for granted within the studied culture and thus reveal its hidden meanings and enable the researcher to perceive 'what it is all about'. Many of the games researchers of today have been gamers long before they started to do research, which is also highly visible in their writings. Having a background as a gamer may be positive insofar as it gives a familiarity and knowledge to the field, and it may also give valuable access points. But on the other hand, this familiarity may also lead to blindness to the specific character of the culture and a biased understanding of the field. To sum up: for games researchers with a background as gamers, the main problem may not be to attain an insider's perspective, because that they already have. Instead, the challenge lies in being able to move away from habitual perspectives and look at gaming cultures with the eyes of a stranger.

## GETTING CLOSE

Working ethnographically involves trying to reduce the distance between oneself and the individuals in the studied field. Thus one important ingredient in ethnography is closeness—but how close to the studied individuals is it appropriate for a researcher to go? One may here understand closeness in several respects. When a researcher gets close to the informants and spends time with them, personal relationships emerge. In a way, this is what ethnographic researchers seek. But researchers often do not reflect upon what kind of relationships these are, how to handle them, and most importantly, how to relate to them in their role as researchers, and in the written results of their research. Focusing on romantic feelings, desires and relationships between ethnographers and informants, Kendall (2009a), Sundén (2009a) and Campbell (2009) point out that even though such feelings and relationships have probably always occurred between ethnographic researchers and their informants, the praxis has been to not mention them in ethnographic writing. These authors all offer insightful discussions on the potential consequences of concealing such background knowledge, because it is indeed part of our understanding and it also does influence the kind of knowledge we as researchers get from the field (see also Sundén, Chapter 5 in this book).

The word 'closeness' can be understood in other senses as well. The meaning that has most often been implied in ethnographic writings concerns how involved and immersed researchers should become in the cultures they study. On the one hand, ethnographic participant observation is associated with an approach where the researcher seeks to attain an insider's perspective on the activities or the group. On the other hand, we are also frequently warned of the danger of getting too close and of becoming *too* involved in the group's world views, thus losing our objectivity and analytical perspective, what has been called 'going native' (Patton 1987, 76). The kind of reasoning that draws on the need for objectivity and analytical distance can in a sense be seen as a residue of positivistic ideals that for a long time remained also in qualitative studies, where ethnographers sometimes wished to be like 'flies on the wall'—observing without being seen and without affecting the research situation. Nowadays, most ethnographers have ceased to see this as possible (or even desirable) (Sveningsson et al. 2003). Instead, closeness to the studied culture is generally seen as valuable—it is only through our own experiences that we can attain an understanding and knowledge of other people's social reality (Ferrell and Hamm 1998). Here, I would argue that even subjectivity may be a good thing in ethnographic studies, or at least one of the potential strengths, if handled properly. If the researcher is careful to document his/her subjective experiences made during the participation, and is able to use the field notes for a thorough analysis—not just a description of things that happened—s/he will have access to research material that goes deeper than most interviews manage to reach.

How is it possible to be an insider in the group, sharing its perspectives and world views, but at the same time keeping the analytical distance? The answer is that it is not. As Boellstorff (2006) says, one cannot fully participate and fully observe at the same time. The solution to the problem of analytical distance, as I see it, is not to stay out of the interaction and maintain distanced and detached during the whole research project out of fear from getting too close. That will not give an understanding of the culture. The solution must instead be to oscillate between different positions on the insider—outsider continuum. Sometimes this corresponds to different phases in the study: the researcher starts with seeking the insider perspective and develops it during the course of the study. When s/he is finished with gathering research material, s/he leaves the field site and goes home, starts to write, and thereby moves closer to an outsider's perspective. However, as Sveningsson et al. (2003) point out, this is an oversimplified image of the procedure, because the gathering of material and the writing often occur simultaneously. In reality, we must alternate between positions: letting ourselves go with the game and the experiences we have there, and then in the next phase, take a step back to analyze what really happened.

There are those who would say that I have gone too close to my informants and my material. In a way they are right: during my activities when in the guild, I often felt like one of them, and I came to see the gaming world in much the same way as they did. But when I sit down in front of my computer, to write down and analyze my experiences, and those of the informants, I do this with the eyes of a researcher, interested in gender issues. Time is also a key factor here: during my time in the guild, my ways of playing and taking part in the activities have varied, so that during some periods I would play if not as a true hardcore gamer, at least something reminiscent of it—like a casual hardcore gamer, I guess. During other periods, however, especially during periods with much to do at work or at home, I did not participate in guild activities at all, meaning that I somehow moved out of that particular mode of thinking and acting. Moreover, the guild changed over the years and by the time I write this, it was not anymore what it was when I collected my data. Many of the members had quit, changed guilds, or taken breaks, meaning that both the people and the group culture were different from when my field notes were written. In the end I even left the guild.

Thus, when I sit down and write about my experiences, I look at them in retrospect. The field diary that was written when I was immersed can be read and analyzed as if it was the diary of someone else, which allows me to look again at my experiences-as-insider, now through the eyes of an outsider. I then try to put myself outside of all the things that I have come to 'know', and question all the things that I have started to take for granted. The field diary thereby allows me to travel in time, to meet the person I was before I became immersed in the culture. It also permits me to follow myself during the process.

Another aspect of closeness with the studied group concerns what happens when the researcher is finished with the fieldwork. Can s/he, or should s/he even, remove her/himself from the studied group and just 'go home'? In a paper on how to draw the boundaries of research, Lori Kendall (2009b) addresses this question. In my work, I have sometimes thought that my close relationship with the group under study made my research less scientific, that I was getting too close and had become too immersed in the culture that I wanted to study. Also, when thinking ahead about the termination of the study, I realized I had no intentions of quitting playing, at least not yet. I felt like I had found a place where I felt at home and people whom I cared for and enjoyed spending time with. Altogether this made me feel guilty as well as a bad and subjective researcher. Thus it was with relief that I read Kendall's piece, in which she discusses these questions. When she was performing her ethnographic study, one of her informants once asked her if she was going to leave after she had finished her studies. She did not. In fact, she stayed with her informants in the studied online environment for several years after her research was finished. In my case, I stayed in the guild for a year and a half after my material was collected. Kendall's text made me think in a new direction and made me look at research from another perspective, namely that of the informants. Because, as Buchanan (2009) says, we, as researchers, tend to discuss ethical guidelines at length and how they apply to our studies, but we seldom stop to ask ourselves what our informants get out of it. These two texts read together made me realize that, in the end, staying in the field after the work is finished may not be a bad thing after all. It may instead be a way to demonstrate respect towards the group members and show them that they are important and interesting, also after we have got what we came for, and had our research papers written and published. Remaining in the field just for a little while longer is a way to communicate this to the group and to counteract a hit-and-run mentality that does not benefit the business of research in the long run.

This chapter has addressed questions on how to do ethnography in games research. Many of the issues are not new; they have been treated in other ethnographic writings before. But what is occurring now is a process similar to the one that took place in Internet studies in the late 1990s, when novel environments gave rise to new questions, or perhaps rather, old methodological questions re-emerged in new ways in the new research fields. In Internet studies, questions often dealt with the disembodiment of the medium: for example, how we as researchers can deal with the fact that the places where we interact as well as the people we meet online are mediated through computers. In game studies, questions that are being treated as specifically central and problematic deal above all with immersion—in the games and in the gaming cultures. In this chapter I have discussed this and other related questions, and reached the conclusion that for the ethnographic researcher, a certain amount of immersion is absolutely crucial in order to reach an insider's view and an understanding of the culture under study. However, there are no clear cut answers. As is always the case in methodological issues, the researcher must constantly be reflecting upon what he or she is doing, why s/he is doing it, and with what consequences.

## NOTES

1. In this text, I will use both words 'gamer' and 'player' in partly different ways. When I talk about 'players' it is in a general sense, including anyone who plays computer games. When I talk about 'gamers' on the other hand I understand this as players with a pronounced interest in gaming, who spend much time playing computer games, reading about games, or taking part in gaming cultures.
2. The gaming communities were fuska.nu, goodgame.se and gameplayer.se.
3. The use of the word 'insider' may give the impression that I see the group under study as homogenous. This is not the case. All members are different, and have different relationships to each other and to the group. They may also look at their participation in different ways, and see themselves as insiders or not. When using the word, I mean it in the sense of trying to place oneself in the same situation as those who usually are there, to be able to see what they see.
4. All names of guilds, guild members, and characters have been changed.
5. The local connection of the guild, as well as the fact that many of the members knew each other offline, had certain repercussions on the interaction and group dynamics, as will be discussed later on.
6. As the character levels up, it gains talent points that the player chooses how to place. Some talents increase the damage that the character does, while others protect it from various sorts of damage, or give it special abilities. The 'spec' refers to the way the character's talent points are placed.
7. Admittedly, the server was a role-play server that did not belong to the larger ones, but the guild's ranking was still high.
8. This evokes questions of researchers getting too close, which will be discussed further.
9. I knew the gender of all the guild members. Being made up by groups of friends who knew each other in real life, the guild had strong real life connections,

which made virtual cross-dressing within the guild very unlikely. In the list of members, all players' real first names were added, and visible for all guild members. In addition to this, the guild used voice chat Ventrilo, which was obligatory to use during raids, and many members also used it outside of raids, for social purposes.

10. Referring to Lombard and Ditton (1997), Carr (2006b, 53–54) distinguishes between perceptual and psychological immersion, perceptual immersion dealing with "the degree to which a technology or experience monopolizes the senses of a user" and psychological immersion dealing with "the player's 'mental absorption in the world'". When I speak of immersion, it will be in the latter of the senses.

# 2 The More the Merrier!

*Malin Sveningsson*

*Ulrika:* Being a woman you often get a lot of appreciation in gaming communities. Just because you're a female player. [ . . . ] I guess people have ideas of gender, like you're supposed to contribute something special.

When one reads research about gaming women, the image one gets is often of computer game culture as a misogynist sphere, where girls and women are actively or symbolically excluded (Bryce and Rutter 2002; 2003a; Burrill 2008; Carr 2006a; Delamere and Shaw 2008; Dovey and Kennedy 2006; Schott and Horrell 2000; Taylor, Jenson, and de Castell 2009). However, there are other stories to be told. In an initial study of the project (Sveningsson Elm forthcoming), I discuss how the overriding image of women as being subject to harassment and exclusion from gaming communities has to be questioned. An analysis of three Swedish forum discussions showed that the responses to gaming women can also be understood by how their gaming activities relate to a number of contexts: cultural context, context of game genres, and gaming scene. With very few exceptions, the discussants expressed an overwhelming consensus of female players as appreciated within gaming communities, saying things like "gaming girls are the coolest", "it's a pity there are so few girls", and it would be better if more girls started to play—"the more the merrier!". Thus, at least among Swedish gamers, many boys and men seem to strongly welcome girls and women, especially in casual and non competitive gaming.

As this chapter will show, alongside the well-documented sexism and harassment of female players, there even seems to be some positive discrimination. But what does this positive discrimination consist of? What is it that makes the male players appreciate the female players they meet and wish for more to start playing? As the opening quote indicates, are there certain qualities that women are expected to bring to gaming worlds, and certain positions that they are expected to occupy? These are questions that I shall take a closer look at in this chapter.

## "YOU BECOME KIND OF UNIQUE"

During my fieldwork, especially during the first year, my general experiences were that I received a very warm welcome by guild mates, and, I believe, considerably more attention than a male newcomer would get. I received help from my male guild mates (as well as the one female guild member who was active when I leveled up), who willingly answered my endless questions on anything that had to do with the game—from what gear to use to issues of game strategy. I received gifts—some symbolic items without much value for my character's performance (pets, pretty dresses, bracelets, bouquets of roses, and a wedding ring), but also more valuable items such as gems, equipment and weapons. Guild mates with crafting skills made equipment for me—sometimes I provided the material needed and sometimes not. Some guild mates gave me the material to train my professions, or loaned me the gold needed to buy mounts and better equipment in the game, and quite a few of these debts were remitted. They assisted me on quests and boosted me through instances[1]—sometimes I asked for the assistance but just as often it was their initiative: "Is there anything I can help you with today?" At times the assistance was accompanied by comments like "Anything for a damsel in distress" or "I'd do anything for you, hun".

My experiences are echoed in the interviews:

*Sanna:* On the whole you get a lot of discrimination, both positive and negative from being a female player, in online games. When I got to know people in my guild, they thought it was fun that a woman joined and you would get gifts in the game. And maybe you'd get milder treatment too.

*Malin:* Do you think there's a difference between game genres? That it's being seen as more natural that there are only guys in war or shooter games, for example? Because it's a context that has been so male dominated IRL too.

*Ulrika:* No, I think it's rather the opposite, that the more male dominated it is, the more appreciation you'll get as a woman. The more hullabaloo there'll be, like "wow, a girl!". You get appreciated for your gender and, you know, you get free cred, you don't have to work for it. Everybody, just like "Wow, are you a girl?! That's so awesome! Can't you come and play with me?" And everybody, just: "Can't you be my friend?" sort of.

The special treatment of female players sometimes reaches beyond the game. For example, one of the informants, Lisa, told me that on several occasions, she had been offered what she called 'sponsoring' from her male guild partners to be able to join them in offline activities:

*Lisa:* Well, you sort of become the little mascot. I've seen this in several contexts in different guilds. For example, in one hardcore guild I was in, the guild planned to meet one summer, in England, because the guild master owned one of those paintball/gaming halls where we could sit and play. And well, he wanted to pay my ticket so that I could make it there, because we were only two

> women out of 60 players. And when I said "Why, I can't afford it, I'm a student, I can't go to England for a week and pay for my living there"—then you know, "But we've got to have you with us". So you become kind of unique—just because you're a woman who plays.

As these stories show, being female in a straight, male-dominated, gaming context can carry advantages—which some users choose to utilize. General, an 18-year-old male guild member told me that in his previous guild, he had even pretended to be a girl in order to get the special treatment that came with being female. Other male guild mates who also take on the role of female characters, have told me about the advantages they get from players outside of the guild, players who do not know them, and who assume them to be female also in real life.

It may of course also be that these male players behave in certain ways when they play their female characters, which could explain the positive discrimination. I have, for example, observed Erik assume what I considered a very flirty attitude towards other players in pick-up groups. And I have heard David bragging about the way his female alt character manages to get various in-game items by appearing help-seeking and vulnerable.

The sense of receiving special treatment may also have grounds that go beyond gender. In my case, some of it may be explained by personal chemistry and by me compensating for my lack of routine with trying to show a nice personality and a good sense of humor—generally a useful strategy for new players (cf. Sundén, Chapter 5 in this book). The guild in which I did my fieldwork also was generally very friendly towards both old and new members. I, in turn, adopted this approach, and did what I could to reciprocate. Nevertheless, as Jerry, a young male guild member with a character roughly the same level as mine, once jealously remarked, it was generally a lot easier for me than for him to get help with group quests or to get people to boost me through instances, even though he, too, showed gratitude when someone helped him.

One first conclusion, then, is that the discrimination of female players does not need to be negative and excluding as it can also be positive and inclusive. As General explained: "The girls got this special treatment because the guys wanted them to be happy in the guild so that they'd stay there". Thus, as one of the female informants stated, even if one does not deliberately play on gender, appear help-seeking, ingratiating, or flirtatious, female players may get advantages anyway, just because of being women. However, this does not mean that they get favors for free: as will be shown, female players have to pay for the advantages they are given in other ways, in currencies that are not obvious, but where the prize may still be quite high. These currencies have to do with the specific values that they are expected to bring into the gaming communities, and the positions that they are expected to occupy.

## MAKING THE (GAMING) WORLD A NICER PLACE

In the analysis of the three forum discussions, interviews and observations, four themes emerged that point to values that gaming women are expected to bring to the gaming cultures. The first theme consists of the idea of women as being nicer and friendlier than men. In one of the discussions analyzed, one participant asked the others why they wanted to increase the number of female players. He was answered by arguments such as the following:

*Muziel:* because in general girls are much nicer than guys . . . (Goodgame)

This post was probably meant at least partly as a joke. Still, the idea of women adding a nice and friendly touch seems to be quite widespread, and I have seen various manifestations of it. During informal in-game interviews with male guild members, several of them have confided to me that they like it when there are female players in guilds and raids. With female players present, they say, the tone gets less aggressive in raids and the ambiance generally gets better—"nicer and more civilized". Williams, Consalvo et al. (2009) make similar claims. Their results showed that the female respondents claimed to be more socially motivated whereas the male players claimed to be more motivated by achievement. Female players also showed significantly lower levels of aggressiveness than male players, especially those who played with their romantic partner. Williams, Consalvo et al (2009) explain their findings with gender role theory, according to which women are encouraged to be social and caring, and to maintain relationships.

Not only are female players believed to make the gaming community a nicer place by being there and acting less aggressive than male players, but the presence of women in gaming communities, says one female interviewee, may also result in the guys monitoring their own behavior. What this recalls is a practice often used in schools—namely that of using girls as balancing elements, which, placed between noisy boys, can calm down entire classrooms (Walkerdine 1990). In my view, the way the male guild members talk about female participation has something to say about the way they see themselves and other male players—as troublemakers or unruly boys, unable to steer their behavior on their own without women to keep them on track. It also says something about the expected behavior of female players, and the ways they are being positioned.

A position, according to Harré and Langenhove (1999, 1–2) is "a complex cluster of generic personal attributes, structured in various ways, which impinges on the possibilities of interpersonal, intergroup and even intrapersonal action through the assignment of such rights, duties and obligations to an individual as are sustained by the cluster". 'Positioning' can be translated as the way others look upon an individual, or a group of individuals, how they talk about and treat them, or the way the individual or the group looks upon, talks about and treats itself. Thus, the concept can be seen as a more dynamic alternative to the concept of role (Langenhove and Harré 1999, 14). The position determines the way the positioned person is expected to act and what s/he can do. For example, someone who is positioned as incompetent in a certain area will not be accorded the right to contribute to discussions in that area, or at least, his/her opinions are not taken as seriously as someone who is positioned as more competent. Positions are also dependent upon each other, meaning that when one individual is positioned as powerful, others will fall into a position as powerless relative to the first one.

People can acquiesce in the way they are positioned, contest it or subvert it. To refer to such occasions, Langenhove and Harré use the terms 'first' and 'second order' positioning. First order positioning refers to the way persons locate themselves and others, by saying or doing things that make themselves or others appear as certain kinds of persons, or as holding certain rights or obligations vis-a-vis each other. When a first order positioning occurs, the positioned person can accept the way s/he is being positioned, for example by acting the way such a person is expected to act (or, when someone else is positioning him/herself, the persons before whom the positioning is done may accept it and act in accordance with the positioning being made). In these cases, the storyline will evolve without any questioning of the positioning. However, individuals can also object to what is said or done. In such cases, a second order positioning occurs in which the first order positioning is questioned and has to be negotiated. In other words, second order positioning happens when the first order positioning is not taken for granted by all of the persons involved (Langenhove and Harré 1999, 20). If those who object to the positioning then proceed to discuss it with other persons, this is referred to as 'third order positioning'.

Returning to the theme of women being positioned as 'nicer than men' and used as 'calming elements', one can ponder how fun women think it is to play a game where they are not allowed to be truly playful and let loose, but where their role is seen as to maintain order and create a nice atmosphere for the male players. The interviewee Paula reflects on the role of computer games for her, as a way of relaxing:

*Paula:* Well, my son has ADHD and it's good to get away from that reality for a while some times, you know. To forget about your troubles for a while.

*Malin:* Yeah? I can feel that too some times, as a mother of small children. To get a little time for yourself.

*Paula:* Yeah. I believe that this would be good for all women. Because unfortunately we live in this model that we conform, we want to please everyone and make everyone happy, and because of that we become worried and distressed. And then, to get that moment

> for yourself . . . You've only got to look at economy, if you're not so well off, as a woman you always see to that the others in the family get what they need first, above all the children. The woman always steps back. At least I do. But in any case, I take the time to just sit down and just care for myself for a while. Because it means so much.

In his book on masculinity and computer games, Burrill uses the concept of 'boyhood' which he defines as "the regressive nature of first-world, capitalist masculinity", which offers an escape away from the pressures of the external. Videogames in the 21st century, says Burrill (2008, 2), serve as "the prime mode of regression, a technonostalgia machine allowing escape, fantasy, extension, and utopia, a space away from feminism, class imperatives, familial duties, as well as national and political responsibilities".

Even if I do agree with Burrill on the potential of computer games to offer relaxation from the constraints of everyday life, I find his gendering of the concept 'boyhood' problematic. It is true that Burrill states that 'boyhood' can be accessed by anyone engaged in digital technologies, thereby opening up the position also for non-males. However, at the same time, he states that the position is articulated in the sense of fulfilling 'male' fantasies, which again excludes women. In Paula's case as described previously, for example, the games are definitely a way to escape the constraints of everyday life. But there is nothing male about her fantasies—they rather stem from a strongly female point of view.

The function of computer games as escape and relaxation is not and should not be reserved for men. As Paula's story illustrates, for many women too, computer games fill an important role as they feel they can get a moment of time for themselves, when they do not have to care for others. In this respect, games fill the same need as has been provided by women's magazines (Hermes 1995) or romance novels (Radway 1984). Computer games have indeed the potential for providing women with a room of their own,[2] where they can get some relief from their tasks and duties of everyday life. However, when they are inscribed into the 'nice position', with expectations on them to act nice and care about other people, much of the beneficial effect of the games for these women is lost. For some women, the reward that lies in being seen as 'good', 'calm', 'stable' and 'mature' persons may be enough, and they may accept the position as 'nice' and as calming elements. They may also be eager to fit into an appropriate female gender role. However, others may contest such positioning.

## THE PROBLEMATIC POSITION OF THE 'GUILD MOM'

In my fieldwork, I once experienced becoming subject to an unwelcome positioning of the kind described previously. I was talking to Miles, a

40-year-old male guild member, one of those who I had had most contact with, and who I felt that I had become friends with. We were talking about my role in the guild and Miles said: "Why, you've become sort of like a guild mom".

I did not take this as something positive, even though I know that this was the way Miles meant it. On the contrary, I remember the resentment I felt over being categorized as a mom. A *mom*, for Christ's sake, despite the fact that the person with whom I was talking was just about my age, that my raid performance was well in the same class as that of any of the other players in the guild, and that I had never done anything to keep order or shown any caring tendencies except just being nice and friendly in general. So why then should I be singled out as a mom? Was I not a co-player, participating on the same conditions as everybody else?

I imagine that for many other women too, this kind of positioning and the tasks associated with it resemble too much ordinary everyday life with its duties and obligations. Or, it may be that, like many others, I am inculcated into a certain way of looking upon mothers—as people whose whole existence circles around self-sacrifice and of being there for others without ever seeking any pleasure or fun for themselves (cf. Enevold and Hagström 2008, in their discussion of the discrepancy of the gaming mother and the Victorian ideal woman described as the "Angel in the house"). What I did in this situation was to contest the positioning that I was being subjected to, in a second order positioning towards Miles who put me in the undesired position, but also in a third order positioning in my discussions about the conversation with other guild members on later occasions.

Several months later, when going through my field notes, I started to reflect upon what it was in the concept of 'guild moms' that had made me feel so disturbed over the positioning. In order to find out what the concept really stood for, I discussed it with Dragon, a 27-year-old male guild member, who I had also heard using the expression, but in another context and in a negative sense. He attempted to explain it by giving examples from his previous guild experiences, and finally stated that a guild mom can be two different things. The guild mom is a female guild member who can be caring and see to that things work smoothly in the guild, that everyone does his/her job, that everybody is feeling alright and that the ambiance is good between all members. Or, she can be someone who wants to decide, one who meddles in other people's business and their discussions, and who wants to be at the center and have a say in all matters that concern the guild and its activities. If the guild mom is self sacrificing, she is seen as a good mother (or an 'Angel in the guild' perhaps), but if she aspires to power for herself, it is rather the fairytale image of the evil stepmother that emerges. It struck me that even though Dragon saw this as two separate ways of being a guild mom, I interpret it as representing two sides of the same coin. In order to see to the wellbeing of the group as a whole, the guild mom may sometimes have to meddle into the business of individual players, as well as make her voice heard in discussions. The guild mom is here seen from different perspectives—on the one hand, from the perspective of the group as a whole, and of weaker members in need of protection, and on the other, the perspective of the stronger members who the guild mom might try to steer away from their dominant position vis-à-vis the weaker members. However, the guild mom seems to be always seen from someone else's perspective, not her own, and furthermore, she often does not get the appreciation that should go with her efforts to satisfy the common good.

In my discussion with Dragon, I tried to develop the subject by asking if there was any male equivalent to the guild mom. Would it be possible to talk about guild dads? Dragon just laughed at my question and said, "No, no, that's not possible. That would be a guild master". The two concepts speak for themselves. A 'master' is one who manages and masters his environment, one whose authority is irrefutable. A 'mom', on the other hand, is a caring if meddlesome woman, whose authority is often contested. When I pointed out the injustice of male and female players being valued so differently for something that is basically the same job, Dragon told me, "In a way it's only fair, because female players get so many other advantages. Like it's extremely easy for you to get help from others if you need to".

In a way this is true. As was discussed in the introduction of the chapter, in a (straight) male-dominated gaming context, female players often do find it easier to get help from other (male) players, and I guess this can be seen as an advantage. But the situation can also be seen as part of a larger pattern, where the advantages that are available to women above all are found in situations where they find themselves in a weak position vis-à-vis the male players. The old narrative structure of the 'damsel in distress' never seems to cease repeating itself: in a heterosexual context, women are expected to be the vulnerable ones in need of protection and assistance, while the men are expected to be the strong ones who offer the protection and the assistance. Or, as Svahn says about ideals of femininity: "The weak woman, who needs to be cared for and protected by a man is considered a positive femininity. The man thereby gets his manliness confirmed. However, the opposite, i.e., a strong woman who wants to have her own way, tends to be a threat to the man's authority" (Svahn 1999, 122, my translation).

When girls and women make their voices heard and claim a space, this space is often apprehended as larger than it really is, by both men and women (Adelswärd 1991). If women do not keep a low profile, they appear as if they take too much space and/or are provocative (Svahn 1999). Men, on the other hand, are expected to take the leading positions and are accepted in them more easily, hence the problematic position of the guild mom. The woman who aspires to a leading position becomes positioned not as a master but as a mom—on the one hand her position is relatively strong, but at the same time she is put into question. During my fieldwork, I have, for example, heard several guild members talking about having left—or thought about leaving—previous guilds because of too dominant female guild members and leaders, but I never heard anyone question male members or leaders for being too authoritative. Of course, this does not mean that it never happens. There are likely male guild leaders who scare members away by being too authoritative too. However, when they do, it does not seem to be an issue that people discuss to the same extent—an authoritative style may be what is expected from them, or in any case it seems to be more tolerated than when a woman is experienced as being too dominant.

The subject of guild moms also came up in my interview with Lisa. Lisa had encountered the expression 'guild moms' in several guilds: one Dutch, one British and one Swedish. She, in contrast to Dragon, had also encountered the expression 'guild dads'. Lisa elaborated the definition by stating that a guild mom or dad is someone who may not be a guild leader or officer, but *who might have been*. It is someone who may be older than the majority, someone who is mature, stable and responsible, and influential in the guild. It is someone who other members want to point out as being special. From this follows that Dragon's comparison of guild moms with guild masters do not tell the whole truth. A guild mom may be a guild leader, but the epithet does not aim at her title, but her personality, and at the fact that she is influential, regardless of her formal position.

## "YOU WANT DADDY TO DO THE TANKING MOW?"

Looking closer at the concept of 'guild dads', I recall that I once saw Miles referring to himself as a 'dad' in his gaming activities. The specific occasion occurred during one of our LAN parties, where I made one of my very first attempts at tanking.

A 'tank' in gaming contexts is defined as "the front-line soldier built to tolerate heavy attacks and protect the other members of the group" (Corneliussen and Walker Rettberg 2008b, 294). Tanks are designed to have armor values high enough to make them survive attacks, and they use their abilities to force the enemy to attack them, which leaves the other members in the group free to attack the enemy without receiving so much damage themselves. The tank is thus, together with the healer, the most important character in raids and instances.

Until the occasion I am referring to, my character—a female night elf warrior—had been designed to play dps, i.e., I had been a plain damage dealer. However, when in the spring of 2009, Blizzard introduced the dual spec (i.e., the possibility of permanently having two different sets of abilities that one could easily switch between), I wanted to try the tank role too and see what it was like. Lacking previous experience, I was uncertain of how to do; I made mistakes and the group's progression was not as fast as it could have been. So when we got to the last and most difficult boss, the question was raised whether we should switch roles and let Miles (who had more experience) switch from healer to tank while I went back to my regular dps role. I remember Miles' way of saying: "Ok, you want daddy to do the tanking now?" Obviously, unlike my unwillingness to identify as a mom, Miles had no problems with referring to himself as a dad.

Burrill (2008) states that although what is happening on screen is not real per se, computer games require an investment in and a commitment to a type of masculine performance that is based on the real. This is visible in the occasion referred to previously. Here, characteristics ascribed to gender are reproduced from the RL world to the game world. In this specific situation, a 'daddy' seems to represent security, assurance, protection, and quite a lot of muscle power. In a way, these ideas of a dad are very similar to the role and tasks of a tank (however, see also Sundén, Chapter 6 in this book, in which she discusses tanks and tanking along the lines of female masculinity). It also seems as the role of the tank is the one furthest away from and hardest to incorporate into the ideals of normative femininity, a fact that is also reflected in female players' choices of classes. According to an American survey (Weathers 2008), female players primarily choose to play support classes such as healers or possibly ranged damage dealers (the most commonly chosen classes among female players are priests, druids and hunters). According to Duchenaut et al. (2006), priests especially are associated with femininity. Melee damage dealers—and most notably tanks—on the other hand, do not seem to be nearly as popular among female players. One explanation for this can be sought in Adams and Rollings' (2007) claim that women seek to identify with their avatars to a greater extent than men do. One possible interpretation is thus that women try to shape their avatars in accordance with prevailing gender ideals, which prescribe a nurturing rather than violent orientation in women.[3]

## COUNTERBALANCING THE LADDISH ATMOSPHERE

In my discussions with male guild members, several of them have told me that they feel that with female players, conversations can deal with other topics than gaming activities. Quite a few of them have also discussed sensitive topics with me, for example asking for a woman's opinion and perspective on feelings and relationships. This leads on into the second theme found: that of female players challenging masculine values.[4] According to the male guild members, the ambiance generally gets more 'laddish' and 'crude' when there are no female players in the guild and the raid group. When I asked Sergey, a 30-year-old guild member to develop what he meant with 'laddish' he was not able (or willing?) to formulate it in words. However, according to General, the 'laddish atmosphere' refers to diverse behaviors: misogynous, homophobic, aggressive, or just generally crude. In other words, it is the kind of practice that can be observed in other same-sexed contexts such as the military or in sports teams.

Jesper Andreasson is a Swedish sociologist who has studied how masculinity is 'done' and negotiated by the members of a Swedish handball team (Andreasson 2003). He uses Eve Sedgwick's (1985) concept of homosociality, which develops when men gather in same-sexed groups. The aim of homosociality is to create an intimacy between men by excluding that which is not defined as manly. The members strive at strengthening the experience of manliness within the group, while simultaneously drawing and maintaining firm boundaries against the 'Other', which is not included in the concept of manliness. The 'Others' in Andreasson's case were, above all, represented by women and gay men. In a first phase, according to Andreasson, the woman is excluded, and in the second, she is transformed into an object, a trophy, which reinforces the men's feelings of manliness and superiority. In a similar way, men who do not meet the ideals of hegemonic masculinity are excluded or ridiculed.[5]

In the male collective, Andreasson has observed a certain type of humor which is central and recurring. He sees such joking around as a way to deal with issues of masculinity and sexuality, by drawing boundaries. Homosocial relations must always be balanced between, on the one hand, the longing after male closeness, and on the other, the establishing of a marked distance from the closeness that is associated with homosexuality. Sometimes the male collective in Andreasson's study performed make-believe homosexual situations, where the homoerotic performances were interpreted as caricatures rather than real overtures. The strategy, says Andreasson, is to dramatize homosexual behavior, make fun of it, and defeat the threat that it represents by making it a spectacle.

Looking at the guild activities and their ambiance with the gaze of a woman who has managed to gain entrance into a game-space equivalent to a locker room, I recognize some of the practices that Andreasson writes about—but not all. In the guild, I seldom if ever saw any derogatory or openly sexist comments aimed at women. It may be because of my presence and that of the few other female members, or the guys may have internalized a politically correct perspective on gender, one that fits within the Swedish equality discourse (see, for example, Gemzöe 2004; Sundén and Sveningsson Elm 2007). Or, maybe Andreasson's picture of men taking every opportunity to run women down as soon as they are among other men is simply not accurate or applicable to all settings. However, if the men in the guild appeared to be respectful enough towards women, the kind of jokes and make-believe performances that make fun of homosexual desires and actions were abundant during raids and group activities, and in the guild chat. The following excerpt shows one such occasion where General, who is just about to graduate from high school, is pondering the current job situation.[6]

*General:* Let's see how long I have to stay at home before I begin to eat my furniture ;)

*Keilna:* what kind of job would you want??
*General:* Just about anything :p
*Dragon:* Pimp
*Keilna:* sounds nice
*Spurge:* you could clean my house, I'll pay you an awesome salary.. . . . you can have my bitch Bourbon whenever you want to
*Bourbon:* what the f . . . how the hell did my name get into your whoretalk =)
*General:* haha Spugge sure, I'll be right there
*Spurge:* he might have a few diseases though so be sure to protect yourself
*Keilna:* lol
*Dragon:* I guess you know that Spugge :P
*Spurge:* no, but I heard Boreal caught something last time
*Bourbon has demoted Spurge to Centurion.*
*Bourbon has demoted Spurge to Initiate.*
*Bourbon has demoted Spurge to inactive.*
*Dragon:* haha
*General:* hahaha
*Spurge:* hahaha

This excerpt exemplifies what Andreasson writes about: neither the woman nor the fag fits into the collective, and so they are symbolically disarmed and made innocuous so that the men can create a phallic domination which cannot be questioned by new sexual practices. The excerpt also shows an example of how the technology is used as a communicative resource, when Bourbon (who is one of the guild officers) demotes Spurge and takes away his guild rights (these rights were given back afterwards). When talking to Bourbon later, I learned that the situation was a bit more complicated than would be immediately apparent to an outsider observer: Bourbon may be a guild officer, but Spurgeon is his superior at work. Thus, even if the excerpt shows a jokey, playful situation, there may still be tensions and negotiations over RL power and agency lurking in the background, or maybe the existing RL hierarchy is what made this situation possible. After all, it is the RL superior, Spurge, who refers to his subordinate, Bourbon, as 'his bitch', even if Bourbon resists the positioning by taking advantage of his superior position in the guild hierarchy.

The guild members' gabbing on the guild chat and Ventrilo often included sexual innuendos, such as when one player's concentration and performance once was called into question by the phrase "Hey, do you still play with one hand in your pants?". Such bantering is also often used as a way for the men to show affection towards each other, such as when Gol and his friends yell: "Asshole!" to each other, or when General and Dragon, who are friends, go into name-calling, tell each other to "feck off" or pretend not to be on speaking terms: "goodnight to all except for Dragon".

In Andreasson's account, the kind of activities referred to previously is seen as a liberation, as a way for the men to 'be themselves' outside of the forced demands from wives and girlfriends.[7] Andreasson distinguishes between the actions that take place in public, in the handball field, and in the back region—in the locker room: "In the locker room, the men do not have to worry about the demands that they have on them outside of the club. Here, they can be boys who make jokes and take life easy. They find themselves in a back stage region where they do not have to feel threatened or called into question" (Andreasson 2003, 31). But, one wonders if this 'laddish' masculinity ideal is not just as forced and restrictive as the more politically correct one which is displayed when women are present. The statements from those of the male guild members with whom I have discussed the issue tend in this direction. Maybe it is a question of who the interviewing researcher is. It is likely that with a male researcher, especially one who is involved in the informants' activity and part of the subculture, informants would say that they like it when there are only men there, and that they appreciate the specific atmosphere created under such circumstances. With a female researcher such as myself, on the other hand, the statements may be biased in the opposite direction, so that informants say that in reality they do not appreciate the 'laddishness'. The truth is probably that the same-sexed environment holds both liberating and restraining elements. The male bastion may be experienced as liberating for some, but it may also be experienced as restricting and demanding by men who do not feel quite at home with the ideals of hegemonic masculinity. Even if hegemonic masculinity is something that they always have to relate to, these men will likely welcome elements that break or challenge it. Thus, at least some male players may see the presence of female players as a way to loosen up too strict masculinity ideals.

## HANDLING SOCIAL SITUATIONS

The third theme found deals with social situations and relationships within gaming communities, which female players seem to be expected to be more interested in and adroit at handling than men (for a more thorough discussion on this subject, see Sveningsson, Chapter 3 in this book). But the fact that women often focus on social situations and relationships does not mean that they always enjoy it:

*Ulrika:* When I played Diablo, sometimes I just had to stop talking. Some days I would make up my mind that "today I'm not gonna talk with anyone". Because as soon as I started to talk to people I kind of "hm, now I have to be nice to him" and I have to wait until he wants to play and so on.

*Malin:* You mean people you met in the game?

*Ulrika:* Yeah. Because when you start to play with people you get those tendencies—starting to care about other people, acting nice and so on. And then you're back in the real world. Because there, you always have to show consideration for other people and so on. And I think there may be a gender aspect here too, you know, women tend to be leaders in mmorpgs, they take those roles. They are over-represented as leaders in proportion to their numbers. And I believe it's because women have a tendency, when they get into contact with others, to take the responsibility for the relationship, you know.

Here, the interviewee is referring to the social expectations she feels are laid on her as a female player. These expectations exist as a power from outside, but are also, to a great extent, something that she has internalized as a woman. She has grown used to behaving in a certain way, in accordance with her gender (cf. Williams, Consalvo et al. 2009). In the gaming activities, this means that women players often take, or are given, the role as a listener, specifically in areas that deal with feelings and relationships (cf. Enevold and Hagström 2009). The informant quoted previously says that she, like other female players, may then sometimes choose to play alone to escape such demands and expectations (cf. Nardi and Harris 2006).

The phenomenon of women taking on the responsibility for social situations in gaming communities is nothing new but can be observed in all aspects of everyday life. In heterosexual relationships, it is more often than not the woman who does the relational work such as keeping in contact with family and friends, organizing birthday parties and holiday events, writing Christmas cards, buying the Christmas presents for both spouses' families and so on. Gaming communities do not seem to differ from the general picture. For example, when *Mercenaries* was to organize a RL party, the initiative came from the two female members:

> Now, I think this has dragged on long enough . . . all these anonymous friends of friends, who are they? What do they look like? How will I be able to tell their voices from each other at Ventrilo?
>
> 6th December is the plan. Seche enjoys fixing parties. We can use my parents' house. The plan is a party with some kind of fantasy-wow-theme, live-costumes appreciated. We'll make something to eat and drink, you can bring more drinks if you like. More thorough planning to be announced.
>
> Right now I just want signups. :P There's more than one month left so you should have time to get babysitters etc. if needed. Looking forward to seeing you.

The previous text was posted to the guild web site by Renee, one of the two female members at that time. Seche, whom she mentions, was the other one. At the time of the posting, both of them lived in relationships with two of the central figures in the guild; although being an officer, Renee also qualified as one of the key figures. The RL party took place and was all along planned and organized by these two women, and judging from the postings to the web forum, it was much appreciated by those who attended the event. A few weeks later, a new RL meeting took place in a pub. This time, the initiative was taken by one of the male members who had appreciated the previous RL party. However, despite an initial self-assured tone in the men's postings to the guild web site, only three of them eventually turned up, leading to this slightly sarcastic post from Renee:

> My, it's strange how people get ill all of a sudden ^^
>
> Bourbon and Miles on the one side and Dark on the other stood watching each other for 20 minutes without daring to say hi . . . the solution came when Miles got Gol to mms a photo of Dark :P
>
> Seche turned up and these four did their best to drink beer for the whole guild. Three hours later I joined them. Fun to get to see two new faces anyway!!

Judging from these two occasions, one could draw the conclusion that social events as related to guild life are mainly the responsibility of female members. The image one gets of the men is of them being shy and socially awkward characters, in need of female members to steer up their social life.

But upon closer scrutiny, the situation is not quite as simple. During my time in the guild, I have taken part in a few LAN parties organized by guild members in their homes, and also organized one myself. We would gather a group in one member's home, meet up with our computers by noon and play together during the whole day, evening and night, taking only short breaks for bolting down some hot dogs, beer and pizza. Occasions such as these are indeed social events too. Playing instances and raiding together in a MMORPG is a social activity per se, but so much more when the players share a physical space, crowding themselves and their computers, screens and cords together around a kitchen table, topping up with energy drinks and beer. In a way, it can even be described as intimate. So what, then, is the difference between these two types of occasions? What makes the men more willing to organize LAN parties than ordinary ones? And when the men do organize ordinary parties, why is it that they take place in the pub rather than in the members' homes?

As for the location of events, the home is commonly coded as a women's space, while public places have been more associated with men (Fullerton, Morie, and Pearce 2008; Lewis 1993; McRobbie and Garber 1976). This may be one reason why the RL party that was organized by a man took place in the pub, while the one organized by the women took place in the home. As for the LAN parties, it is true that they took place in the homes of the members. However, here the technology may be an important factor to consider. The technology can be seen as representing masculine values enough to outweigh at least some of the feminine values of the home.[8]

The two types of parties—the LAN party and the ordinary one—while both being social, are framed in slightly different ways. The way the female members organize more traditional parties with homemade food, candles, and nicely set tables, makes it possible for them to assume the roles of technologically skilled gamers, while still managing to keep up their normative femininity. Likewise, the connotations between LAN parties and masculine culture may facilitate the men's enjoying sociality and intimacy, while still acting in line with hegemonic masculinity (for discussions of how gender identity may be balanced, see for example Sveningsson Elm 2009). Nevertheless, the masculine values brought by technology did not seem to be enough, there was a need to add further ones. These were provided in an abundance of demonstrations of masculinity as manifested in a general roughness, lack of table manners, and in derogatory jokes about gay men and to some extent about women (had I not been there, there would surely have been more sexist jokes). I interpret both these demonstrations and the technology as something that may be used to legitimate the closeness and physical proximity between the participants in much the same way as Andreasson's handball players used roughness, misogyny and homophobia (see previous section). In his article on e-sport, Nick Taylor (2011, 236) is onto something quite similar. He describes how the physical space in e-tournaments is often very limited, and therefore, the young males' close proximity to each other is strongly 'policed' in order to maintain and reaffirm participants' heterosexual identities:

> At each event, participants negotiated the tight physical boundaries of the LAN apparatus by positioning themselves in ways that minimized intrusion into one another's spaces; their default posture during play seemed to be leaning forward in their chair, elbows resting on knees, head and neck craned towards the game terminal.

My observations made at LAN parties speak in the same direction. The computer equipment is given a prominent place, and is almost demonstratively used—it takes up more or less all the space on the table, and cords coil all over the kitchen floor so that participants have to navigate carefully between them to avoid tripping. In a way, the computer screens and other equipment can also be seen as walls being put up between the participants to prevent too much physical closeness. Thus, the LAN party demonstrates much of what was said about homosociality in the previous section—a longing for closeness between men that has to be balanced in various ways in order for the participants to still live up to the ideals of hegemonic masculinity.

## "GUYS LIKE TO FLEX THEIR MUSCLES BEFORE GIRLS . . ."

During my first months in the guild I asked a lot of questions about the game, and in return I received a lot of advice and assistance from my male guild mates. Now and then I worried that I asked too many questions and that people would get tired of it. Miles then assured me: "Don't you worry, guys like to flex their muscles before girls". This utterance leads us to the fourth theme, which deals with women as constituting an audience for the men's performances of skill.

It is said that communities require something that is outside of them, in order for the members to apprehend themselves as insiders (Sveningsson 2001). In the same way, in order for someone to appear as an expert, he needs others to demonstrate his expertise in front of. Here is where the women enter the picture. If the male or the masculine represents technical expertise, then the female or the feminine represents an absence of such expertise. This may be yet another reason why men enjoy the presence of female players—they represent an audience before which they can demonstrate their skills and their expertise.

Men's assumed technical expertise is actualized, among other situations, when they do favors for female players. Some of the informants have reflected on this practice:

*Ulrika:* But there's like the idea that women don't cope as well as guys. And then guys may help them by giving them diamonds and running after them and protecting them and so on (laughter).

*Malin:* OK, so you think that the positive discrimination is because they think women need help to manage?

*Ulrika:* Yes I do, but I also believe that the guys really want to be heroes you know. Even if a woman obviously isn't bad, because she's got good characters, you still might want to play the hero. You know, be the one who supports. So sometimes it doesn't need to be that they think the woman is weak, but that in some way, they want to appear like . . .

*Malin:* Like gentlemen?

*Ulrika:* Yeah, exactly.

By offering the female players helping hands, the male players position themselves both as players who are competent enough to be able to help, and as gentlemen, which is a type of masculinity that is often highly valued in Western societies. But at the same time as they position themselves this way, another positioning also occurs—that of the women towards whom they act. As Langenhove and Harré (1999, 18) point out, "Positions may emerge 'naturally' out of the conversations and social context. But sometimes an initial seizure of the dominant role in a conversation will force the other speakers into speaking positions they would not have occupied voluntarily". In this specific instance, this means that when the guys position themselves as competent helpers and protectors, at the same time they position the female players as individuals who are not capable of handling things for themselves, and who are in need of help and protection. In gaming contexts, this means that they are positioned as less competent players—even if they may be just as skilled as the men who offer the help. Through giving assistance, the guys also position themselves as helpful and generous, while the female player who receives the help is put into a debt of gratitude—she is expected to return the favor in some way, or at least show gratitude (for discussions on reciprocity, see, for example, Shibutani 1986). In this way a tie is created between the giver of the favor and the receiver.

If the woman accepts the help, she also accepts the positioning, as well as the demand for reciprocity. However, if she resists the positioning, a second order positioning occurs, in which the offered position is contested:

*Ulrika:* [ . . . ] like they feel this is the right thing to do, you know. I should help her because she's a woman and so on. Even if the woman plays really well. But this implies that the women play along, of course.

*Malin:* Yeah?

*Ulrika:* Because if you get sour, then it becomes really complicated. If people try to help you and you don't want the help, I've been into that a couple of times.

*Malin:* Yeah?

*Ulrika:* If for example . . . If you turn them away and clearly mark that "I don't want to", then people can be quite upset. And they think that: "Why, I'm just trying to help and what's the matter with you? I'm just trying to be friends". So they don't see their own actions from the outside, what they really look like.

This is something that I, too, have reflected upon, especially when I was new to the game and leveled up:

> I feel that right now it's not so fun to play with Erik. His character is at a so much higher level than mine. Being a hunter he also uses ranged weapons while I'm melee, meaning that he kills all the mobs before I even get to them. So what I do is basically just walk after him and loot. Last time we played, I even had to tell him, "Stop! I want to kill some of them too", because I didn't want him to do the whole quests for me. I guess that it's the same thing as Ulrika talked about in the interview, about guys wanting to be gentlemen, but this sometimes ruins your own experiences of the game. And then it's hard to say 'no' without hurting the feelings of people. (Field Diary, 10/01/08)

The informant previously quoted reflects upon what happens when she tries to resist her being positioned as in need of help, i.e., when she turns down men who are trying to help her in the game. What she does is not only to engage in a second order positioning to resist being positioned as less competent, but her resistance can also be seen as a new first order positioning, in which she appears ungrateful to the person who offers her his help. She then positions the male as a helpful, kind and misunderstood person who is a victim of misdirected feminism. Hence, the type of positioning of female players as less competent that builds on men's attempts to help them is one that is very hard to escape from.

There are many co-existing kinds of masculinity that relate to each other. Hegemonic masculinity has been defined as the kind of masculinity that is the most highly valued within a society, and the ultimate reason why men's superior position in relation to women can continue (Connell 1995). Characteristics that have been pointed out as integral to hegemonic masculinity have above all been connected to (physical) strength, hardness and toughness, speed and skill in certain tasks (Connell 1995; Frosh, Phoenix, and Pattman 2002; Laurel 2008; Svahn 1999). However, I hold that the 'gentleman' manifests just as much of a hegemonic masculinity as the tough guy, if not even more. As Holin Lin (2008) puts it, the treatment of female players reflects traditional gender roles in heterosexual relationships, with males as providers and females as dependent. The ultimate effect of men helping women is that it constructs them as weaker than men and needing help and protection. This indeed contributes to preserving men's dominance over women, even if the dominance is hidden within actions that appear respectful and caring.

The theory of hegemonic masculinity deals with relations and hierarchies between men. Heterosexuality has often been seen as central in the concept, leading to the importance men place on demonstrating their (sexual) interest in women. Being popular among women is one thing that increases one's status in relation to the other men, and so, the female companion in the online game becomes an attribute and a status symbol, especially in contexts where the women are few and far between. To return to the opening quote of this section, if guys like to flex their muscles before girls, it is because they like it when the girls notice their muscles and admire them—but probably even more so if they do it in the presence of other men.

## BRINGING FEMININE VALUES INTO GAMING COMMUNITIES

To sum up, there seem to be certain qualities that female players are believed to bring into gaming communities. Female players are believed to add a new and different perspective and may therefore enrich the gaming experience and make it more varied for the implied 'default' player, who is white, Western and male. Female players are also believed to make gaming worlds a better place—more friendly and civilized, and less 'laddish' (in the sense of being loaded with traditional masculine values such as hardness and toughness). For male players who feel uncomfortable with the rough sides of hegemonic masculinity, the presence of female players is here seen as valuable. Female players are positioned as being more interested in and are also assumed to take more responsibility for the social and relational aspects of the gaming activities than their male counterparts.[9] They often accept this positioning and do take on such duties, for example as guild leaders and officers, however, they do not seem to get full credit for it. Finally, being positioned as less technically skilled, female players may also serve the role of positioning the male players as technical experts, providing an audience in which the men can mirror themselves. The presence of female admirers will also likely strengthen the men's status in other men's eyes.

What the themes have in common is an essentialist view of gender. Despite the fact that both the participants in the analyzed forum discussions and male informants expressed a view of female players as being equally skilled (or at least with equal opportunities to become skilled if they have enough interest; (Sveningsson Elm forthcoming), different qualities are ascribed to men and women, and bringing in female players in the gaming worlds is seen as a way to incorporate such 'feminine' values. The specific qualities that are seen as feminine and are desired have to do with softness, nurturance and social competence.

Judy Wajcman (1991) brings forth some of the critique that has been raised against the essentialist perspective. First, she says, the values being ascribed to women originate in their historical subordination. The association of women with procreation, nurturance, warmth and creativity, lies at the very heart of traditional and oppressive conceptions of womanhood. According to Wajcman (1991, 8), nurturance, associated with motherhood, came to be culturally defined as feminine within a male-dominated culture. Rather than asserting some inner essence of womanhood as an a-historical category, Wajcman contends that we need to recognize the ways in which both masculinity and femininity are socially constructed and constantly under reconstruction.

It is a fact that women tend to be overrepresented as guild leaders, in relation to their numbers in online games (Yee 2009). It is also a fact that female guild members (including myself) seem to put much more time into the social aspects of guild life and to relational work with other guild members than most male members do (even if there are of course exceptions). If this depends on an inherent aptitude for and interest in social relationships, or if it is rather that they—we—fall into expected roles and positions, is hard to tell.

There are numerous ways in which the positions offered to women are challenged (which will be further developed later on in this book), but the positions are also often accepted. Maybe the position as a 'social engineer' is one of the strongest positions available for female players at the moment, and this is the reason why some women accept the positioning they are subjected to. Another argument for why women players accept such positioning is that these positions do carry rewards. After all, it is tempting to be put on a pedestal and seen as a 'good person'—an 'angel in the game' of sorts. However, accepting these positions may ultimately contribute to reconstructing old cemented gender hierarchies. It is true that women's entrance into male-dominated areas, in this case the computer game culture, seems to be viewed as something positive. All my data sets, and perhaps most of all, my own observations, pointed to lots of good will from the male players. Of course this is a good thing. However, men and women still end up falling into certain roles that follow patterns from the real world, where they are expected to act in certain ways and take up certain positions vis-à-vis each other. In the end, because of the male players' underlying rationales surrounding female players, and the positioning of female players, women's entrance in male-dominated gaming contexts may instead counteract their ultimate power and agency by inscribing them into positions that raise expectations regarding their behavior and ways of playing—expectations that are very similar to the ones we have tried to get rid of in the RL world.

## NOTES

1. Getting 'boosted' refers to a practice where a low-level character gets help from a high-level character to run through an instance to get loot and experience points fast and easily.
2. Using the phrase "a room of their own" invokes associations to Virginia Woolf's famous essay from 1929. Here, Woolf addresses the limitations that women writer's face, and argues that a woman needs a room of her own (as well as money) in order to create, think and write—actually to work. In my text, I have rather used the phrase "a room of one's own" to denote a space (physical and/or symbolical) where one can engage in leisure activities and relaxation. Maybe this is significant of how women's conditions have changed. At the time Woolf's essay was written, it was not self evident for a woman to be able to study, let alone spend time on thinking and writing. In most Western countries of today, access to higher education is seen as an evident right. However, what is missing for many women is the space and time to be alone, to engage in leisure activities, or just relax. Women, in their capacity of being women, have duties that result in a more restricted access to leisure activities in general, and to masculinity loaded activities such as technology and computer games in particular (Bryce and Rutter 2002, 2003a, 2003b, 2007; Delamere and Shaw 2008; Enevold and Hagström 2008; Holmberg 1993; Royse et al. 2007; Schott and Horrell 2000).
3. It is, however, important to keep in mind that there are cultural differences as to what can be incorporated into a normative femininity, and also that not all female players wish to conform to that. I, for one, am similar to the average female WoW player in certain respects (my characters are slender and beautiful night elves rather than stubby dwarves) but not in others. I prefer melee, plate-wearing classes, who deal physical rather than magical damage,

and after having started out as a dps I increasingly took on the role as a tank, even though I never came to feel fully comfortable with it.

4. The use of the concept masculinity can be criticized. Hearn (1996), for example, argues that the concept has often been used too widely, too imprecise, and in a way that conflates gender and sex. In the following text, masculinity will be understood as referring to the cultural construction of men as gender, or what is commonly associated with 'manliness' in the given cultural context.
5. The concept of hegemonic masculinity is defined as "the configuration of gender practice which embodies the currently accepted answer to the problem of the legitimacy of patriarchy, which guarantees (or is taken to guarantee) the dominant position of men and the subordination of women" (Connell 1995, 77). Hegemonic masculinity is the form of masculinity that is the most valued in a certain society at a given time. What is valued depends on the societal context, and what is hegemonic is therefore changeable with time and space. It is important to note that far from all men fit into the ideals of hegemonic masculinity, which should rather be seen as an ideal to relate to. As Connell (1995, 78) says, "hegemony relates to cultural dominance in the society as a whole. Within that overall framework there are specific gender relations of dominance and subordination between groups of men". Some masculinities are for example seen as complicit, i.e., consisting of men who take advantage of men's privileged position without themselves living up to the ideals of hegemonic masculinity. Other masculinities are seen as subordinated, i.e., those that are associated with femininity, among which homosexual men are the most obvious (Connell 1995).
6. The excerpt is translated from Swedish.
7. This perspective is quite similar to Burrill's (2008) view on computer games as offering men an escape from external demands.
8. Peterson and Munters (2007) are into similar thoughts when they conclude that the activities that constitute the play in The Sims are an equivalent to the dollhouse, and as such connote girls' play styles. Playing with a conventional dollhouse would often be seen as inappropriate for boys to do. However, because the activity takes place on the computer and in a computer game, attributes commonly marked as masculine, it passes without questioning.
9. Such ideas find support in a study by Yee (2006a), according to which female players are significantly more likely than male players to form stronger friendships in MMORPGs.

# 3 The Straight Game

*Malin Sveningsson*

In the previous chapter, I discussed some values that female players are often expected to bring into the gaming worlds, which can be described as dealing with softness, nurturance and social competence. At the side of these 'feminine' values, female players are adding other things to the game environments as well. For example, the presence of women in the gaming communities can sometimes also be seen as bringing romantic potentials.

Sexuality, romance, and the creation of romantic relationships in online settings have been addressed quite thoroughly (see, for example, Adamse and Motta 1996; Baker 1998; Daneback 2006; Kaufman 1996; Lea and Spears 1995; Schofield Clark 1998; Sveningsson 2002). To some extent, such research has been done in relation to computer games too. For example, for romance and sexuality in story driven games, it has been argued that they often follow strongly gender stereotypical patterns (see, for example, Burrill 2008; Consalvo 2003a). However it also seems to occur quite frequently that real players meet, fall in love and create romantic and sexual relationships in online games. Such encounters and relationships is something that researchers have begun to address (see for example Linderoth and Olsson 2010; Kroløkke 2007; Nardi 2010; Wu et al. 2007; Yee 2006a).

In this chapter, I will take a closer look at the *World of Warcraft* game world as a site for romantic and sexual encounters. I will specifically address the tensions and sexually charged situations that may occur between players who meet in the game, and the relationships that sometimes follow as a consequence. These encounters and relationships often have a great importance for the players' gaming experiences as a whole. As the chapter will show, they also fill an important function in the players' gender work, the regulating of norms of gender and sexuality, and ultimately in upholding gender hierarchies in the game.

## FLIRTING IN AZEROTH

When playing and moving around their characters in the game world, flirtatious behavior seems to be quite widespread among players, even though the extent and expressions may differ greatly between different player constellations. This is something that the female guild member Renee reflects upon:

*Renee:* Sexual innuendo and that kind of things is kind of a jargon, a way to express yourself. It doesn't occur so much in this guild—it may be that people blow kisses to female toons. But the flirtatious atmosphere and allusions to sex that I'm used to from previous guilds can be quite fun, it's a way to communicate. You know, there isn't much to build contacts on in WoW otherwise, but the gender of a toon or a player (if you know it) can be one such thing.

In her research on a male dominated MUD,[1] Lori Kendall found flirtation and sexual innuendo to occur quite frequently, suggesting that it offered a diversion that made the long hours by the keyboard easier to bear (Kendall 2002; 2009a). It is true that a 3D game such as *World of Warcraft* offers more diversion in the form of audiovisual content than did MUDs in their time. Still, flirts and sexual innuendo can be seen as a game within the game, something that enriches it, and adds a further touch of tension and excitement to the gaming activity. As Renee states, the flirtatious jargon can also be seen as a communicative resource that allows players to extend their means of communication just a little bit more in an environment that she sometimes experiences as too poor. I can see similar thoughts reflected in my own field diary:

> Something that I've found quite fun is that as you get to know people, the tone often gets more flirtatious. You always keep within the limits, like, both of you know that you're married and have kids so it's not like it's serious, but precisely this may be the reason why you can sometimes take the corners wide. Or if it's just fun to include some innuendo when you know that you're a woman and they're guys. Not too much, just a little. Anyway, this heterosexual game within the game is a potentially quite fun thing that may enrich the game further. Even if you're not after flirting or picking someone up. (Field diary, 12/28/08)

The in-game flirt can be staged in various ways. One common way is to let the characters act. There are various ways in *World of Warcraft* in which players can express themselves through their characters: through how they move around and how they use certain pre-programmed sequences, commonly called emotes. Emotes can consist of text, vocalization, character animation, or combinations thereof.[2] To use an emote, the player types an emote command, for example "/laugh". This makes the character laugh, at the same time as the chat display shows the text "NN laughs". If the player types "/shy" the chat display will say "NN smiles shyly" at the same time as the character looks down and shuffles his/her feet. The command "/silly" makes the character tell a joke. There are a number of pre-programmed jokes, which are created with respect to the character's gender and race. Likewise, the command "/flirt" makes the character say a pickup line, that too being constructed with regard to the character's gender and race.

The pickup lines are constructed after quite gender stereotypical patterns where the male characters are consistently more pushing than the female ones, even if there are certain races where the female characters show their intentions more explicitly. Symptomatically, it is the races whose appearance deviate the most from Western beauty ideals that do this. In her post-colonial analysis, Langer (2008) describes the tension between the two factions as that between familiarity and otherness (rather than good and evil). She demonstrates the similarities between the Horde races and the otherness as found in non-Western civilizations, reflected in the architecture and soundscapes of the races' territories, and the characters' names, accents and bodies. Langer also found the races of the Alliance to be closer to and the Horde races further away from Western beauty ideals.

Langer's argument about familiarity and otherness can be applied to gender and sexuality (which we discuss in the introduction to this book). In general, not only are the Alliance races closer to Western standards of beauty (even if the dwarves, gnomes, and the more recently added worgen can be seen as exceptions), they also behave in ways that are more consistent with normative femininity and masculinity. The Horde races, on the other hand (especially female trolls and orcs, and male blood elves) diverge from such ideals in ways that can even be seen as queer (see Sundén, Chapter 8 in this book). Hence, while flirting night elf females may say things like "If I wasn't purple, you'd see I was blushing", and "There's nothing like sleeping in the forest under the moonlight", the female dwarves may say: "I'll have you know I can flatten steel with my thighs", and the female trolls: "When enraged, and in heat, a female troll can mate over 80 times in one night. Be you prepared?"[3]

If one, while typing an emote, has another character marked, the actions appear to be directed to that character. So, for example, if another player marks my character and types the emote "/sexy", my chat display will show the text "NN thinks you're a sexy devil". Characters can greet each other, cheer, applaud, cry, make rude gestures, wave, bow, dance, hug, blow kisses and perform many other actions.[4] Players can also create their own customized emotes by typing "/e" followed by the action they want the chat display to show. When the player hits enter, the "/e" is exchanged for the name of the character. Thus, if, when playing my character Lore, I type the text "/e looks at the beautiful sky" and "/e thinks it's a wonderful day", the chat display will show the following text:

> *Lore looks at the beautiful sky.*
> *Lore thinks it's a wonderful day.*

The WoW emotes build on a heritage from text based MUDs—the customized emotes are even constructed in exactly the same way, with the command /e—but they clearly have a role to fill also in graphical environments, especially for communicating feelings and thoughts. Emotes are said to be used especially frequently by role-players (MacCallum-Stewart and Parsler 2008) and by people engaging in cybersex (Valkyrie 2011). In the latter case, creative re-interpretations may be done, so that emotes that were designed to depict certain acts are used to denote something quite different. For example, Valkyrie reports of users having found that if they sat down, facing another character, the emote /cry (which makes the character burst into tears) looked like giving oral sex. To make the new meaning more explicit, they could also accompany the animation emote with a customized text emote (as in "Player A goes down on Player B" (Valkyrie 2011, 84).

In previous online environments aimed at social interaction, such as MUDs and chats, flirtatious jargon was abundant, although the contracting parties were reduced to using only words. It is true that the words could be, and also were, used to describe actions. There are accounts of how MUD and chat participants made creative use of the language, creating make believe scenarios which researchers sometimes compared to improvisational theatre (Danet 1998; Danet, Ruedenberg, and Rosenbaum-Tamari 1998; Ma 1996; Reid 1995; Sundén 2003; Sveningsson 2001). However, the fact that in 3D virtual worlds such as *World of Warcraft*, players interact through characters, which they can watch and move around, implies a difference compared to previous, text based online environments and virtual worlds. The players can maneuver their characters and act vis-à-vis each other, both through words and spatially, creating a sense of embodiment which sometimes increases feelings of intimacy.

The visual environment and the game's soundscape are aspects that may affect the interaction between players, influencing the ambiance and adding an extra dimension to the game and its activities (Carr 2006c; Jørgensen 2009). In my own gaming, I have especially reflected on the soundscape's, notably the extra-diegetic[5] music's, potential of changing the ambiance. The melodies that are played as a background to various geographical areas in the game to a large extent contribute to their specific character: landscapes, cities and villages can be magnificent, menacing, melancholic, idyllic—and romantic (see also Sundén's discussion on these issues in Chapter 6 of this book). In most cases where the music has affected me, it has been when I have returned to places which I have not visited for some time. The music would then inspire me with feelings of nostalgia, transporting me back in time to experiences I have had in the game, and situations that I have shared with other players (see also Sundén, Chapter 5 of this book). But the extra-diegetic music can also create moods in that it frames the performed activity in various ways. In the following field note I reflect upon one such occasion:

> Often if you go on a quest together, just two persons, the situation can get quite intimate. And this can be further reinforced by the soundscape. As today when I helped Reilly in the caves near Grizzly Hills, the one with the giant spiders. It was especially one moment, we ran uphill in the tunnels after having defeated the spiders, and the music changed to string music. It felt just like being part of a romantic movie. (Field diary, 02/19/09)

The preceding quote may need some contextualizing. When I leveled up my character, I was one of extremely few guild members who did not have a max level character with which I could access endgame content and join guild raids to play with the others. Thus, with the exception of the times when guild members boosted me through instances or helped me with group quests, during my first three months I was mostly solo playing. When my main character was about level 50, I met Reilly, a 29-year-old Irish guy, whom I came to play with quite a lot over the following months. According to Yee (2006a), through requiring the cooperation between players, MMORPGs contribute to the strong potential for the creation of relationships. There may be some truth in this. In any case, it is clear that over these months, Reilly and I came to be quite close. Most of the time was spent questing, but while doing that we also talked a lot about life, by and large. At least I experienced a tension between us, but since we were both married, and in addition to that lived on different continents, the relationship was kept on an amicable level.

When the diary entry just quoted was written, I had just helped Reilly finishing a quest. As we ran up the winding path to get out of the cavern, the music suddenly changed from the menacing melody that belonged to the cavern, to the melody that belonged to the landscape outside of it. This melody was beautiful and idyllic, featuring string instruments, and it sounded like the classical lead motive to a romantic movie. As our characters ran beside each other towards the sun lit entrance of the cave, the ambiance at once changed from adrenaline filled combat to a romantic excursion in the forest. In my view, the impression of a romantic movie was further enhanced by the look of our characters. My companion's male character was a paladin of the race draenei—player choices of race and class that result in a large, muscular and powerful-looking character. My female night elf warrior, on the other hand, while wearing heavy plate armor, was still tall, slender and graceful in comparison. Needless to say, perhaps, these are body shapes that at least in a Western context are seen as suitable for men and women respectively, and judging from the looks of our characters, they would definitely have fitted into the standard model of protagonists of romantic movies.

When experiencing flirt and romance through a game character, one can discuss what it really is that one perceives. Other authors have described both the agency (Burn 2006) and the gaze (Burrill 2008, 55) of the player as being characterized by a doubleness:

> The player is seeing the self on stage, thus the gaze is returned from the stage in the form of a spectating (re)directed gaze, breaking the hierarchy formed in Western performance, and therefore, culture in general (sic!). The gazer is thus made unsure of whether she or he is the one doing the gazing. This indeterminacy is fuelled by the fact that the player looks on to the avatar who (that?) is in turn looking into the world of the game, a world filled with objects that return not only the gaze of the avatar but the gaze of the player. This double reflexivity can create levels of desire and anxiety that would not only split the subject but cleave it into two, into a purely gazing entity and a purely gazed entity.

Even though I do not agree with Burrill's generalizations of Western culture to culture in general, the previous quote is interesting in other respects. In her article from 1975, Laura Mulvey writes about what she terms 'the male gaze' in film, arguing that the cinematic apparatus generally puts the spectator in a male subject position, while female characters on screen are seen as mere objects of desire. Mulvey has received criticism due to the heteronormative bias in her theory. As we write in the introduction to this book, a queer perspective opens up possibilities of the function of the female body in films and games other than that of being eye candy for male spectators. Still, Mulvey has an important point when she writes about women's 'to-be-looked-at-ness' that can be observed in media. This is also a perspective that many women appropriate in their everyday lives, practiced in a habit of constantly placing them outside of themselves, in the position of the spectator, to figure out how others experience them. As John Berger (1972, 45) puts it, "Men look at women. Women watch themselves being looked at". Thus, the double gaze that Burrill is referring to may not be so new after all—women have always in some sense had to handle this double, almost schizophrenic, state of at the same time looking and watching themselves being seen. However, judging from the quote, it seems like in computer games, men too have started to experience this state.

The double gaze of the player means that when flirting through characters, there can sometimes be a fuzzy boundary of whether it is oneself who is the one flirting, or if one is rather only a spectator who watches a romantic scenario happening on the screen, just like a movie, in which characters flirt and interact with each other. In a way, flirting through the character and through emotes can also be seen as a safe way to express emotions without really risking anything (see also Nardi 2010). The physical player is protected behind the screen and the character, and can easily explain away the flirt saying that "it was only for fun", "it was part of role-play", or "it was the character who flirted—not me". However, it should be noted that 'virtual' interactions can have 'real' repercussions, as was discussed already in 1993 by Julian Dibble in his article on rape in cyberspace (Dibble 1993). As the chapter at hand also will show, what happened to my character in the game, or rather, how I/my character was treated by other players, was something that I felt very strongly about. Thus, depending on the extent to which players identify with their characters, their online interactions cannot that easily be separated from their real life identities and feelings.

Not only the player as a subject is troubled with this double state, but also other players/avatars with whom the player interacts. In his research on construction, representation and commingling of gender identity on a German *World of Warcraft* server, Schmieder (2009) shows how the linguist markers of gender (for example pronouns and inflected forms) were used in an inconsequent way—sometimes they reflected the gender of the player and sometimes that of the avatar. To describe this amalgam state, Schmieder uses the term "player-avatar-hybrid". In Chapter 5 in this book, Sundén leads a similar discussion, when reflecting on the target for her romantic feelings. Who or what was it really that she was in love with? Was it the player she had met offline, now being mediated through the game and through the character? Was it the game, with its richness of experiences and meetings? Or was it the character itself—who at that time was much stronger and powerful than herself, a figure to look up to and admire?

During my years as a player, I, too, have had romantic feelings for other players. In most of the cases I was not attracted to the physical person. My feelings were mostly concentrated to the game context and the avatar. Of course, as in other online romance, personality played a great part (Sveningsson 2002), and in one case, I was attracted to the voice, as I heard it on voice chat Ventrilo. But in addition to that, looking at it systematically, I see that the attraction I felt was in most cases for players who had more experience than I and whose avatars were stronger than mine. I felt admiration for the abilities of the avatars, powers that my own avatar did not have at the moment. But above all I admired the unhampered way with which the more experienced player carried himself and his avatar through the game space and its challenges. Thus, inside the game the avatar can sometimes replace the outward form, and a well geared and well played character can provide the player with an attractive appearance (cf. Tronstad 2008).

## DATING IN DALARAN

My observations were made on an RP server, i.e., a server where many players engage in role-play. Role-playing inside the game means that players take on the role of their characters, think out a background for them, and, in general, try to talk and act as if they were their game characters (see, for example, Bennerstedt 2008; MacCallum-Stewart and Parsler 2008; Mortensen 2008, 2007). However, far from all players on RP servers actually do role-play, but there are other reasons to join. Talking to original members of *Mercenaries*, I learned that the main reasons why the guild moved to this server was that it was less densely populated than the one where the guild was first started, and the players' average age was higher. The tone is generally also said to be more civilized on RP servers (cf. Bennerstedt 2008).

In the previous section, I discussed how I got to know the player Reilly. When we met, our characters were roughly the same level, and we had been playing the game for the same amount of time, so both we and our characters were quite evenly matched in abilities and skills. We also had the same degree of gaming interest, meaning that we would stay attuned with each other as we leveled up. In the course of three months, we went from level 50 to 80, questing and doing instances together. Once we reached max level, however, belonging to different guilds that required our attention, we drifted apart, although now and then, we would still play instances together. After one such occasion, around midnight on a summer's night, Reilly took the initiative to another in-game activity:

*Reilly whispers:* r u off now or not?
*Lore whispers:* staying a little while longer
*Reilly whispers:* cool me to
*Reilly whispers:* u know what, we havent done any RP me and u
*Lore whispers:* thats because i dont rp :-)
*Reilly whispers:* Y?
*Lore whispers:* dont know
*Lore whispers:* guess im more of a raiding person :-)
*Reilly whispers:* wana give it a try u can pick the topick
*Lore whispers:* ok what the heck, let me get a dress and we can go get sth to drink.

I do not belong to the role-playing population of the server, but have mostly seen that activity as slightly silly and as something that would have taken valuable time off what I saw as the essential parts of the game, i.e., playing my characters to max level, and then successively through participations in raids acquiring better and better equipment, at the same time as increasing my own player skills. However, since I was playing on an RP server, I said to myself, I should at least give it a try. It might be a valuable experience and I should try it at least once in order to learn more about the game world in which I did my research.

Inspired by others that I had observed role-playing, I changed my regular plate armor for a dress, which had no armor values at all, but was used solely for the sake of the appearance of it. I had once received it as a quest reward and saved it in the bank for future use. The dress—a "lovely black dress"—was very low cut and revealed more of my character's skin and shape than I was used to, and to be honest, I felt quite uncomfortable with it (cf. Taylor 2003b; 2006b). It is possible that Reilly interpreted my choice of clothes as a choice of topic for the role-play, something that steered the role-play in a flirtatious direction. Or, it may have been his intentions from the start.

Our first stop was a lawn in the city of Dalaran, where we headed for a picnic. While getting there, Reilly walked behind me/Lore, and while doing so, he commented on her body, especially her behind. Even though it was all compliments, I still did not like that he was watching and commenting on my/Lore's rear and asked him to stop (which he did not do). Here, the connection between player and avatar is again evident. I guess that some may consider it irrational of me to become annoyed by the fact that another player commented the body of my game character—after all, it was not *my* body that was the focus of the attention. However, apparently, an identification occurred between me and my character, which made me feel ill at ease with getting the shape of my bottom appraised (or praised) (see also Sundén, Chapter 6 in this book, where her informants expressed the bond to their characters as a matter of identification and desire). I was also disturbed by Reilly's behavior, which I at the time found quite sexist. I had never experienced this side of him before, when our shared gaming activities had focused on goal-oriented gameplay and chatting about RL issues. Here, one can draw connections to Burn's (2006) discussion on identification between player and avatar. Drawing on socio-semiotic theory, Burn distinguishes between three layers in a game: representational, interactive and organizational. Using a quote from an interviewee as example, Burn illustrates that when the interviewee talks about the narrative parts of the game (representational level), the acting subject is the character (as in 'he' does so or so). However, when the interviewee starts to talk about aspects of the game that are more focused on gameplay (interactive level), she switches so that the acting subject is the player (as in 'I', or 'you' do so or so). If one looks at role-play as being closer to the narrative aspects of the game than to gameplay, this may give a clue to what I saw as a changed behavior from Reilly. It may very well be that while in his gameplay mode, he thought of his offline self as the acting subject, and thus acted in accordance with that role. When in the more narrative mode of role-play, however, it was rather his character, or an amalgam between the two, a player-avatar-hybrid, who was the acting subject: a subject that could take more liberties. This model can also be used to explain the fact that Reilly had always acted nice towards me, but now suddenly I found him behaving like a male chauvinist towards my avatar. Maybe he saw us as two separate entities, as two different persons. I, Malin, was a respectable Scandinavian researcher, while Lore was a scantily clad female game character and, as such, fair game.

On the other hand this may all be over interpretations. Role-play is role-play, and one of its essential purposes is to open up for the engaging in activities and perspectives other than what one would normally do (Tynes 2007). Role-playing also carries a multitude of conventions. Especially in role-play that takes place in fantasy or medieval-like settings, it is relatively common to see gender roles being exaggerated, transported and displaced to something quite stereotypical, in line with an imagined past (Åsberg and Axelsson 2007). Despite the fact that Blizzard has designed male and female characters to have identical sets of strengths and abilities, this seems to be true for role-playing in *World of Warcraft* too. Thus, as I had noticed when doing group quests with role-players: even though Lore was a hard hitting warrior in plate armor, the male characters would still adopt a chivalrous attitude; addressing her as "fair lady", and saying things like "the forest is dangerous and full of beasts, but with us you will be safe".

Returning to my role-playing date in Dalaran, while sitting on the lawn, a male blood elf character approached and started to hang around us. Either he was curious of what we were doing, or he may have wanted to sabotage for what he thought of as silly role-players, who, in addition, belonged to the opposite faction. Annoyed as I was over Reilly's behavior, I started to make emotes to the blood elf character, like flirting and blowing kisses to him. I also wrote a few customized emotes, such as "e/ thinks kell is kind of cute" and "e/ has never met a blood elf before". At that time I did not know that the player behind the blood elf character would not be able to read my customized emotes,[6] but Reilly did, got sour, spat on the blood elf and made rude gestures (by using standard emotes). I told Reilly that there's for going on about my behind.

Here, something could be said about my way of trying to resist the sexist comments that I felt I was being subjected to. On the one hand, I did make an effort to signal my discontent with the way I/Lore was treated. While still trying to speak in-character and continue with the role-play, I ended up acting out another female gender stereotype—that of the scantily clad temptress who flirts around and turns men against each other. Thinking of the situation now, almost two years after it occurred; I realize that there were a number of other ways in which I could have resisted the sexist treatment while still staying in character. I could for example have objected by targeting Reilly, and written emotes like "/disappointed", "/angry" or "/slap", which would have resulted in the text "Lore frowns with disappointment at Reilly", "Lore raises her fist in anger at Reilly", and "Lore slaps Reilly across the face. Ouch!". For some reason these alternative options never came to my mind. One reason is that at that time I was not familiar with all emotes. But I was also faced with the same paradoxical situation as is often the case in real life. In order to keep in line with normative femininity, a woman needs to keep a low profile in sexually charged situations, and not appear too promiscuous. At the same time, normative femininity prescribes a civilized, pleasant and pleasing conduct (Ambjörnsson 2004; Bäckman 2003; Svahn 1999). The awkward balance between these instructions is obvious—because how does one reject sexual advancements without being seen as rude or disagreeable? The situation is especially awkward when the man who makes the advancements is a friend. The solution, as in the case described previously, is often found in escaping to evasive maneuvers.

I never got to feel comfortable in the role-play, so after a while I steered the conversation out of it. Talking out-of-character, the commenting on my/Lore's body ended. However, the conversation continued to have a flirtatious undertone. When after some time I had to log off, Reilly asked me if I wanted to be his 'WoW girl friend'. When I objected that we were both married, he answered "what you don't know doesn't harm you", and that "everything would be kept solely in-game, over the waist and respectful". I know that it is not uncommon for players to have such arrangements, and it was not the first time I was asked by a player to be his WoW girlfriend. Such in-game relationships may be part of role-play, and is then something that is only performed in-game. Or it may be a way to form closer bonds with a player of the opposite sex, to get an in-game companion (which will be discussed further in the end of this chapter). However, I have always been a person who takes things that happen online quite seriously. While it is true that the interaction between *World of Warcraft* players takes place inside a game world, and while many of the activities circle around fictional stories, I personally see other players, the interaction and the relationships that can be created to them as definitely real. So, in a situation where some players would have let go and role-played a make-believe in-game romantic relationship, I declined. At the time, I lacked the attraction that I felt was necessary to enter into a romantic relationship. I also saw our RL commitments as a hindrance. In the end, my way of understanding player interactions meant that I did not find such an arrangement respectful to any of the persons involved.

I interacted a lot less with Reilly after the incident than I had done before. Just then, I did not think of it consciously, but now, while writing this, I realize that it was at least partly because of the role-playing date and the awkwardness I experienced in it. When I was close to publish this text, I asked for Reilly's permission to tell the story, and sent the text to him. He was then shaken to learn how I had experienced the situation, apologized and said that he had no idea that I had become offended. This illustrates very clearly how players may sometimes experience and interpret situations in quite different ways, which may sometimes be related to their gender and their previous gendered experiences, but also to their ways of understanding the game world and the interaction that takes place in it.

## WHEN BOUNDARIES ARE TRANSGRESSED

It is probably without risk to say that all players who are known to be female at least at some occasion are met by romantic or sexual advancements by other players in the game. These advancements may be of various kinds on a continuum—from 'innocent' flirt, to pickup attempts or sexual harassment. Players may be serious or not in the advancements, they may mean to keep the romantic or sexual liaison solely between characters in-game, they may have the intention to include the real person or eventually even take the relationship offline. At least some of these situations are experienced as fun by at least some female players, who welcome the attention and the added tension to the game activity. But the line between flirt and harassment can be thin, and as stated previously, the situation may be perceived differently by the different persons involved. This is illustrated in the quote from my field diary, referring to an experience I had during my first few months as a player:

> Yesterday, I wanted to do this instance Sunken temple, so I entered a group with Reilly and three other guys from his guild. At one occasion something strange happened. After having taken down the first boss we sat down for a mana break, and one of the guys started to talk about seeing naked persons,[7] and he said that it looked nice. I felt slightly uncomfortable, so much more since an instance is a secluded area that no other players can enter at the same time.
>
> My feelings of discomfort grew stronger as his character started to flirt and dance with mine. Some of the other guys joined as well. I do know that this habit of letting your characters dance is something that players often do when they wait for each other and want to kill time between the boss fights, at the same time as signaling that they're ready and waiting. It's like rolling your thumbs actually, or tapping you fingers against the table. But I still felt uncomfortable and exposed, being the only woman in the group. Finally, I said to myself that enough of this, and if they don't stop, I'll just leave the group or log off. So I/Lore stood up and said "Hey, did we have work to do here or what?" That made them wake up and after that there were no problems. We went through the instance and killed all the bosses.
>
> When we were leaving the instance, the guy who had been talking about the naked persons and I were the last ones to leave. When we were to teleport out of the instance he blew a kiss to me. I chose to just let Lore wave back and bow. He let his character bow too, and wrote "I guess that will have to do'". At a later occasion, I discussed the event with Reilly. He said that this guy always goes on like that and that I should not take it personally. But then, how should I take it? (Field diary, 11/12/08)

In the preceding field note, it is obvious that this specific player and I experienced the situation in very different ways. What for him was a playful use of the environment and the game's built-in means of communication, became for me an awkward or even menacing situation. This partly has to do with the fact that at that time, I was relatively new to the game. Being a newbie was for me tightly associated with feelings of insecurity, and of anxiety of making mistakes and not performing well enough, at least in the more demanding situations of playing instances and raids in groups (cf. Taylor 2010). This means that my approach was often defensive, and I felt tense and vulnerable already from the start. This was especially the case since I was the only woman playing with four men I did not know (although at the occasion, I had met and quested with Reilly a couple of times before).[8]

As a beginner I was also unfamiliar with the gaming culture and how players behave in the game. I did not know that the kind of situation described before is quite common and would be considered perfectly normal within the game. At the same time, players' experiences of the game are absolutely gendered, in that their previous experiences (both online and offline) form a basis for their reactions. A male player in this situation would probably not feel exposed the way I did, even if he had been a newbie.

The preceding situation is not my only experience of being exposed to unwanted advancements in the game. In the following field note, for example, I had just created a brand new alt character, one that I planned to use at a LAN party with my closest guild mates:

> I had just created a new character, a human rogue with long black hair in a pony tail, and I had just started to learn how to handle her in the starting village. After a while, a male character that I had never met before approached me, and asked me if I wanted to strip before him. I had never experienced such things before in the game, although I had heard of similar events from other female players. I was first consternated, but quickly came to my mind and answered: "Are you totally fucking out of your mind?" Then I continued fighting the quite harmless monsters that meet players in the starting village. After a while, I saw that the player had managed to persuade another player with a female character to undress; she was standing there in her underwear. (Field diary, 12/18/08)

The Internet and its online arenas have often been described as liberatory places, where constraints and prejudices can be overcome. This perspective has been criticized by for example Brookey and Cannon (2009). In their study on *Second Life*, they demonstrate how users employ their agency to create content that reproduce, or even exaggerate traditional gender roles, where female avatars are consistently shaped to be available and submissive in sexual contexts. It is true that all this takes place on a voluntary basis. However, Brookey and Cannon point at the problematic issue with this voluntariness, both in terms of what kind of content is made available (and affordable), and the opportunity for male users to create female avatars solely for the purpose of exposing them to sexual violence and other humiliating acts. It is true that a sandbox environment such as *Second Life* does offer greater opportunities for users to influence the environment and create objects, thus it has a greater variety of items that are symptomatic of the objectification of female avatars than *World of Warcraft* has. Also, *World of Warcraft* is not only a virtual world, but first and foremost a game, whose focus of game-related goals makes sexual encounters a side effect, or a diversion from the ordinary gameplay.[9] Still, despite its focus on gameplay, *World of Warcraft* shows plenty of occasions where female avatars are objectified and assumed to be available to sexual advancements, just as *Second Life* and other virtual worlds. For example, according to Valkyrie (2011), male players' performances of hegemonic masculinity included blatant advances towards female avatars (who claimed a female IRL gender identity):

> Comments such as "Strip bitch," "Get naked," "Dance whore," and "Show me your boobs" were common forms of expressing desire toward female avatars. The scripts in the virtual world paralleled the hegemonic constructions of male and female sexuality in the solid world: men are aggressors and supposedly initiate sex while women are required to act reserved and encouraged to carefully choose their partners (Valkyrie 2011, 88).

When I look back at the preceding field notes, about two years after I first wrote them, I see both situations in another light. When they occurred, I had only been playing for a few months. Looking at the field notes in retrospect, I almost find it hard to believe that I took things so seriously, and that my reactions were so strong. I remember that at both occasions, I felt very ill at ease, even though, as the field notes show, I tried to put up a tough façade.

In certain respects, my change of perspective has to do with my development as a player, which is reflected in the development of my character(s). My main character is, at the time I write this, a top geared warrior, who would certainly not be asked by a stranger to strip. Her level, and notably her gear, signals that she belongs to an experienced player, one who has repeatedly played the most difficult raid instances of the game. The guild name tag shows that she is not alone but has friends in the game world.[10] On the other hand, had I played a low level character, moved around clumsily, and acted as if I did not quite know what to do, I might very well be targeted again. Still, the fact that I now have several max level characters and have gained more gaming experience has given me the self confidence I did not have when the field notes were written. Had any of my characters been asked to strip today, I might get disturbed over it, but not intimidated.

Nardi (2010) suggests that male players sometimes choose to play female characters as part of 'girl-watching', something that they do alone when watching their characters during play, but also together, as players watch each other's female characters. The in-game strip tease may be one manifestation of this. Over my three years as a player I have seen several such scenarios, to the point where I have ceased to react. I still do not like it when players with female characters offer to let them strip for in-game money (sometimes as part of a role-play). But nowadays I see it more as a nuisance than an offence. One can say that I have learned to see the gaming culture from within, and know how to interpret things—what is significant and what can be ignored. But in this 'normal culture' lies a number of values and world views, which I have also grown used to. One can wonder which of the perspectives is better to have as a female player: is it to be a beginner, who holds low status in the game, but who still has a clear view on how gender hierarchies are enacted in the game, or is it to be an experienced player, who is respected by other players but has largely grown blind to such aspects and take them for granted without opposing them? If we, for example, go back to my statement that the first of the preceding scenarios is a perfectly normal one within the gaming cultures, one could ask how it became seen as normal to make constant passes at female characters, especially those whose players are known to be female in real life. Here the boundaries that constitute what is normal are clearly being pushed to reflect the interests of the dominant group (i.e., the male players).

Delamere and Shaw (2008) write about gender in relation to first person shooter games. They state that female characters are often subject to a sexualized objectification and abusive behavior. Female players, too, they say, are frequent targets of abusive behaviors and discriminatory actions during game play. Male players may engage in abusive verbal comments in the form of 'trash talk', which often center on sexist, homophobic and derogatory remarks related to non-hegemonic traits (examples provided are "you pussy" or "you fucking faggot get out of my way") (see also Nardi 2010). Female players, on the other hand, are much more likely to be the targets of both verbal and other forms of abuse. The talk and actions of some of the male players, say Delamere and Shaw (2008), result in a stigmatized environment that female players have to negotiate in order to happily play.

Even if Delamere and Shaw's account reflects one part of the gaming culture, it is important to take into account the context in which the gaming takes place. The way female players are met partly depends on factors such as game genre and gaming scene, for example if the gaming activity is casual or hardcore and how competitive the level is (Sveningsson Elm forthcoming). Specific player groups (and specific players) also differ much in their general attitudes towards female players. The context that Delamere and Shaw studied was a very competitive one. The context in which I gather my material may be competitive insofar as it is quite focused on players' performance, but it also stresses the importance of the game as a social environment. The specific game culture of *World of Warcraft* is also described by informants as considerably nicer and kinder than that of many other games, where especially shooter games are pointed out as being hostile towards both female players and newbies (cf. Nardi, 2010). In my gaming, I have never experienced, nor heard of, any really serious harassment or attacks at female players, such as those that Delamere and Shaw report of, or that those of my interviewees who play first person shooters told me about. That being said, there are certainly occasions when I as a female player have experienced how boundaries are transgressed and one's integrity is violated, just because one is a woman. The excerpts from the preceding field diary notes show two such occasions. Why on earth would I want to strip before a perfect stranger, even if it was not me but only my game character? And what gives 'him' the right to ask me about it? Another aspect that is interesting to discuss is what he would get out of it. My game character is not a real woman but only an assembly of polygons. Moreover, the graphic rendering is not very advanced, and the resolution is quite low. There are also limitations as to how much characters can undress—they will always have their underwear on. In the end, undressed characters look very much like cut-out dolls.

One can speculate in what it is that makes it so fascinating and titillating to get another (female) character to undress. Or, for that sake, what is the allure of real life strip tease. It is likely that it is not the nudity per se that is the main thing, but rather the enticement lies in the fantasy, and the sense of power and control that the strip tease may inspire the spectator with. It can also be seen as a reflection of gendered power structures in society and gendered expectations, where men are expected to be the predators who take sexual initiatives while women make up the prey and are expected to be available to romantic and sexual advancements (see also Brookey and Cannon 2009). Such structures, setting up conditions for how men and women should relate to each other, are surprisingly tenacious and hard to get rid of. As Fiske (1989, 4) states, as in culture as a whole, in popular culture too, power is unequally distributed among categories based on social differences such as class, gender, and race. Popular culture therefore always "bears within it signs of power relations, traces of the force of domination and subordination that are central to our social system and therefore our social experience".

## SELF DISCLOSURE AND SOCIAL CONTROL

The game with its characters and milieus can be used to stage various forms of meetings, including romantic ones. But flirts are also carried out through written messages between players, in their capacity of 'real', physical persons, through public channels such as the general chat, semi-public such as guild chats or party chats and through private whispers.

In the first excerpt of this chapter (p. 61), Renee states that flirt occurs relatively seldom in *Mercenaries*, compared with what she was used to from previous guilds. This can have several reasons. One explanation is proposed in the composition of this specific guild, being made up of individuals who have relationships to other players, which precede and exceed the gaming context. No one knows everyone, but everyone knows someone, and most members have RL connections to at least some other members. According to Renee, this may lead to a situation where people are cautious about what they say to other guild members, and what kind of information they disclose about personal situations, feelings and opinions—because what one says may eventually reach the ears of the wrong person. I for one, had a RL connection to Erik, whose partner knew my husband. Thus, even if Erik was my friend, there was still a risk that what I said or did in the guild would leak out and get to my husband's knowledge. Many of the other players had similar relationships—they were connected to each other through friendship, kinship or through their places of work. This lead to a social control—for good and bad. Serious conflicts were few and far between, as was unpleasant behavior between the members—those who misconducted themselves disgraced not only themselves but also their friends who had first introduced them to the guild. The drawback with this social control is of course, as Renee also points out, that it lead members into being less open-hearted vis-á-vis each other.

In the 1990s, Internet environments were often claimed to lead to decreased inhibitions and increased self disclosure (Dubrovsky, Kiesler, and Sethna 1991; Lea and Spears 1995; Sproull and Kiesler 1991). Some positive consequences that were stressed were that users could become close to one another, and that they disclosed personal information to a greater extent and much sooner than in RL meetings (Sveningsson 2001; 2002; Van Gelder 1991). It was also believed that people would be assessed for their personality and the strength of their arguments, rather than for outward signs of success. More recently, these thoughts have seen a revival in the context of game research. For example, Linderoth (2008) talks about the opportunity that online games offer for people to be judged for their internal rather than external sides. And in a study about player motivations, Yee (2006a) found that the respondents claimed to display a higher degree of self disclosure towards friends in the game than to real life friends.

It is true that computer-mediated communication to some extent can inspire users with a sense of being protected behind the screen, making them more daring to say and do things they would not have done in 'real life'. Nonetheless, as I have argued previously (Sveningsson 2006), I hold that it is not the medium per se that is the only, or even the most important reason why users' inhibitions decrease. What is crucial is instead the extent to which users are anonymous or known by each other. Those who know other members of a group and interact with them on a regular basis have reason to conduct themselves in a way that allows them to continue to interact with the group (cf. Sveningsson 2001). This applies if users are only known by their user names (what Donath 1999 termed 'pseudonymity'), but even more so if their RL identity is known and they share circles of offline friends and acquaintances.

Much work on online identity and (dis)embodiment was done in the early to mid-90s by authors such as Balsamo (1995; 2000), Hayles (1999), Stone (1991; 1995), and Turkle (1995). At that time, Internet communication was based on written text, the only way to represent physical characteristics being to describe them in words. Today, the conditions for presenting the body online are quite different. Increased computer speed and bandwidth allow for the inclusion of photos, sound files and video-clips. With the technological innovations, a shift occurred in the ways people use online social arenas. While the cybercultures of the 1990s were characterized by their anonymity—the anonymity was even seen as one of the main allures of the medium (cf. Myers 1987)—the online social environments of today are largely anchored in the local and the familiar. Today, people use the social spaces of the Internet to keep in contact with people they already know, not to meet strangers (Bromseth and Sundén 2011; Dunkels 2005; Enochsson 2005; Krueger and Chamberlain 2005; Thiel 2005). Here, MMOs can in a sense be seen as a step back to the anonymous (or pseudonymous) online spaces of the 1990s. Even though some guilds (such as *Mercenaries*) are made up by people who know each other offline, most guilds are not. Furthermore, most players at least now and then have to interact with strangers, for example in pickup groups. Hence, the revival of the discussion on online identity may have its reasons in the characteristics of MMOs as a medium—characteristics that in some respects are very similar to the online social spaces of the 1990s.

## FALLING IN LOVE IN THE GAME

According to a survey made by the Daedalus project (Yee 2006d), 80% of the female and 60% of the male MMORPG players claimed to at some occasion have flirted with another player. About 50% of the female and 22% of the male players had developed romantic feelings for another player, and about 40% of female players and 15% of male players had told another player about their romantic feelings for them. Finally, 29% of female players and 8% of male players had physically dated someone who they first met in the game.[11] What these figures show is that it does happen that romantic relationships are created in the game worlds, and they are also taken offline.

It is quite easy to fall for someone that one meets in the game. Explanations to the ease with which players can let themselves go has been offered in the anonymity (or pseudonymity) of the game worlds, and the absence of physical cues that make users drop some of their inhibitions as well as their fears of getting rejected (Hill 2010; Yee 2006b). Like in other online environments, the computer screen can be seen as a mask, giving the users increased opportunities over their impression management, as they can decide what aspects of self to display (Sveningsson 2001; 2002). The absence of physical information lets users create (perhaps ideal) images of themselves and other users, in a way that makes physical attraction irrelevant, at least while still interacting online (ibid.).

During my years of fieldwork, I have had romantic feelings for a handful of other players. Most of these were not more than occasional flings, and kept on a platonic level, but one relationship was taken further and developed into a RL relationship. When I had been playing for a year, I got to know a player in my guild. We talked and played together, in instances and raids, and over time our friendship developed to a romantic relationship. By then, I was going through a divorce.

For those who play with their partner, or who are creating a romantic relationship within the game, the game world with its rich environments and vast landscapes can offer many venues for romantic meetings. In the beginning of our relationship, Shy and I often went fishing together, to be able to talk among ourselves, while at the same time having something to do so that the pauses and silences would not feel so awkward. Eventually we started to actively look for nice places within the game, where we could be alone. There were of course pubs and bars where we could sit down at a table and have a drink together, which we did a couple of times. But to me, the magnificent sceneries and landscapes offered far better sites for romantic rendezvous. We enjoyed one of the most beautiful views in the game sitting on a balcony of a tower in Ecodomes in Outland. Another favorite site was in the night elf area Ashenvale, where we had found a tall tree leaning over a lake. There, we would climb up and sit on a branch over the water, protected from malevolent monsters, and talk whole evenings away.

Having the game as a site for romantic meetings had several repercussions on our interactions with the rest of the guild during that first period. Since one of my guild mates had RL connections to my ex-husband, for a long time I wanted to keep my relationship with Shy a secret. This was easier said than done, as messages that were intended to be whispered between us sometimes by mistake were sent to other guild mates with which we had recently whispered, or at times even to the guild chat. As a last resort, we created new alt characters outside the guild, which no one else knew about, to be able to talk without risking MTs (mistells, i.e., posting a chat message to the wrong channel). This meant that we entered a new mode, and a new way of playing:

> I haven't been raiding for a month now, and if log Lore or my DK (Death Knight) at all, it is only to do some cooking or jewelcrafting quest. I am still online every night, but I don't play, at least not the way I used to and not the way the game was meant to be played. When I have been online the last month, I've almost only been with Shy. We have been fishing in Wintergrasp, been to the pub in Shattrath, looked at the northern lights in Hellfire and had picnics in Ecodomes in Netherstorm. Just been going to the most beautiful spots we could find in the game. After some time, it began to be hard to find excuses for why none of us participated in the guild raids any more. And after one MT too much, we decided to play alts outside of the guild instead. So, here we are now, with two level 21 druids that will probably not gain so many more levels. Sometimes we log our mains to play an instance

together. I guess that sooner or later we'll start raiding again. But right now, this is so much more interesting. (Field diary, 10/22/09)

Eventually, our relationship was taken offline and we started to see each other IRL. That meant that we turned back to normal guild life with its raids and instances. However, the game continued to play an important part for us as a meeting place during periods when work and family commitments made it difficult for us to meet face to face.

## IN-GAME RELATIONSHIPS AND GENDER

Statistical surveys show that a higher percentage of female than male players have romantic relationships in the game, play with a partner, or date someone they have first met in the game (Williams, Consalvo et al. 2009; Yee 2006a). This could be taken to support the claim that women are more oriented towards relationships than men in their gaming activities. However, I am not sure that I fully agree with this claim—at least it deserves more discussion.

It does seem to be the case that more women than men put forward social interaction and relationships as motivations for playing MMORPGs (Williams, Consalvo et al. 2009; Yee 2006a). However, if there is a causal relation, we do not know which way it works. In Yee's (2006a) survey, for example, a very large part of the female respondents (26.9% compared to 1% of the men) reported to have been introduced to the gaming activity by their romantic partners. Furthermore, 59.8% of female respondents participated in the environment with a romantic partner and 39.5% with a family member.[12] Thus, for many female players, the gaming activity is inscribed in a relational context already from the start, which may explain at least part of their focus on relationships. As Yee (2006e) acknowledges, given this fact, it is not surprising to find that many of the women who play computer games do so together with their partner, and think of the gaming as a way to socialize and spend time together. The social motivations may also be something that women stress to make the gaming activity more compatible with ideals of normative femininity.

Research has been made that highlights the fact that respondents tend to give answers that are in line with social expectations. In her research on boys' and girls' Internet use, Enochson (2007), for example found that even when the boys and girls were doing basically the same thing (i.e., played computer games online), they termed it in very different ways that were consistent with expectations based on gender (i.e., playing vs. communicating). For a researcher who had not been observing the children, but only interviewed them, a conclusion would have been that the boys used the Internet to play computer games, while the girls used it to communicate (which is also a quite common representation about boys' and girls' Internet use).[13] The discrepancy between the respondents' answers and their actual behavior is addressed by Williams et al. in relation to one of their questions: When the female players' self reported estimations of time spent playing was compared with their actual playing time, they found that the heterosexual female players were three times more likely than the men to underreport their playing time, for which they suggest the explanation that gaming is not consistent with an appropriate female gender role. One could ask the same question about the ways respondents answer other survey questions as well, and reflect upon if they, too, are answered in lines with gender ideals.

As the previous chapter highlighted, female players are often expected to be oriented towards sociality and relationships, thus, female respondents' answers to survey questions that put forth sociality as a player motivation could be a reflection of such expectations. The social aspects of the game may also function as an alibi against what many non-gamers consider an anti-social and utterly futile pastime, or as Yee (2008) puts it, the time spent playing can be thought of as a way to nurture one's (romantic) relationship. I, for a one, have often found myself stressing exactly the social aspects of the game to justify the hours I spend playing, along with my fascination with the graphics. It is true that male players do this too—I have for example heard Erik defend the gaming to his partner stressing the social character of the activity, and the opportunities that the game gives him to socialize with his (offline) friends. However, for him, the issue was to counter imperatives such as "get a life", and to show that his gaming did not make him anti-social. I, on the other hand, being a woman, needed to address both these issues and in addition also try to incorporate the gaming into the frames of normative femininity. One way of doing this is to claim that one is motivated by the game's beautiful graphics, its storylines, and above all, its opportunities for sociality and friendly cooperation, rather than, for example, competitive play.

## FLIRT AS REPRODUCTION OF GENDER HIERARCHIES

Game worlds offer places for players to meet, communicate and interact with each other. The interaction takes place in several layers and through various modes of communication. Players can interact through their characters, take part in role-play, or talk as themselves in their capacity of real life persons, through typed chat or voice chat. They can also engage in many different types of interactions, from instrumental, goal oriented instructions and co-ordinations of raids and instances, to social small talk and flirting with other players.

Flirt, romance and sexual encounters can be seen as representing a game within the game that offers other kinds of activities than was intended by the game's developers. It can thus to some extent be seen as subversive play (for a more thorough discussion on subversive play, see for example Mortensen 2008, or Sundén, Chapter 8 in this book). In her discussion on deviant strategies in *World of Warcraft*, Mortensen concludes that the most deviant are not the players who break the rules, but those who decide not to care about the rules at all. Thus, she says, the deviant players are those who take part in activities outside of the arena of rules, who "use the game to chat, to take pretty pictures, to have cybersex in an inn in Goldshire, to have a group of researchers meet in a cave in Durotar" (Mortensen 2008, 220).

When discussing role-play as a form of deviant play, Mortensen (2008) states that it does not help the player to achieve better in the game—it is counterproductive and may even be a hindrance for one's progress in the game as such. The same goes for the flirt, in that it constitutes a diversion, or a side activity that is not rewarded in any form of achievement points in the game (although it may feel rewarding for the individual player). However, it is important to acknowledge that Mortsensen's discussion of deviant play (and also my own labeling of flirt as potentially subversive) focuses on *World of Warcraft* as a game, or more exactly, it defines deviance in relation to the game's rule-based or ludic qualities. The role-play and the flirt both exist at the side of these activities, and are closer to what Caillois (1961/2001) terms paidia, a more playful and freeform activity without rules and predefined goals. However, even if the ludic aspects are what distinguish a game from other virtual environments, I feel that they are sometimes receiving too much focus in explanatory models, at the cost of other qualities of the games (see also Sundén's discussion on this issue in Chapter 8 in this book). This is especially true for a game as multifaceted as *World of Warcraft*. Players are motivated by different aspects of the games (see, for example, Bartle 1996; Yee 2006a). While many players may be focusing on achievement and overcoming obstacles in the form of computer generated enemies or other players, others find it more interesting to explore the game world—as a system or as an aesthetic experience. They may be deeply fascinated with the game's narrative aspects as they appear in game lore. Still others tend to see the social interaction with other players as the main allure of the game. If we look at *World of Warcraft* as a social arena, the occurrence of flirt at once seems entirely logical and not particularly subversive at all—it is on the contrary highly likely that flirt and sexual encounters would occur in any multiuser environment where users meet and spend time together, as has been the case in previous online arenas such as MUDs, chats or *Second Life* (Baker 1998; Brookey and Cannon 2009; Daneback 2006; Kendall 2002; Lea and Spears 1995; Lipton 1996; Parks and Floyd 1996; Schofield Clark 1998; Sveningsson 2002).

The romantic and sexual encounters per se are not only expected, but they are also often quite conventional. In most cases, they tend to reproduce traditional gender hierarchies, in that they reflect the interests of the dominant group (i.e., the straight men). Thus, although much of the flirtatious interaction is playful and experienced as fun by both male and female players, it can also be seen as a reflection of gendered power structures in society and gendered expectations.

Heterosexual desire is commonly listed as one of the most important ingredients of hegemonic masculinity (Connell 1995). As Svahn (1999) demonstrates, the 'real' man is supposed be interested in and sexually oriented towards women. One way to 'do masculinity' is thus to demonstrate the heterosexual interest, for example by making advances at women. The previous chapter suggested some reasons why male players embrace the presence of female players. Yet another reason lies in the potential that female players bring for heterosexual love and romance. Regardless of whether or not any such relationships are actually created, the presence of gaming women leaves room for the male players' demonstrations of a heterosexual interest. This stance is taken also by Taylor et al. (2009). In their research on large scale LANs, they state that booth babes can be seen as guarding an intensely homosocial space from homosexual desire: "the presence of highly sexualized women ensures for the male attendees that their heterosexual desire is firmly secured and on display: even more so given that these women are 'available' to take pictures of/with" (2009, 248).

The need to demonstrate heterosexuality is likely experienced as larger the more male dominated the environment is. This assumption finds some support in my interviews. For example, talking about how female players are met in male dominated games, the informant Ulrika states (Chapter 2 in this book) that many male players welcome the advent of a female player; they will want to talk, play, be friends and start some kind of relationship with one of the few female players who are around (see also Linderoth and Olsson 2010). From this follows that even though female players are the ones ascribed with the interest in romance and relationships, it is an open question if the issue is not just as central, or even more so, for the male players.

This chapter is called "The Straight Game" because of its focus on heterosexual romance. In the field note quoted in the introduction of this chapter, I also called the flirt a 'heterosexual game within the game'. When I wrote this, I termed it this way because I wanted to be specific; I did not want to take my observations about heterosexual flirt, and the gender conventions that are put to play in those situations, and generalize them to non-straight relationships. Flirting and creating relationships is of course something that non-straight players do in game environments too (as Sundén's chapters in this book clearly show). Furthermore, players of the same sex who are known to be straight also sometimes do flirt with each other, especially by using emotes (for example "/lick" is very commonly used). This could be seen as a way of queering the otherwise so heteronormative atmosphere, and for some it may be. However, for most players, when flirtatious in-game behavior is performed, it is expected to be between players of opposite sexes. If the heterosexual is the general norm in society, this is even more the case in gaming contexts, which can be observed in the abundance of derogatory remarks that focus on non-straight orientation or other deviations from the hegemonic masculinity (cf. Nardi 2010, and Sundén, Chapter 8 in this book). The environment is coded as masculine and straight, and as is often the case in computer games (Consalvo 2003a), much of the content is based on heteronormative assumptions and world views.

Talking about heterosexuality as opposed to a non-straight orientation may give a dichotomous view of sexuality, as if I saw it as consisting of two opposite polarities—that people are either heterosexual or homosexual. This is not the case. Lori Kendall (2009a) leads a discussion on these matters, suggesting instead a view of hetero/homo-sexuality as something of a continuum, where no one is entirely at the one end, but always somewhere in between. I would personally side with this view, as this is how I believe that things work. However, people's social constructions of sexuality work in other ways—many, if not most people seem to want to set up firm limits that regulate what is a man or a woman, what they should be like, who they should desire and how this desire should be expressed. This was quite visible in the parts of the game world and the player cultures that I got into contact with during my research, where the perspective that was taken for granted was always a straight one.

Admittedly, I myself may have had part in this. My use of the phrasing 'heterosexual game' reflects my own position as a straight woman—it is the heterosexual game that I have seen and been involved in. But it has also something to say about my frames of reference, because being who I am indeed influences what I see. Thus, something should be said about my own position as a researcher. Even though I have tried hard not to, I know that I have still sometimes slipped into heteronormative interpretations of other players' actions and interactions. As the Swedish social anthropologist Fanny Ambjörnsson (2004) notes in her study on high school girls' gender work, what is said or done between two persons is generally interpreted according to their genders. Thus, intimacy and closeness between two women is generally interpreted as a close friendship, while if exactly the same actions are observed between persons of the opposite sexes, it is interpreted as a romantic relationship and/or flirt. In my case, this means that if any of my male guild mates or quest partners greeted me with "kisses", wrote me equivocal messages, called me "love", "sweetie", "honey" or "Hotlips", or emoted that they thought I was a "sexy devil", I saw this as flirtatious. However, if my guild mate Lisa or any other female player would do the same, I would rather interpret it as an expression of friendship. I do not have all information about other players, and it is very likely that at least some of the players that I have come into contact with are not 100% straight. What I saw may then have had another meaning. Also the fact that when interacting with strangers in the game, their gender is unknown may also call for alternative interpretations. For example, if the player who once asked me to strip (see p. 72) was female, what would this do to my interpretation and analysis of the incident? Another aspect is that, both because of the actual gender distribution of the game, and the general assumptions of the implied player as being male, it is not unlikely at all that the strip tease seeker thought that I was a male, playing a female character. Seen from that perspective, things are starting to look less clear cut.

Finally, even though heterosexuality is generally regarded as the norm, this does not mean that heterosexuality is always the more normal and that homosexuality the more transgressive alternative. Even within the seemingly homogenous label of heterosexuality, there are important differences. For example, those with preferences in sadomasochism see themselves (and are seen) as very different from those interested in vanilla sex (and vice versa). As Sundén shows in Chapter 8 in this book, the same can be said about the varying subcultures that are formed around sexual preferences and practices among non-straight people too. However, as she shows in her discussions on gay masculinities, the grammar of what is 'normal' and desirable may look quite different from the one exercised in a straight context.

The variety of sexual desires and practices means that also within the norm (of heterosexuality), some desires and practices are seen as 'normal' while others are seen as deviant or for that matter queer. In her classical essay "Thinking sex", Gayle Rubin (1993, 11–12) states that modern Western societies appraise sex acts according to a hierarchical system:

> Marital, reproductive heterosexuals are alone at the top of the erotic pyramid. Clamoring below are unmarried monogamous heterosexuals in couples, followed by most other heterosexuals. [ . . . ] Stable, long-term lesbian and gay male couples are verging on respectability, but bar dykes and promiscuous gay men are hovering just above the groups at the very bottom of the pyramid. The most despised sexual castes currently include transsexuals, transvestites, fetishists, sadomasochists, sex workers such as prostitutes and porn models, and the lowliest of all, those whose eroticism transgresses generational boundaries.

From Rubin's discussion we can conclude that merely being heterosexual is by no means always equivalent to being normative. What within heteronormativity is seen as 'normal' and desirable is *a specific kind* of heterosexuality, one which includes specific desires and practices. It also includes specific kinds of masculinities and femininities (Bäckman 2003). Thus, heteronormativity is something that also heterosexual men and women have to relate to, live up to and perform, in their everyday lives offline, and, as this chapter has shown, in their game spaces online.

## NOTES

1. Multi User Domain.
2. See, for example, http://www.wowwiki.com/Emote.

3. http://www.wowwiki.com/Flirt.
4. http://www.wowwiki.com/List_of_emotes.
5. In film and, more recently, games, it is common to distinguish between diegetic and extra-diegetic sound. The diegetic refers to sounds that are part of the story, whereas the extra-diegetic sound comes from a source outside of the storyspace. It can be the voice of a narrator, sound effects, or mood music with the function to create the proper atmosphere.
6. Players belonging to the opposite factions cannot chat with each other. However, players of opposite faction who want to communicate can to some extent do this through emotes. The standard emotes (http://www.wowwiki.com/List_of_emotes) will be understood by players of the opposite faction, while the customized emotes that players themselves construct will appear in the chat display as "NN makes some strange gestures".
7. I learned afterwards that the player in question had a bug, which made characters appear without their clothes. At the time I thought that the comment referred to the use of a pair of goggles (maybe the "Gnomish X-ray specs") that allow the player to see other characters without clothes and armor.
8. The men in the group knew that I was female IRL (or at least that I claimed to be).
9. Here, it should be noted that different player constellations differ from each other. In Sundén's chapters, for example, we see how in the queer guild she studied, issues of sexuality were pushed to the forefront and became intimately connected to the specific gaming community as well as to gameplay. For them, sexuality was a central part of the game and its activities. Furthermore, as my field notes show, even if players in 'ordinary' guilds do not reflect on or negotiate them, hierarchies of gender and sexuality are still very much present. Here, as in so many other contexts, 'neutral' means that norms are taken for granted and mostly reflect the perspective of the male, straight members.
10. Furthermore, well-geared characters are often assumed to belong to male players (for example, one female guild member was once told by the participants in a pickup group that "Why, you can't be a girl, your gear is way too good for that").
11. These numbers should be seen in relation to the actual proportion of players. In Yee's study (2006e), the gender ratio was 85:15. Taking the singles rate into account, Yee concludes that for every single woman in an MMO, there are 10 single men. It is thus likely that the average woman player meets romantic or sexual situations in the game to a much higher extent than the average male player, and that this is part of the reason why more women than men report getting romantically involved with other players.
12. The corresponding numbers for male respondents were 15.8% and 25.5%.
13. It is true that the boys and girls did play different games—the boys' games included more shooting and the girls' games were more oriented towards exploration and social interaction. However, as Enochson observed, the shooter games required quite a lot of communicating and the girls' games included gameplay—something that the gendering of the activities did not let them express.

# 4 Playing Along

*Malin Sveningsson*

It is not unusual that women who try to carve out a career in male-dominated professions face difficulties. Researchers have, for example, written about the obstacles that meet women in professions such as the military (Pettersson, Persson, and Berggren 2008), journalism (Djerf-Pierre 2005; 2007; Melin 2008) and the music industry (Ganetz 1997; 2008; Gavanas 2009). Women in these professions have been found to develop various strategies to cope with the male-dominated environment, to be accepted and create themselves a space there. For example, one common strategy is to compete for a place in the male culture, to become 'one of the boys' (Djerf-Pierre 2005; 2007; Melin 2008). Another is for the women to play on their femininity, or to focus on 'female' interest spheres within the profession, thus positioning themselves as 'one of the girls' (Djerf-Pierre 2005; 2007; Melin 2008). The women may also try to escape the competition altogether, in what Melin (2008) terms 'flight', resorting to other, less competitive ways of practicing the profession (such as free lance). Discussing the strategies of women officers in the Swedish armed forces, Pettersson et al. (2008) distinguish between two major perspectives, described as the individual and the structural one. The individual perspective means that the women accept the established gender order in the organization, and if they challenge it, they do it on an individual basis. The structural perspective involves a questioning of the structural conditions of the organization altogether.

Taking part in computer game culture on a voluntary basis in one's leisure time should perhaps not be compared to practicing and striving to make a living out of one's profession. Still, both the professional and the gaming context hold strongly gendered power structures that all women who wish to make themselves a space and a 'career' there have to deal with in one way or another. In this chapter, I will take a closer look at what strategies are used by women in the male-dominated computer game cultures I have come into contact with.

## STATUS AND SUBORDINATION

In their study of women officers of the Swedish armed forces, Pettersson et al. (2008) found that the women's perceptions of gender relations varied with time, age and rank, and so did the strategies they used to cope with the gender inequalities they faced. They found that the young recruits tended to lean against the individual and the older veterans towards the structural perspective. I can see this process being reflected in my own 'gaming career' as well.

It is said about *World of Warcraft* that it is relatively easy to learn but difficult to master. Thus, even if I got into the gameplay after only a couple of hours, during my first year as a player, there were still lots I did not know about the game and how it was played (and after almost three years, there still is). Furthermore, when I started to play, it was in a guild in which my only connection was Erik, who was also a relatively new member. Thus, for me it made sense to adopt a humble attitude, try to adapt to the prevailing culture and be prepared to learn from those who knew more than I did. In doing so, I voluntarily entered a subordinate position vis-à-vis the other guild members, who had been playing for a longer time than I had. An example of how I reasoned is provided in the following field note:

> Yesterday when I was fighting some raptors in Wetlands, one male guild member whispered and asked me if this was my first WoW character. I answered him that "well, I tried a couple of classes before deciding on this one, but it was only up to lvl 10 or so, so I guess I'm pretty new". "Right", he said, "not like the likes of me who have played since the game was released". "No", I said, "not at all. I've mostly played console and single player games before". "Well, I guess we've all been beginners", he said.
>
> I don't know why I got disturbed over this, after all he was just trying to be nice. But at the same time I felt that his tone was a little superior, as if he had to make sure that I knew that he had a lot more experience than I did. Sure, it's true that I'm a newbie, I know that. But still. However, I said to myself, it's better to just accept the situation, so I just answered "better begin late than never". He agreed and said that if I needed help with anything I could just ask him. I continued the polite track and answered "thank you, I really appreciate it, there's a lot of things here that I don't know".
>
> I don't understand why so many guys feel that need to assert themselves, like letting you know for how long they've been playing or how many max-level characters they've got. I've seen a lot of people, mostly guys, do that. Anyway, I'm glad I took the polite road and accepted the positioning of me as new and ignorant, because it turned out that the guy who whispered me was one the officers. (Field diary, 10/15/08)

In a previous study on chat users, I found a pattern where users with much experience held higher status than those with less experience (Sveningsson 2001). As the excerpt from the previous field note points to, there are similar patterns to be found among *World of Warcraft* players. Here too, there are hierarchies between players, where those with more experience hold higher status (or think of themselves as holding higher status) than those with less experience. Experience comes with practice, meaning that if you want to estimate how experienced a certain player is, you need to know for how long time s/he has been playing, and how much time s/he devotes to it.[1] Thus, in their struggles over status and power in the game, a very common way for players to assert their superiority is to point at such factors. However, the value system is not unambiguous. The updated knowledge that extensive play gives about the game as it looks today—both concerning gameplay and narrative content—is indeed a form of cultural capital in the gaming cultures. However, new knowledge can be overtrumped by old knowledge. Hence, if one player tries to establish his position by making it evident how much he knows about the game and its recently added content, his assertion may be successfully countered by other players who make comparisons to what the game was like in the old days, commonly called 'Vanilla WoW'.

*World of Warcraft* contains three expansion packs: *The Burning Crusade*, *Wrath of the Lich King*, and *Cataclysm*. 'Vanilla' or 'Classic WoW' refers to the initial, original release, where characters' max level was set to 60.[2] Vanilla WoW is said to have been much more difficult than the game is today. Thus, to establish oneself as someone who was a *World of Warcraft* player already in the Vanilla days, means to position oneself both as an experienced *and* a skilled player.

The skill of a player will show with time to those s/he is regularly playing with, at least if those persons are experienced enough to be able to tell the difference. But there are also other ways to try to position oneself as a skilled player. One can, for example, link lists that show the performance of the players in the group. Such lists are provided by specific add-ons (for example Skada or Recount) that keep track on various aspects of the play, for example how much damage or healing each player does and takes, how many interrupts or dispels are done by each player, and how many deaths each player suffers during the playing session. What kind of list a player chooses to post depends on what role s/he has in the group. If someone posts a list, it is most likely because s/he performed well and wants to make others aware of this, but it can also be a way for users to taunt and admonish others in the group who performed less well.

Even if add-ons such as those mentioned before provides one way of measuring skill, they are quite blunt. It is true that they give a measurable comparison of players' performance, however, they do not take into account all factors that are essential for the group's success. A player who seeks to maximize his or her dps will often take risks, for example by hitting too soon and/or too hard, or failing to move, which makes the project more difficult for tanks and healers. If the dps player attracts 'aggro' (the boss starts to attack him or her instead of the tank), s/he will very likely die, thus reducing the group's chances at succeeding. In the worst case, the aggroing player may cause the group to 'wipe', meaning that the whole group dies and has to restart.[3]

Experienced players are aware of that dps or damage done lists do not tell the whole truth about how well a player performs: high dps numbers are not very important if they can only be upheld for a small part of the fight. Players also have to survive and do the right things at the right time. They also have to be able to work as a team. Such aspects can be monitored by other add-ons, such as Failbot, EnsidiaFails, or BigBrother. With this help, raid leaders can spot which mistakes are made, and by whom, and thus they can instruct players and make the raid group as a whole more successful. The add-ons can also be used to monitor participants' performance to punish or exclude those who are not performing well enough (cf. Nardi 2010; Taylor 2008c). Although not used as frequently as Skada and Recount for such purposes, these add-ons too can be a way for players to demonstrate their skill, or to demonstrate other players' lack of skill. In this way, add-ons can be used as a resource in players' struggle for power and status within the gaming communities.

## THE PYGMALION PROJECT

In Chapter 2, I discussed how male players may sometimes help female players, something which I experienced especially during my first year. Here, my guild mate Miles is probably right in his statement that "guys like to flex their muscles before girls". However, it seems like some guys also like to help the girls flex *their* muscles. In my case, this manifested itself in various situations. For example, for a long time, Shy conducted what he wittingly called his "Project Lore",[4] where he helped my characters with group quests, loaned me the money to buy mounts and equipment, and crafted items for me that would have been expensive for me to buy, such as gems, potions and flasks. On a few occasions, he also looked up new specs for me,[5] which helped me improve my characters' performance.

There were other players, too, who engaged in my progress, to the point where I sometimes even felt like a Pygmalion project[6] for them. One such instance was when I learned how to tank. As mentioned in the previous chapter, in the spring of 2009 I invested in the dual spec,[7] but since I felt uncertain of how to play as a tank, I rarely used it. During the summer vacation when many players took a break, however, it became difficult for the raid leaders to get players to fill all tasks. Thus, one night they called me in as an off tank[8] in Ulduar, which was the most difficult raid instance at that time:

> We were talking about Ulduar but we needed one more tank. And then someone said: "I heard Lore got some good tank gear recently". "Haha, you want a good laugh?" I said. "But the only way to learn is

> to practice" Kafir said. "But Ulduar for God's sake", I replied. "But sure, if there's no other tank online I can try, but in that case I want instructions".
>
> We tried but it didn't go so well. When we had wiped twice, Morning came up with the idea that we'd all go to Naxx so that I could practice. So we did and it went much better. It's really fun to tank, actually. But I feel somewhat like a Pygmalion project, they seem to think of it as a fun new project to help me out and show me how to play. (Field Diary 05/19/09)

Four of the officers became my 'tanking teachers' over the summer: Morning, Dark, Wasai and Thad. I do not think it was a coincidence that it was these specific players who helped me—they were all among the most experienced players in the guild and, taken together with the fact that they were officers, their status in the guild was very high. Someone with less status, or whose performance was not as good, might not have invested so much time in improving the skills of another player. Gender may also be a contributing factor. Talking about it with Thad almost one year later, he stated that he did not think that gender had any relevance in this specific case, but rather attitude and personality were determining factors. He added that he would have done the same for a player like Ziggy, for example. Still, being only 15 years old, Ziggy was not even half the age of these four officers. As he would self-ironically put it: "Hey, what do you expect from me, I'm only a child!"

But Thad may have a point in his reflection on personality and attitude. My tanking teachers noticed that I appreciated their help, and that I listened to their instructions and acted in accordance with them. When I improved, it was to a large extent thanks to them. In a way, I was a product of their work. However, Pygmalion projects have expectations on them, too. As Lisa put it, reflecting on the help female players may receive:

*Lisa:* I believe that should a woman turn up and really play on her feminine helplessness, she wouldn't last for long.

*Malin:* You mean the others would grow tired of her?

*Lisa:* Yes.

*Malin:* So what you are saying is that in reality it's only interesting to help people who don't really need the help?

*Lisa:* Well, in principle, yes! (laughter) But seriously, that's what I think. Because if you're new and don't know what to do, and someone helps you, then you learn quite fast. But I know, I've got female friends who are so helpless in all situations—they never learn how to change tires on their cars, for example. But they would never get away with that in the game. You may get more help when you're new, and you may get more help if you're a woman. But you can't go on playing on it forever.

*Malin:* Sometimes I've felt sort of like a Pygmalion project. That the guys think it's fun to care for you and help you improve, but . . .

*Lisa:* Yeah, but in that case, if you're Eliza, you have to make progress too (laughter).

When I look back at my gaming history, I see that when I was new I used certain strategies to be accepted in the guild. During my first year as a player, I held a low profile and largely positioned myself as someone who did not have full control over how to play the game, and who also readily accepted help and advice from others. This made sense as I was less experienced, and knew a lot less about the game than most other players in the guild. However, as experience and skill is so connected to status in the game world, my positioning as less experienced meant that I also entered a subordinate position relative to the other players. I believe that this was part of the reason why I got accepted so easily—for someone to be superior, they need others who are subordinate. Someone who voluntarily enters that position will strengthen the position of all other players, thus it is likely that s/he is welcomed into the group (even if not admitted to join its more difficult tasks). However, as Lisa said in the previous excerpt, it was probably also helpful that I made efforts to learn, and actually made progress. For those who were my 'teachers', my progress could count as yet an achievement on their part, especially since I was careful to show appreciation for the time they dedicated to sharing their knowledge with me.

## THE CONFLICT BETWEEN GENDER AND GAMING SKILLS

As time went on, my gaming skill increased. The question of gaming skills and gender may sometimes involve a tricky balancing act. Players who are not skilled enough will in most cases not be allowed to join raids (unless the purpose is to train them). And those who doubt themselves and openly admit their insecurity may inspire others to adopt a view of them as less skilled than those who are more self-assured. However, my impression is that being female, one should not be too self assured about one's skills and performance either—or one might face comments such as "She's so stuck up" and "She thinks she's special", comments that I was told that at least one guild member had made about me behind my back. Thus, for a female member to have her gaming skills acknowledged, she will sometimes have to abstain from the confirmation that lies in being liked by the other (male) members.

This ambivalence is mirrored in the inconsistent responses that I feel my performance elicited over my years as a player. At times, especially when I was new, I received what I felt was undeserved credit. As the female informants quoted in the introduction of Chapter 2 said, I too sometimes felt that I received milder treatment than the male members, with less criticism for my mistakes and more praise when I performed well. Sometimes, I even received compliments for doing things that were very easy (see also Sundén, Chapter 8 in this book). This can be interpreted as if I performed better than they expected from a female player, or from a relative newbie, but it can also be that these specific players were just trying to be friendly and supportive. However, on other occasions, when I knew what I was talking about, or if I ever tried to assert myself, I felt that my knowledge was not taken seriously, where at least certain players preferred to continue seeing me as a newbie who did not know anything about the game or how to play it. Maybe they were just used to relating to me in that way. As one male informant said—one will always be seen as a newbie in the guild one started out in. However, gender may have contributed, as representations of female players as less skilled and less interested in games than male players still seem to be quite prevalent (Enevold and Hagström 2008; Nardi 2010; Sveningsson Elm forthcoming).

The positioning of me as inexperienced meant that I often, especially during my first year, felt that I needed to prove my gaming interest and skills:

> Maybe it's stupid of me, but I sometimes feel like I have to do better just because I'm a woman, that otherwise people would think that if I screw up, it is just because I'm a girl. And also because the few of us who are female get noticed so much more—like you can't hide among the others. (Field Diary, 04/28/09)

When discussing this with male guild members, they would just look bewildered at me, assuring me that for them, the gender of other players did not matter. So why did I have these feelings? Why have I consistently felt that my gender made me less genuine as a gamer, and less likely to be skilled? Is it just a question of personal characteristics, of me having bad self-confidence, or are there deeper structures to be found that my co-players and I are not aware of? Similar thoughts came up in the interviews too, even from one of the hardcore gamers:

*Josefin:* Well, there are these places in my town, adventure halls and a LAN place where they've got games, but that's nothing that I would consider, going there to play.

*Malin:* Why not?

*Josefin:* Why, I dont know. I like the home environment and to play with just my friends or alone.

*Malin:* You've got any idea of why you prefer that?

*Josefin:* No . . . Maybe you get more shy when you get out among people that you don't know, and you don't want to show them "look how good I am" you know.

*Malin:* Yeah? Even though you've been playing for so long? Or is that the reason? Because, in my case, I wouldn't walk into a game store and play because I feel people would think "What an amateur.

She can't play". But you mean that it's the other way around for you, that you would feel as if people thought you came there to show off?

*Josefin:* No, I often feel quite crappy myself too. If I play with others around me. I don't like to show others how I play. Because then you feel quite small, for some reason. I really don't know why.

*Malin:* No? Maybe that's one of the reasons why you don't see women gamers. They sit at home and play because they don't want to show others how crappy they are.

*Josefin:* Yeah, because that's the feeling, you don't want to stand there and show, well, as you say, walk into a game store and try something new, because you don't want to show how lousy you play.

*Malin:* Especially if it's the first time you try that game.

*Josefin:* No, but maybe you're good at it, you don't know. But then, you don't think so, for some reason.

Judy Wajcman (1991) has discussed the relation between gender and technology. Referring to Cockburn (1985), she states that men's affinity with technology is seen as integral to the constitution of male gender identity, whereas femininity is incompatible with technological competence (in Chapter 5 in this book, Sundén makes a similar point in discussing how the culturally intimate connection between masculinity and technology creates a paradox for women who are passionate about technologies). Wajcman shares Cockburn's view that women's reluctance to enter into technological domains has to do with the sex-stereotyped definition of technology as an activity appropriate for men: "as with science, the very language of technology, its symbolism, is masculine" (Wajcman 1991, 19) . Following Wajcman's arguments then, the question why women are underrepresented in gaming communities is not so much because of the ways they are socialized into gender roles, but more because the language and values are already written so as to define the activity as 'male'.

Being female seems to work as a hindrance for girls and women to be seen as real 'gamers'. Kerr (2003) for example found that when trying to solicit 'female gamers' for her study, she got very few responses, something which she explains by saying that women do not feel at home with being classified as gamers—a gamer is by definition male (c.f. Bury 2011, who found the same about female 'geeks'). Thus, one way for women to enjoy technology, and to carve out careers in such areas, is to abstain from, or lose some of their association with feminine values, or as Wajcman (2004) puts it, these women have to forsake their femininity.

## TO BECOME ONE OF THE BOYS

In my interviews with female gamers I saw several signs of how the informants tried to position themselves as being less feminine, for example by dissociating themselves from other women, traditionally feminine interests and ways of being.[9] They also invoked associations to masculinity. Without being asked, most of them at some point mentioned the experience of having been considered tomboys when growing up. I brought this up with one of my interviewees:

*Malin:* Do you think that there are certain positions in gaming contexts that girls and women can take more easily? I was thinking about what you said earlier about your being a tomboy. That your family always said you were a tomboy. 'Cause when you look at forum discussions online, other girls and women who play often say they are tomboys too.

*Paula:* I guess many of them do. Absolutely. The fact that I do is not because of that but because I always had that interest. When I was little, I didn't like dolls and such, and if my mom brought me dolls, you know "Eew!" I preferred cars, and my dad was a truck driver. I spent a lot of time with him and I've always been interested in technological things. I've always tinkered with my own cars when I could. And I build my computers myself, for example. So technically I may be a tomboy. Fall into that category. But then in the gaming, I don't think you have to be a tomboy but many female players put themselves there anyway.

Femininity and masculinity should not be understood as binary opposites. The content of both concepts may also be open for change, so that as the number of gaming women increases, it may eventually be possible to talk about a kind of gamer femininity—one that makes it possible to combine femininity with technological interests and skills (cf. the closing chapter of this book). However, this did not seem feasible when the interviews were conducted, or at least, most of the informants did not seem to see such possibilities[10]. Instead of emphasizing their femininity *and* gaming interest, they used the appropriation of masculine traits as a way to legitimize their interest and skill, and to get away from the stigma that femininity would bring them. Looking back at my field notes, I notice that I have done precisely the same thing:

> Yesterday I went to my first LAN, at Erik's place. Matt and I arrived first, at noon, and then David and Andy turned up by 3 o'clock. Even if I had been talking to the other guys in the game, this was the first time I met them face-to-face; Erik was the only one that I knew IRL.
>
> The whole thing was really interesting from a gender perspective. Already from the start I felt the need to distinguish myself from women in general, and to position myself as a non-typical female. I believe part of the reason why I did it was to signal to the guys that they could be as relaxed in their gaming as they would, had I not been there.

> That I was not like their wives and partners, whom I knew opposed their gaming interest and tried to restrict it. I guess that my gaming interest makes me different from those other women already from the start. But our efforts to position me as 'un-girlie' came up in relation to other areas too. For example, when the guys found out that I have a bad simultaneous capacity, this was pointed out as something that made me different—in reality, said Matt, I might even be a man, I only looked liked a woman. The fact that I turned up on time while Andy and David were too late was brought up as further evidence of my inner masculinity. Finally, we agreed that I could pass as an 'honorary guy'. (Field Diary, 01/11/09)

Even if my appointment as an honorary guy was a joke, there still lies something in it: in order to enable me to pass as a true member of this specific gaming community we joined in a common effort to make me appear more masculine, to make me 'one of the boys'.

Just like my efforts described in the previous field note, the female informants' positioning of themselves as tomboys can be seen as a way for them too to become 'one of the boys': to blend in, and to be seen as more authentic as gamers. This was done by using masculinity as a resource: by explicitly calling themselves 'tomboys', and by bringing up other interests that are traditionally male dominated and/or loaded with masculine values. Thus, 40-year-old Paula brought up her vivid interest in cars, 23-year-old Sanna in heavy metal music and playing hockey, and 30-year-old Ulrika told me about her experiences of being a female rock musician and web designer, both in male-dominated contexts. Almost all of the informants talked about having a general interest in computers, and of having played with boys instead of girls in their childhoods (c.f. Bury 2011 and Cassell 1998, who report of similar results in their research on gender and technology).

A further explanation may be offered in Burrill's analysis of masculinity and computer games. He explains the function and main allure of computer games by the notion of 'boyhood', which he defines as "the state of premature masculinity that is accessed by males seeking to re-engage their youth/virility/power/dominance over forces that appear to be encroaching on their former footholds" (Burrill 2008, 137). Boyhood is a state that allows the individual to escape from the constraints of everyday life—to be a boy again, without commitments and duties. However, an adult cannot enter this state without a proper alibi. Computer games provide one such alibi, constituting an arena in which the state of boyhood can be accessed and lived out.[11]

It may not be so difficult for a male adult gamer to step into the imagined role of a teenage boy. As Burrill (2008, 15) states:

> boyhood, particularly within the digital sphere, is the privileged site of power that the subject accesses to successfully understand, navigate,

> and play both virtual and real games. It is a position that I believe the male (sic!) subject can access throughout his life, using it when needed, as a carpenter would use a specific set of tools at hand.

In my previous discussion, I stated that female players may sometimes try to appear more masculine in order to blend into the gaming community. However, according to the quotes from Burrill, it may not be enough to be masculine, but the subject may even have to be *male* to be able to access the privileged site of power that 'boyhood' offers. At first I thought Burrill's use of the word 'male' was unintentional slips of the tongue. However, it may be just an accurate description of the state of affairs in computer game culture. In any case, it is for certain very problematic for women to enter, even when they do have a passionate interest in computer games and are skilled at playing them.

So, what do female players do when they wish to enter the state of 'boyhood' that computer games provide? Maybe they do exactly what the informants previously mentioned do: position themselves as tomboys. In their tales of having 'male' interests, they represent themselves as, if not male so at least more masculine, and in their evoking of their childhoods, they also enter the adolescent state that the notion of 'boyhood' refers to. In this way, the position that male players carry with them as a 'set of tools at hand' is something that the female players try to re-create by invoking associations to masculinity and youth.

## HANDLING THE HEGEMONIC DISCOURSE

In all cultures, hegemonic discourses emerge that reflect the interests and perspectives of the dominant group. The hegemonic discourse that one meets in computer game cultures varies with gaming context, and with specific persons and player constellations. Still, it is generally the men's perspective that is taken as the evident point of view—the 'laddish' interaction style that was described in Chapter 2 is but one example. This specific way of interacting with each other in the game has largely become the norm, to which female players have to conform. In order to play with the boys, female players have to accept and adapt to a jargon that may be 'crude but cordial', quite competitive, and include frequent putdowns of women and gay men (Delamere and Shaw 2008; Nardi 2010).

One can wonder why gaming cultures look like this. One possible answer is that male players were the first to adopt computer games, and for a long time made up a dominant part of the players (and still do in many gaming contexts). But the proportion of women players has steadily increased during the last decades. Would not the computer game culture change with the advent of so many women players? Well, not necessarily. A number of studies show that when women enter male-dominated professions, they tend to adapt to the hegemonic discourse. As van Zoonen (1994) writes about female journalists, they tend to accept and internalize the demands of the profession. Thus, the fact that an increasing number of women enter the gaming cultures, or even start to design computer games, does not necessarily lead to an increased equality or a change in perspectives.

The extent to which female players adopt the hegemonic discourse varies, from a more passive way of relating to it (growing used to it and ceasing to react) to a more active stance where they contribute to the discourse, and thereby take part in recreating it. In my own gaming, I have found myself doing both. Being a feminist and a researcher, I consider myself to be relatively conscious about gendered power structures, and also eager to break with them. Despite this, I have found it very easy to fall into the dominant pattern. For example, in Chapter 3 I mentioned that I have become so used to situations with sexual advancements being made at female players and characters, to the extent that I hardly react anymore. I have heard similar accounts from other female players. For example, in *Mercenaries*, some male guild members had the habit of engaging in certain gender exclusionary practices, such as greeting the guild with the words "Hello guys" and praising it after raids with "Good job chaps!" (see also Sundén, Chapter 8 in this book, where she describes similar experiences). I felt disturbed over this exclusionary practice, notably the constant use of the word 'chaps'.[12] To me it did not matter whether the exclusions were intentional or not, because the consequences of making us women invisible were very real. I also experienced the situation as somehow problematic. How should I deal with the exclusion I felt that I and the other female members were being exposed to? And how should it be interpreted? One interpretation is that the specific players greeted only the male players, but not the female ones. As if they did not care to get to know us. Or worse, that they did not even want to admit that we were there. Another interpretation is that since a gamer is per definition male, a female player needs to identify (and be identified) as "one of the boys" to be defined as a gamer. Seen from that perspective, the addressing of us women as 'chaps' would perhaps be interpreted in a positive way (if we were included in the address, which I do not know).

When I discussed this issue with the female guild member and officer Renee, she answered me that she had ceased to react on such comments long ago, that the persons involved probably did not mean any harm, and that they meant to address everybody, it just took too long to write out "guys *and girls*". This stance is probably a good survival strategy if you want to play with the boys. But to me, even if the persons may not have meant any harm, I could not and would not let the practice pass unnoticed. At the same time, I did not want to make a fuss—it is seldom appreciated among men when women complain about inequalities, and I might instead end up being labeled a whining feminist. To avoid this, while still making my point, I tried to make use of humor. Thus, when someone said "Hello guys" or "chaps", I took as a habit to answer that person with the words

"Hi there little lady", to make it show (by my presence) that not everyone was male. I also thought it might make them understand how it felt to be forced to choose between either being addressed as belonging to the wrong gender, or not being spoken to at all. Eventually, some players got the hint and started to add "and girls", although not all of them did. One player even started to say "Hello chaps and else",[13] possibly in protest. All in all, I am quite sure that at least some guild members thought my comments were exaggerated and right out silly.

## TAKING THE HEAT

In their article about women officers in the Swedish armed forces, Pettersson et al. (2008) found that one strategy often employed by young recruits was what the authors call 'take the heat'. In order to be accepted, the women accepted and adapted to the prevailing culture and did not protest against inequalities, at least not on a structural level. The informant Ulrika reflects about similar issues:

*Ulrika:* Well, you've got to be thick-skinned, you can't keep on getting upset over things and become fretful, because if you do, you won't get accepted at all.

*Malin:* No?

*Ulrika:* And you can't . . . You've got to be thick-skinned. And not so . . . As a girl you must . . . I guess the best for a girl is to have some distance. To be able to just turn such things off. Maybe that's why it's difficult for me to talk about it now because I've been doing it so much. Because if you'd get upset over each and everything there is to be upset about, then you wouldn't do much else than just being upset pretty much all of the time. So I'd say it's easier to play if you get into that, what should I say? Not disrespectful, but detached attitude to it all. That you catch onto racist jokes and sexist jokes, and . . . But this doesn't mean that you can make jokes about anything, and that's the tricky part of it, if you believe that. Because if you start to make jokes about guys in the same way they do about women, they don't think it's fun anymore.

The excerpt points at several interesting issues. First, Ulrika talks about getting blunt almost as a necessary stance for a woman to be able to enjoy the gaming. If the gaming woman would get upset over all inequalities, it would be just too much and it would not be fun to play at all. Instead, she has to be thick-skinned. She needs to be able to take the heat, and look away from inequalities like racism and sexism in the gaming culture. Finally, Ulrika notes that even if the jargon can be described as crude, it does not strike evenly in all directions—it is not acceptable to talk about men the same way they talk about women (and gay men). From this follows that if a woman wants to be part of a male-dominated gaming culture, she needs to conform to the men's rules. I, too, have reflected on this in my field notes:

> There was some crude jargon during the evening, and I recognized what both Sanna and Ulrika had been talking about in the interviews, that you need to deal with this jargon in one way or another. If you're a woman and want to be accepted in the group, you need to signal that you don't mind the jargon, and that you don't take things personally. And thus, you find yourself sitting and laughing at things you wouldn't normally laugh at. Things that in other contexts wouldn't be fun at all. And there were other things that I just pretended I didn't hear. Sometimes, if I wanted to mark my discontent, while still not making a fuss about it, I would just say "I didn't hear that". (Field Diary, 01/11/09)

> [ . . . ] The tone can be quite crude, and sometimes even sexist. I guess it is like Ulrika says, that you have to distance yourself from it. If you're to be able to play as a girl you have to play along. You have to signal that you can take the heat, and that you don't get offended by the crude jargon. And then you're not supposed to be too 'girly' yourself, meaning sensitive and dapper, but it's a good thing if you use a bad language yourself. (Field Diary, 12/29/08)

In her anthropological study of *World of Warcraft*, Nardi (2010) discusses the laddish interaction style among *World of Warcraft* players. Overall, she states, she found the jargon to be relatively sexist and homophobic, but to her surprise, the female members seldom protested, or showed their discontent. We can see the same patterns in my diary entries, where I hesitate about whether and how to mark my discontent with gender exclusionary practices and sexism. The informant Ulrika too has reflected on how difficult it can be to protest against the liberties that male players sometimes take against female ones, especially since these acts are often masked as 'jokes' and coded as 'fun':

*Ulrika:* I've heard a lot of times when I play that "it was only a joke!" They'd say like "Ok, see you tomorrow. Kiss" they'd say. And I say "Why, Kiss?!" And they'd say "Why, can't you take a joke?" So the thing about harassments is that they may happen, and then the thing about 'jokes' are used as an excuse, like it was only for fun and then it's ok to do just about anything.

Being female in a male-dominated environment often requires some balancing acts. Van Zoonen discusses the ambivalent position that female journalists often fall into. On the one hand, they are judged primarily as women, "being subject to continual comment on their appearance and invitations from male colleagues" (van Zoonen 1994, 54), but if they accept this role, they will lose prestige as professionals. However, if they ignore or criticize the comments and invitations, they will not be accepted as 'real women'. Thus, the female journalists have to choose between being either professional *or* women, they cannot be both at the same time.

In the case of computer game culture, many female gamers may not be so eager to be seen as 'real women'—on the contrary, many of us would rather want to be seen as 'one of the boys'. However, neither this stance is compatible with resisting or criticizing sexism. Paradoxically, if you try to resist or criticize sexism in computer game culture, you may not be seen as a 'real woman', but even less will you be seen as 'one of the boys'. Instead, you will stand in opposition; many players will see you as a kill-joy who does not allow 'people' (i.e., the men) to have 'fun' and 'make jokes'. Maybe the most fitting metaphor would be as a meddling mom, one who threatens the state of 'boyhood' as described previously.

The problematic position of the guild mom was discussed in Chapter 2. As I wrote there, at least I felt that this position was none that I wanted to take. I too wanted to feel young, mischievous and playful—and not be a rigid and orderly mother who tried to restrain and keep the unruly boys in order. In the choice between 'boyhood' and 'motherhood', I never hesitated about which position was the most fun and desirable. Thus, I, as many other female players, largely chose to put a bold face on it and keep quiet about inequalities, exclusionary practices and sexism. This paradoxical situation is something I believe is crucial to explain why female players find it so hard to merge into the male gaming cultures. Already from the start, it is very difficult for women to gain entrance to the computer games' state of 'boyhood', although they may be able to do so through using masculinity as a resource. However, by exposing female players to sexism, male players put up further obstacles for them. If the 'boys' sexualize and objectify you, you are clearly not one of them. However, if you protest against the sexism you are being subjected to, you are forced into the role as a kill-joy and meddling mom and thereby you move even further away from the desirable state of boyhood (which you could never fully enter anyway).

Women who want to be accepted in a male-dominated environment may not only keep quiet about inequalities, but also adopt the jargon, thereby taking part in recreating it. In their study on LAN players, Delamere and Shaw (2008) found that female players often adopted hyper-masculine power roles, and even used sexist language themselves. Thereby, say the authors, they reproduced the misogynous discourse. It is true that the specific gaming culture that Delamere and Shaw studied was cruder and more explicitly sexist than most *World of Warcraft* gaming cultures. However, I have definitely seen equivalents. In *World of Warcraft* too, female players do catch onto the prevailing laddish interaction style with its crude jargon (see also Nardi 2010). Especially during my first year as a player, when I was striving to create a space for myself in the guild, I often caught myself using a language style that was generally cruder, and with considerably more cursing than I would normally use. This was partly because I was influenced by the surrounding culture, but on a semi-conscious level it was also a way for me to blend in, to try to become one of the boys by acting like them.

Adapting to the hegemonic discourse may not to be too difficult as concerns bad language, but is considerably more problematic when it comes to the sexist jargon, which I have also caught myself taking part in, to some extent. One example is provided in the following entry from my field diary, in the account on how I interacted with a British guy called Demps[14] during an instance:

> I was killed twice and got squeezed under the boss both times. I said "Hey Demps, I don't get it why I always end up under the boss". Demps laughed and said "I think he fancies you". I then answered something like "Well, he's ugly like hell so it's not like it's gonna happen". And then I made a "rude gesture" emote to the boss, who was dead. A little bit like that, you may adopt the sexist jargon, but then you kind of turn it against yourself rather than against someone else. (Field Diary, 12/28/08)

As was discussed previously, in order to be seen as authentic gamers, women have to invest in the masculine culture and discard some of their femininity. The solution for many is to mark a distance to other women (see also Kendall 2009a, 107). But by adopting the sexist jargon they may also mark a distance to themselves, as women, and take a position outside of their gender. Furthermore, to show that they can 'take the heat', they may sometimes even end up directing sexist jokes at themselves. I would call this the ultimate sign that one has been socialized into the prevailing culture and internalized its hegemonic discourse—the dominant group does not even have to do anything to exert its power, but this is done by the members of the subordinated group themselves (cf. Foucault 1979). Needless to say, even if the individual female player may find it easier to get accepted by using this strategy, it does not help to improve the status of female players on the whole.

## GETTING BURNT

The field note that opened this chapter was written when I had been playing for only two months and had just found my way into the guild. At that time there were lots of things that I did not know about the game. Over time, my knowledge and gaming skills increased, and so did my self confidence.

In Chapter 2, I discussed how female players are often offered help, and in Chapter 1, I quoted a field note that showed how Erik offered his help when I was about to start to play. Since I spent considerably more time playing than Erik and his friends, I eventually surpassed them, in level (when we were still leveling), gear, and knowledge about the game. I also managed to create myself a space within the guild, as one of the dedicated players.

When I once presented my research at a seminar, one female Ph.D. student asked me how the men handled the fact that I no longer needed their help, but instead was the one who could help them. As for Erik and his friends, I never experienced this as a problem—however, I was far from helping Erik as often as he had once helped me. Obviously, there were not the same expectations on me to be a 'gentleman', or for him to accept such help. But when I did help, for example by giving information on add-ons or game content, I never had the feeling that Erik, nor his friends, minded getting help from a woman. As for some other players in the guild, however, my transition towards a more skilled stance was not as unproblematic. As stated before, I often felt that my performance was met with mixed reactions. On the one hand, I felt that people saw me as an inexperienced newbie, but at the same time, I could feel that I was expected to perform flawlessly. This inconsistency is partly related to my development as a player. When I was new, I did not contribute very much, but my value was mainly on the social level. As my/Lore's performance increased, however, so did the demands. I was admitted to join increasingly difficult missions, even the so called progress raids that were ran with optimized groups. I would not have been admitted into those groups had I not performed well enough. However, in comparison with most of the other participants, I was inexperienced. I often felt that I was the one who knew the least about the fights and how to play them, and even though I often topped the dps list, I felt that I did not play well enough.

Another contributing factor may lie in the way the guild developed over the time I was a member. When I joined, the guild had a strong focus on social aspects. In Chapter 1, I quoted the officer Thad as he told me to "level up to 70 so you can come raiding with us". In my opinion, this utterance signaled an inclusive attitude, which was also how the guild worked during that first year. Everyone was welcome to join the raids, even those of us who had recently reached max level and not yet had the time to gear up our characters. Most members saw a value in doing things together. They also appreciated being able to do 25-man raids without having to join forces with other guilds. Over time, however, the raiding culture changed, probably for several reasons.

Nardi (2010) discusses the tension in guilds that may sometimes result when new raid content is added to the game. She tells a story about when her guild, which had had a quite inclusive view on raid participation changed to become considerably more exclusive, prioritizing to run progress raids to which only the top players were admitted, while the other players were left behind. I observed a similar development in *Mercenaries*, notably when the raid instances Ulduar and Icecrown Citadel were added in April and December of 2009. Finally, the development may also have to do with the specific dynamic of players and the composition of the guild. When I joined the guild, it was based on networks of friends. However, in the spring of 2009, the guild started to actively recruit new players, and many of them did not have any previous connections to the guild members. Only players who were experienced, skilled, and dedicated were recruited, meaning that those who joined tended to lean more towards the hardcore than the casual end, which was visible in their expectations of the guild and its activities, and sometimes in their interaction style.

Whatever the reason was, over my years as a member, I experienced that the ambiance in the guild became less friendly and cooperative and more goal-oriented and demanding of players' performance and commitment. Raid participation became an increasingly elitist activity where stress was put on taking down the most difficult bosses and on running 10-man raids on heroic difficulty, rather than bringing along more players so that they too could learn tactics and gear up their characters. The focus on progress raids led to a situation where the number of players with sufficient skill and gear decreased, and the gap between groups of players widened. Some guild members approved of this development and pushed it forwards. Others grew tired in sitting at the subs' bench and left the guild or quit playing. As for me, I tried to keep up, but raiding became increasingly associated with performance anxiety.

My feelings of unease eventually also spread into regular 5-man instances. Here, part of the explanation can be found in the Dungeon finder tool that Blizzard implemented in December 2009. Before, players themselves had had to look for participants from their own server and put together groups. This was often very time consuming, but had positive consequences in the regulation of players' behavior. If someone behaved badly during the instance, the other participants would spread the word in their respective guilds, so that eventually the misbehaving player might face difficulties to get invited into a dungeon group. The opposite can be said about nice players, whom one would add to one's friends list to be able to invite them again. The new tool, on the other hand, was used to put together groups from queuing players over all servers in the battle group. The good point is that it became much easier and faster to form groups to play instances with. The drawback is that because the players in a dungeon group do not know each other, and there are small chances that they will ever meet each other again, they do not have to face the consequences of their actions (cf. Taylor 2003b, in her discussion of player accountability). I found that when left unregulated, many players displayed a quite aggressive jargon, characterized by competitiveness, self assertion, selfishness, bad patience, and/or lack of empathy for other people. They also often did not see their own mistakes, but had the tendency to blame others for their own or the group's failures.

Over time, I grew increasingly tired of the aggressive ambiance and overbearing young male players. Even though I rarely showed it, I also got hurt over the criticism I received, whether it was rightful or not. I started to feel burnt out. I felt that gaming became less and less like play and more and more like work, and not even a particularly nice one, where many players were obnoxious and saw it as their evident right to get down on others if they made mistakes. With the advent of the expansion *Cataclysm*, I started to even refuse playing instances unless I had at least one player with me who I knew and trusted. Having finally managed to get a place among the boys, I realized that I was not prepared, nor willing, to take the heat. I realized that I was not thick-skinned, at least not enough to cope with this environment. Feeling sick and tired over the laddish interaction style, the competitive ambiance, and the crude tone, I started to resent both raids and instances to the point where I even started to consider quitting playing altogether (cf. Taylor 2008c).

## CREATING FREE ZONES

At the same time as I struggled with my unease, several of the guild members that I had had most contact with had quit playing, or moved to other guilds. There was especially one guild, which *Mercenaries* had cooperated with during the summer holidays, where several of my favorite guild mates had found a new home. I decided to move one of my alt characters there, in order to continue to play with them.

The new guild, *Eternal Sun*, had a more even gender distribution than *Mercenaries*. It had several influential female members, and a female guild leader, who was very sociable, considerate and eager to make people feel comfortable. She always greeted everybody when they logged on and took an active part in bringing together people for instances and raids, even at occasions where she herself did not plan to take part. In a way, her leader style was very much like that of the social engineer, as described in Chapter 2.[15] *Eternal Sun* did raids too, but not as well organized as *Mercenaries*, and not as oriented towards raid progression. This means that the level was not as high, but also that the ambiance was more relaxed. I also experienced that the members in general were patient and tolerant vis-à-vis each other, and crude and sexist jargon was prohibited. I enjoyed the ambiance, so after a couple of months I decided to move over all my characters. My guild mate Lisa, on her part, had started to play with one of her female offline friends on another server, meaning that we both made a movement towards guilds with more female members in them. I believe that this kind of movement is relatively common among female gamers.

Women who do not want to accept status quo in the gaming worlds sometimes break out and create their own clans, guilds and teams, and play from their own servers where harassment of female players is prohibited and where they can play on their own terms. My informants Josefin and Martina, for example, belonged to the PMS clan, which is described as the world's largest female clan, with the aim to "provide a fun, competitive, and positive environment to female gamers while promoting respect for women in matches and tournaments".[16] Competitiveness is often held out as a typical characteristic of male gaming cultures and men's playing styles. The PMS clan shows that it does not need to be that way. Here, the competitive focus is preserved; it is only the sexism and harassment of female players that surrounds so many gaming cultures that is prohibited. The PMS clan is a multi-platform organization, but for obvious reasons, its strongest position is in first person shooters where the jargon is said to be especially crude.

Josefin and Martina played *Call of Duty*, Josefin as a hardcore gamer and Martina as a semi-professional. They were both very skilled, but this was not enough to make them a comfortable space within regular (male) player constellations. On the contrary, being skilled could even be a hinder:

*Martina:* Often, when guys realize that it's a girl they're playing with, they get pissed as hell.
*Malin:* Why, that's interesting. Why do you think?
*Martina:* Oh, I don't know. Not all guys but a lot of them react in a negative way when a girl shoots better than they do.
*Malin:* Yeah? What do they do then?
*Martina:* Ah, they yell four-letter words and the most frequent expression is "We're gonna fucking rape your ass".

Many female players get tired of the sexism and harassment they meet, to the extent that it even makes them quit playing. Here, groups like the PMS clan make a huge difference. In this environment, the female players can concentrate on the game without having to deal with harassment. In her text on female e-sport players, T.L. Taylor notes that women often are isolated. This isolation is not, as one would think, because they do not have any female friends who play, but that they do not know that their friends play: "Far too often we find that women gamers occupy a kind of closeted gamer identity" (Taylor 2008b, 54). Here, Taylor points at web sites such as Womengamers.com as a powerful resource for female players. In a similar way, for Josefin, the PMS clan, apart from providing a safe haven from harassment, also had a positive impact in that it made her realize that there were more women players out there than she had first thought.

*Josefin:* Actually there are quite a few girls who play. You see it when you join (the PMS clan) but otherwise you never get to meet girls online.
*Malin:* So you mean that they often stay among themselves in their own clans?

*Josefin:* Well, either that or that they play other kinds of games. But now I've seen that they play these games too.

*Malin:* That's one thing I've been thinking about lately. According to statistics, quite a few women play computer games. But you seldom get to see them. How is that? Where are they?

*Josefin:* Yeah, I've been thinking that too, how come you never see them even that you're online quite a lot. And if you're online and people get to know you're a girl they'd say "Are you a girl? How strange" kind of.

*Malin:* Do you think one can draw parallels to how it was when the internet was new? Back then, many women chose not to tell others they were women because they didn't want to get flirted with or harassed. Do you think this could be the reason here too?

*Josefin:* Yeah, absolutely. I felt like that when I started to play. If you told others you were a girl, there would be a certain jargon and it just became so tiresome. And then you started to not reveal that you're a girl.

*Malin:* OK. When you say tiresome, how do you mean then?

*Josefin:* Well, in most cases it would be a sexual ambiance, like they jump on you with certain . . . Well, a sexual jargon, all of the time.

For Josefin, as for many other female players, the women-only game spaces offer an environment that feels safe, where they can get the fun out of playing without having to deal with the negative parts of male computer game culture. It also lets them relax and not only reveal that they are female but even live out those sides of themselves even more. For example, Josefin told me that when she had the choice, she would often choose a pink or red camouflage suits to signal that she is a girl, ultimately to show "that girls like shooter games too". Thus, it seems like female-dominated gaming environments offer more opportunities to combine the gaming interest with femininity, which could allow for a gamer femininity to emerge. Still, talking about 'girlhood' as a state related to computer games (in the same sense as Burrill's notion 'boyhood') may be beyond the reach.

## STRATEGIES AT PLAY

In the opening of this chapter, I mentioned some of the strategies often used by women in male-dominated environments. In her analysis of female journalists, Djerf-Pierre (2005) identified three strategies: the competing, the specializing and the expanding. The competing strategy means to try to become 'one of the boys' and compete for a position on the men's conditions. The strategy of specialization means to use one's feminine gender capital to instead become 'one of the girls'. In Djerf-Pierre's analysis, the expanding strategy means that the women find new areas to spread out into, areas which are not yet gendered. Maybe this can be compared to the strategy that Melin (2008) calls 'flight', where the women find other ways to practice their profession, outside of the established hierarchies, for example as freelance. In any case, both strategies imply escaping to a sphere where they do not have to compete with the men. I can see several parallels to the strategies I have been using in my own gaming. However, as the women officers in the study of Pettersson et al. (2008), my strategies too tended to change over time.

According to Pettersson et al., new recruits tend to use individual strategies, accepting the established gender relations of the organization and adopting the jargon. If they ever challenge it, it is on an individual basis, as in performing well on the running track, thereby proving their capacity. Pettersson et al. (p. 204) states that this strategy is individual in a double sense. First, the woman officer does not question the hierarchies in public when male colleagues make their original statements about women's lesser capacity compared to men, but instead she proves them to be wrong based on her *individual* accomplishment. Second, say Pettersson et al, the result of this accomplishment is that the male colleague may accept her as an individual, however, the view on women officers in general is not challenged.

Looking at my gaming career, the first strategy I used consisted of holding a low profile and voluntarily entering a subordinate position, thereby positioning the other members as strong and powerful. This strategy worked quite well, and managed to get me a place in the guild. Once I became more skilled as a player, however, I passed over into the 'competing strategy', where I tried to become 'one of the boys'. According to Djerf Pierre (2007, 98), women who go for the competing strategy generally do so by bringing in more of the kinds of capital that is valued in the field—"education, contacts, personal networks, etc.". The capital that is most valued in gaming communities are experience and, of course, skill. Over my gaming history, some of my gaming friends have told me that I put too much pressure on myself, which is exemplified in my feelings of having to perform flawlessly as discussed previously. At closer scrutiny, I realize that this demand came from myself just as much as from other players. I had high expectations on my performance because I strived to get a place among the boys, and I felt that the way to achieve this goal was to perform so well so that no one could question my right to be there. In a way, I tried to accomplish exactly the same thing as the recruits of Pettersson et al. did at the running track. However, even if I, to some extent, managed to create myself a space among the boys, this position was always dependent on struggles and competition. It was a space that I was not given for free, but that I felt was contested as soon as I made a mistake.

The two first strategies both include an acceptance of the hegemonic discourse, where I tried to create myself a space within the already existing universe of values and practices. I also strived to get accepted by proving that I could perform better than the boys. Thus, I, just like the recruits of Pettersson et al. (2008) used strategies that belonged to the individual perspective. However, over time I became increasingly critical towards the laddish culture with its aggressive and competitive ambiance, and the ways I saw women being met in it. This resonates well with what Pettersson et al. found about the older women officers, who, as they became more senior, also became more critical towards the gendered hierarchies and tended to employ strategies that question the fundamental structural conditions of the organization. However, say Pettersson et al., this is rarely appreciated. The instances that the informants of Pettersson et al. described as successful in challenging gender relations belonged to the individual strategies when one individual officer manages to get accepted and included—despite of her gender. When the gender relations of the organization as a whole are at stake, however, the resistance is described as massive.

In my gaming, I guess that my ways of trying to resist exclusion and sexism can be seen as challenging the gaming culture on a structural level. However, I experienced that it had very little effect, and also that at least certain players got disturbed over my comments. I felt that there were few ways of fighting the structure from within, so instead I took to another strategy, which implied distancing myself from it. By avoiding raids and instances, and engaging in only casual gaming style activities, I would say that the third strategy I engaged in is best described as flight, where I escaped the competition altogether.

The gaming culture that I have come into contact with is known to be very friendly in comparison with other gaming cultures. Still, as my four chapters have shown, if one scratches the surface, one will still find quite a lot of constraining of women's opportunities to play and enjoy themselves in their gaming activities. Some women may be thick-skinned enough to be able to cope with it, but I was not. In many ways I felt afflicted over my loss. I had loved to be part of a functioning team that took on challenging missions. I had loved playing raids, and most of all, I had loved it when my name turned up at the top of the dps list. Was there not a way for me to be able to do this as a woman? Or was the passion of computer games destined to be forever bound to men and their laddish interaction styles? One strategy that both Melin (2008) and Djerf-Pierre (2007) found in their studies is called becoming 'one of the girls', where the women take advantage of their female gender capital and specialize in so-called female spheres of interest. My movement towards a guild with a more even gender distribution can be seen as belonging to that strategy. In a gaming community with more women in it, I did not have to reshape myself to be 'one of the boys', or defend my right to be there. Furthermore, in this more supportive environment, I slowly came to regain my self confidence and find the courage to play instances and raids again. My guess is that many other female players have had similar experiences, which the number of members of all-women gaming communities such as the PMS clan speaks for.

Creating women-only spaces may be a way to cope with harassment and inequalities, allowing female players to concentrate on their gaming; to increase their gaming skills and self confidence, without having to dedicate time and energy on dealing with sexist treatment or vindicating themselves and their rights to play (cf. Bryce and Rutter 2002). In their interventionist research in an after-school video game club for girls, Jenson et al. (2011) for example found that when the balance of power for the gaming club was shifted to technologically competent female gamers, the girls in the club responded: "they play more, take up more space, police who is allowed in or not, and generally display technological and political competence, interest in games, and knowledge of them. They also acknowledge the dominance of boys and begin to vocalize their presumed entitlement and work to change it" (Jenson et al. 2011, 165).

As positive as this may be, I do not know if creating women-only spaces is the best way to go to make the gaming cultures a better place for women. When women choose to play among themselves, they choose to dissociate themselves from the mainstream, or as Ganetz (1997) puts it (in relation to music industry): *male stream* gaming culture. The creation of women-only 'sanctuaries', or even 'reservations', and for that sake, the fact that many female players do not tell others that they are female, is probably part of the reason why players (both male and female) claim to so seldom meet female players, and believe that 'women do not play computer games', despite the fact that statistics say otherwise. Hence, even if the creation of women-only gaming spaces is beneficial for individual players, it may contribute to the continuous turning invisible of female gamers, and thus not benefit gaming women as a collective. Sadly enough, this can be said for the other strategies as well. Adopting a subordinate position does not benefit either the individual woman or women as a collective. To be 'one of the boys' means to take a position outside of one's gender. The individual woman may gain a position, but it is at the expense of her femininity and of other women, whom she has to betray. Taking to flight or gathering together in all-women gaming collectives means that women can play and live out their gaming passion, but just as long as they accept being invisible and do not threaten the male hegemony. Still, for many female players, it may offer the best solution. And in the long run, with the emergence of more mixed gaming communities, we might live to see a change.

## NOTES

1. These two factors—experience and frequency—were found to be important status symbols among chat users as well, together with the existence of personal relationship to other users (Sveningsson 2001).
2. This corresponds to the years 2004–2007.
3. A wipe is when all participants in the group die during the encounter with the enemy monsters, and the group has to resurrect and restart. Different

games vary in how severe death punishments are (Klastrup 2008). In *World of Warcraft*, the punishment is connected to time and in-game money: one loses the time that it takes to resurrect and get ready for the encounter again, and one also has to pay to repair damaged equipment. Wipes are costly both in time and repair costs, thus players generally try to avoid them.

4. Project Lore is an online hub of various media relating to the *World of Warcraft*, including videos and guides, and it is defined as "the definitive source for all things Warcraft". But Lore is also an abbreviation of my main character's name, and what other players generally call me.
5. As the character levels up, it gains talent points that the player chooses how to place. Some talents increase the damage that the character does, while others protect it from various sorts of damage, or give special abilities. The 'spec' refers to the way the character's talent points are placed. Finding the optimal spec can improve the character's performance in quite a dramatic way, thus, many players put considerable amounts of time and efforts into experimenting with it.
6. In the Greek mythology, Pygmalion was a sculptor who fell in love with one of his own statues. The story was taken up by Bernard Shaw, whose play *Pygmalion* made its first appearance in 1913. In the play, Professor Henry Higgins teaches the lower class girl, Eliza Doolittle, to talk and act like a society woman. The play was later made into the musical, *My Fair Lady*.
7. The dual spec offered a way for players to keep two permanent sets of talents that they could easily switch between. At the time dual spec was introduced, it was quite expensive—1,000 Gold (which is the in-game currency of *World of Warcraft*). The cost was gradually decreased to 100 Gold in October 2010, and 10 Gold in December 2010.
8. In many encounters, the raid group needs more than one tank. There may be several monsters that need to be tanked, or tanks need to take turns to avoid taking too much damage. It is then common to assign one main tank and one or several assisting off tanks.
9. Similar findings were made by Kendall in her study of a male-dominated MUD. There, "each woman's position in the group, her acceptance as smart, funny, and witty (all qualities especially valued on BlueSky), in short as 'one of the guys', depended somewhat on her ability to show that she was *not* like the other women" (Kendall 2009a, 107–108).
10. Josefin was one exception, talking about the constraints of the gamer stereotype. People were often surprised to learn that she was a gamer, she said, as they didn't think she looked like one (she wasn't "fat and ugly with greasy hair").
11. I believe the same can be said about sports.
12. The Swedish word that was used was 'gubbar', as in "Hallå gubbs" and "Snyggt jobbat gubbar". Actually, 'gubbe' is a word for 'old man', but it can also be used in a general sense as 'man' or figure. It is commonly used among members of (male) sports teams, who, after a successful match would probably also say "Snyggt jobbat gubbar" (Great job chaps).
13. The Swedish word was 'annat', which is actually a word denoting objects. Persons as in 'others' would be called 'andra'.
14. Demps was a guild mate of Reilly (see Chapter 3 in this book), and he knew that I was (or claimed to be) female.
15. I realize that in writing this, I too, fall in to the pitfall of describing female players as more social and nurturing than male ones. Maybe they/we are, but if so, I believe that the reasons are because we are expected to take that role, or are socialized into it, rather than because of any inherent predisposition.
16. http://www.pmsclan.com.

# 5 Desires at Play

*Jenny Sundén*

> How bodies are affected gives crucial insight into the research process and the object of study. Including them in the written presentation of the research seems to be a sensible idea.
>
> (Probyn 2005, 135)

Digital games as a media genre aim at and involve the bodies of players in intense ways. Games have a tendency to wind up the body—to rush its heart, to sharpen its senses, to speed up its reflexes. Part of this acceleration is an enfolding of the physical body in game space in ways that expand, or extend the body and its capacities through on-screen representations. Playing bodies are in this sense not only intensely involved in game scenarios, but also most concretely propelled into the unfolding of the game, physically as well as symbolically. As mentioned in the introduction, this entanglement of the bodies of players with the bodies 'at play' in the game has been theorized by game scholars in terms of, for example, affect (Carr 2006c; Colman 2008), pleasure (Kennedy 2006; Mortensen 2004; Taylor 2003a; 2006b), and the phenomenology of play (Bogost 2008; Crick 2011). Interestingly, there appears to be a something of a glitch in the translation from ontology to epistemology in the research of digital games. In other words, even if digital games are understood as an embodied, sensuous media form, this very corporeality seems to leave few traces in the methodological strategies of game researchers and their ways of knowing the field. Literature on games may offer careful investigations of their seductive power, but rarely do researchers themselves admit to ever having been seduced.[1]

This chapter is an attempt to put the sensing, researching body into the picture by providing an ethnographic account of a particular way of being introduced to and of falling for an online game (*World of Warcraft*), a woman, and the ways in which these two were intensely connected. There is plenty of literature on endgame experiences and skilled gamers, but much less on how researchers come to and learn the games they study (cf. Taylor 2008a). At the core of this chapter is a discussion of knowledge production in cultural studies of online games, and in particular an inquiry about notions of closeness and desire in new media ethnography. Drawing on the body of ethnographic work interrogating erotic subjectivity and desire in fieldwork, I make use of personal experiences—in particular an in-game as well as out-of-the game love affair—as potentially important sources of knowledge. By putting into words a particular way of coming to the game/field, questions are raised concerning our motives, drives, and desires as researchers, and what difference it would make if such desires in research were more openly discussed. Or, as Lori Kendall (2009a, 102) puts it in her interrogation of the critical potentials of desire in fieldwork, "How do we know what we know? What do we tell people about how we learned what we learned in the field?" Set against the backdrop of 'the affective turn' in cultural and feminist theory, and in making visible how desire and emotion may circulate through game spaces, I argue for an articulation of desire as intimately related to technology.[2]

My ethnographic work in *World of Warcraft* went through two phases. The first phase, on which this chapter is based, was an affective investigation of queer potentials in mainstream *World of Warcraft* cultures. The focus of this initial one-year ethnography (which began in the Fall of 2007) was on ways of exploring the game world and leveling up, on solo play and play in smaller groups. The second phase was more explicitly focused on queer gamers—or *gaymers*—and consisted of play with a particular guild openly defined as LGBT (lesbian, gay, bisexual, and transgender/transsexual), which in my writing is called *The Others* (Sundén 2009b). The focus all along has been primarily on female players who identify as queer, or by other measures as non-straight. For the initial ethnography, I played and leveled a female green-haired rogue troll with the cover name Bricka. All names of characters and players in relation to this work have been changed for the sake of anonymity. The chapter at hand details my coming to the game as well as to the field, it tells the story of how I was introduced to and began to play and research *World of Warcraft*. This is a love story of sorts, and it made me work with and through notions of attraction and desire—in respect to women, online games, and ethnographies—in ways that were both challenging and difficult. But hopefully, the result points at ways of thinking the personal and the passionate in close conjunction with the critical.

An interesting question is what constitutes 'the field' in studies of new media as culture? The rise of 'virtual ethnography' (Hine 2000), or of an 'anthropology of the virtual' (Boellstorff 2008) can be understood as a response to the 1990s utopian visions of cyberspace as disembodied, placeless, and immaterial (Lanier and Biocca 1992). No longer depicted as a coherent, unambiguous whole, 'cyberspace' has been revealed as consisting of a wide range of particular cultures and contexts, each with its own flavor and each with its own rules (Baym 2000; Correll 1995; Schaap 2002). The idea of cyberspace as placeless was countered by studies of the matter and meaning of the very locations in which online spaces are always produced and consumed (Miller and Slater 2000), and the understanding of cyberspace as disembodied was similarly dismantled by findings according to which the body was consistently reintroduced, represented, and even on demand in virtual worlds (Kendall 1998; Taylor 2003b; Sundén 2003).

As opposed to the kind of fieldwork where being, living, and staying in the field is the only option, new media ethnography brings with it the possibility of moving between different locations and bodies to the point where the borders between them may start to blur. This text positions itself within this very uncertainty of locations and bodies, to investigate its consequences for ways of knowing online game cultures. The fact that the game world is never further away than an Internet connection and a computer with the appropriate game software (such as my own) creates a particular closeness to the field. This closeness has proved to be of a kind that leaves traces in the body. As a new media ethnographer, I potentially carry the field with me everywhere. To be close to the field in this sense means that the field not only stays with me after logging off, but actually never quite leaves my body—or so it seems. During that introductory, intense period of playing the game, I would hear the Stockholm subway at a distance and found myself thinking: "that sounds an awful lot like when my rogue character enters stealth mode". I felt my growing impatience with the elevator ride to the sixth floor where my office was located at the time (at the Royal Institute of Technology), for my body still remembered the speedy elevator rides in various locations in Azeroth. What consequences does this multiplicity of locations—and of bodies—have for the kind of knowledge we can form in online field sites? Is it relevant to make visible experiences that border on the field, but that are not in an obvious way *of* the field? Is it even possible to draw the limits of a field that in intimate ways is part of our everyday media experiences?

This is not to say that there is always a confusion of boundaries for *World of Warcraft* players, or even that it happens constantly in my own play. Within the bounds of my study, I would rather suggest that these might be experiences that are significant in particularly intense periods of play (when the rhythm of the game may stay with the body after logging off), and probably even more so in earlier stages of gameplay before everything turns more mundane, even routine. In addressing the pleasurable, compelling nature of *World of Warcraft*, Bonnie Nardi (2010, 40) speaks of how gaming experiences are "woven of sociality, the visual beauty of the game, and a sense of performative mastery". Similarly, the women in my study talk about falling for the game, using a similar vocabulary to that of a love story ("when I first started to play *World of Warcraft*, everything just clicked and I knew it was the right game for me"). They use this notion of 'love at first sight' to address the seductive qualities of the landscape and soundscape, the avatars, the play with others, the advancements through the game, even if 'to fall', rather than alluding to being *in* control and exercising a sense of mastery may indicate certain loss of control.

Elspeth Probyn (2005) points out that academic writing on affect and emotion is often curiously devoid of the researcher's own emotions. There must be other ways of working, the question is how, and in which language. For how can you put into words the feeling of suddenly being out of breath, of sensing a quickening of the heart only by seeing a particular avatar at a distance? Or, as a woman put it after our very first encounter in the game, "I felt my heart racing when I saw you" (where the 'you' suggests a collapse between the body of the player and that of the avatar, cf. Sveningsson, Chapter 3 of this book, and her discussion of the player-avatar-hybrid). Transmedia desires are an intimate part of many people's everyday lives and media consumption. The question is what researchers make of such intensity when it no longer involves merely their 'informants', but most concretely themselves.

## FIRST IMPRESSIONS

> We are to create science, not porn. (Fine 1993, 285)

I met her in a bar. She was standing alone in a narrow, sparsely lit hallway, leaning nonchalantly against the wall, her pale skin in stark contrast with her all-black tight clothing. It was one of those moments when words are irrelevant, and I could not help but approach her. We spent the night together. She woke up in my temporary home, her dark hair entangled, and gazed at my bookcase. "Is that *World of Warcraft* I see over there?" she wondered, barely awake. "Ehum, yes", I said, "but I only just bought it, it's for a research project on queer women and online gaming". "Aha", she said, wide-awake. "Well, I'm a Blizzard slave, I must confess. I've been playing for two years now". We joked about me interviewing her, and how that hardly could be an ethical procedure. "Well, as long as I'm not in the nude, it should be ok", she concluded. We left it at that. But only a few days later, I got an intriguing text message: "Do you want to meet up in Durotar somewhere this evening?"

I had literally just taken my first steps with my female green-haired rogue troll and I felt a bit reluctant to meet with her endlessly more powerful level 60+ female orc Slap.[3] But my curiosity led me to accept her offer. We did meet, in *World of Warcraft*, and we kept meeting up and playing together. She did not live in Stockholm, or even in Sweden, so scheduling 'dates' (or more spontaneously happening to be on at the same time) in the game became a way of spending time and experiencing the game together (cf. Sveningsson, Chapter 3 of this book). The research on gender and games is heavily populated by boyfriends, brothers, and other men as the ones who introduce women to gaming, and who also moderate and monitor their behavior (see, for example, Bryce and Rutter 2003a; Lin 2005; Schott and Horrell 2000; Yee 2008). In these discussions, gameplay is almost automatically coded as a masculine domain, and online games as somehow inherently sexist. Mine was an irresistibly different story.

Bricka surely had other playmates, both temporary liaisons and more stable relations. With time, she also got the company of other alts (i.e., of other characters belonging to myself). But in this early phase of gameplay, say between level 5 and 25, the initial contact with this particular woman and her avatar/s was by far my most important and intense connection. She gave me a jump-start into the game. Slap protected Bricka with her playing body, introduced her to all sorts of in-game peculiarities, showed her places, and generally showed her a good time. Bricka had things to offer in return. Her good humor and wit, which made orc laughter blend with troll laughter as they ran together over the hills. Of relevance for a research project on emotion, sexuality, and online games, I experienced first-hand the sensation of desiring someone through the game interface. An already enticing, immersive game experience was all the more charged through the ways in which desire and physical attraction came to circulate through the game. I would see 'her', the muscular orc woman, with her white tiger, come running towards me (or Bricka) across the dunes, the sand spurting from under foot and paw. Bricka's heart would skip a beat. Or was it mine? Does it matter? Conversely, when we had drinks at a bar in Stockholm, I would have avatar flashbacks of seeing Slap's gestures in her own physical movements. Even if I had met her 'in the flesh' before meeting her online, due to the sheer volume of hours that we played together compared to the rare encounters face-to-face, the game world became the ground rule and the everyday-like in our contact. This is likely the reason for me seeing the presence of Slap in her physical being, perhaps even looking for her there, since in terms of bodily presence, movements, and attitude, I knew the Orc woman (as an amalgamation of the two) better than I knew her player.

Kate Altork (1995, 110) reflects on the significance of first impressions and of multi-sensorial ways of knowing new places: "It has been my experience that any new locale sends all of my sensory modes into overdrive in the initial days and weeks of my stay". In a similar manner, it is probably during the early phase of gameplay that moving through the landscape is the most enthralling, the music at its most magical, and overall the experience the most powerful. The slightly melancholic soft wind instruments of the Barrens, blending with the sound of a warm wind sweeping through dry grass, became the soundtrack of a brief love story. Bricka's rogue leather attire, including a beautiful leather harness along with her swift blades, resonated in a life and in meetings beyond Azeroth. Perhaps more than anything else, the physical qualities of intense moments of gameplay came to extend and enhance the physical qualities of attraction and desire. Pace, Bardzell, and Bardzell (2010) speak of the permeability of intimacy between real and virtual worlds, and it is very hard to tell what it was, more precisely, that constituted the limits of, or the source of these emotions. Or rather, it is quite clear that it was her, but rather unclear in which form. Was it her, regardless of the game? Was it her *through* the game? Was it her through the orc woman and the ways in which she moved and talked and somehow managed to reach out to me and touch something within me through the screen? Most likely, it was all of these things combined, which makes emotional boundaries coincide with the limits of a field that is not easily defined.

At first glance, questions of sexuality may seem irrelevant to a study of online game cultures. But my own experiences do not seem different from the experiences of many other *World of Warcraft* players. Game studies literature gives evidence of how many players play with people they already know (i.e., friends, family, partners, lovers . . . ; Nardi and Harris 2006; Peterson 2007; Yee 2003, 2008), hence bringing various kinds of intimacy and closeness into game spaces. In *World of Warcraft*, sexuality is performed on multiple levels: as a design feature, as part of players' social practices (flirtations), as a source of imagination (of the physical bodies of co-players), as a property of verbal abuse ("you're so gay"), and as a principle for discrimination. (Krotoski 2006). As a design element, sexuality is simultaneously both on and off. The interface prohibits physical contact between avatars, they cannot even hug each other after a successful battle. There may be textual hugs in the form of emotes, but these gestures do not translate onto the bodies of characters (cf. Sveningsson, Chapter 3 in this book, for a discussion of the function of emotes). At the same time, the bodies of avatars are heterosexualized in ways that, instead of eliminating sexuality from the game, bring the sexual into clear focus (Corneliussen 2008). Avatars can strip down to their underwear, and the dance pre-programmed in, for example, female night elves imitates the moves of pole-dance strippers. And even if there are no ready-made emotes for physical contact between characters, devoted ERP-ers (erotic role-players) have certainly been creative in their ways of making emotes appear as something other than intended by design to display sexual gestures (Valkyrie 2011).

## PASSIONATE SCHOLARSHIP AND EPISTEMOLOGICAL UNCERTAINTY

This is not a confession for the sake of confessing. However, it may share certain affinities with what is commonly referred to as a 'confessional mode' in ethnography (Van Maanen 1988). If the traditional, realist mode of writing ethnographically consists of relatively impersonal, cool, detached language, writing in a confessional mode is, on the contrary, personal and engaged. Although traditionally, confessionals have rarely been part of 'official' ethnography, this is an argument for placing the personal and the passionate at heart of ethnographic work. The text at hand is not self-therapeutic, but it does engage critically with the discussion of the role of the writing 'I' within ethnography. It contains a discussion that makes use of personal experiences and emotions as potentially valuable sources of knowledge. Informants may tell you about online attractions, or of falling for someone in online venues. My story is not qualitatively different, but it does require a fairly intimate disclosure of the researching 'I'. Ethnographic writing in this particular chapter is writing from cultural margins as it brings to the fore culturally marginalized sexualities and desires. It offers a critique of mainstream ethnographic writing in articulating matters that for the most part have remained unexpressed, acknowledging that ethnographers, too, are desiring subjects. Simultaneously, it is an investigation of unclear boundaries of bodies and subjectivities in and through their multiple couplings with game technologies. As such, this text embodies something of a paradox in that it deconstructs the researcher as subject by troubling the border between knowing subjects and objects of knowledge, while at the same time writing out of the position of the 'I', however fractured, incomplete, and partial this position may be.

Writing within anthropology has traditionally been seen merely as an instrument, as a tool for taking notes in the field and for completing the final report. Language in this perspective is transparent mediation of lived experiences and social relations. The same kind of transcendence characterizes the ethnographer—the 'neutral' observer—who comes to represent a disinterested truth. Alongside objectivist claims in traditional ethnographic writing, the telling of subjective experiences has certainly existed. Then again, these personal narratives rarely stand alone, but are usually preceded or followed by a 'formal' ethnography that legitimizes them scientifically. This creates a paradoxical tension within the tradition itself, between subjective and 'scientific' voices, through which fieldwork

> produces a kind of authority that is anchored to a large extent in subjective, sensuous experience [ . . . ]. But the professional text to result from such an encounter is supposed to conform to the norms of a scientific discourse whose authority resides in the absolute effacement of the speaking and experiencing subject. (Pratt 1986, 32)

The 'reflexive' turn in anthropology in the mid-1980s which ultimately problematized ways of knowing and writing anthropologically—certainly performed a shift in ethnographic writing, and can be seen as part of a broader theorizing about the limits of representation itself (see Clifford and Marcus 1986; Geertz 1988; Van Maanen 1988). Then again, as Esther Newton (1993, 5) notes in her article, "My Best Informant's Dress: The Erotic Equation of Fieldwork": "Most 'reflexive' anthropology, which explicitly spotlights how ethnographic knowledge is produced, has rendered sex and emotion between ethnographer and informants more abstract than before". Newton interrogates the reasons why the erotic dimension has been largely absent from the anthropological canon, what this absence does, and what difference it would make if ethnographers were to include it. She traces what she reads as an urge to know 'the other' beyond the reflexive turn, only to find a discussion that in a poststructuralist, discursive manner recedes into a language of bodily metaphors. At the moment when there is an acknowledgment of how ethnographic knowledge depends on, as Pratt has it, "subjective, sensuous experience", there appear to be few efforts to write from and theorize such experiences. Is passionate scholarship an oxymoron?

Erotic subjectivity, experience, or desire in the field is (still) a rare topic in ethnographic writing. Similar to accounts of the more generally personal, written records of (the researcher's) erotic subjectivity have, typically, figured separately from legitimate ethnographies, most notably the posthumous publishing of Bronislaw Malinowski's (1967) private diary, Paul Rabinow's (1977) one-night stand with a Moroccan woman, "thoughtfully provided by a male informant" (Newton 1993, 7), and Manda Cesara (1982), who wrote under a pseudonym of her intimate relation with a male informant. In recent years, there has been a somewhat wider range of publications that in various ways interrogate and break the silences surrounding ethnographers as sexual subjects (see, for example, Jackman 2010; Kulick and Willson 1995; Markowitz and Ashkenazi 1999; Lewin and Leep 1996; Wekker, 2006). In his introduction to the rare collection of essays *Taboo: Sex, Identity and Erotic Subjectivity in Anthropological Fieldwork*, Don Kulick (1995, 18) argues that "desire in the field seems to be one especially poignant means through which anthropologists become aware of themselves as positioned, partial, knowing selves". He suggests that erotic subjectivity in the field is a potentially useful source of insight because it *does* things. Desire provokes questions at the core of anthropological production of knowledge. Desire draws attention to ways of knowing oneself and others, and it highlights the politics of bodily difference.

And yet, the silences around what Newton calls a 'non-subject' in anthropology seem far from resolved. As Kulick points out, there seems to be something more and other at work than objectivist ideals, the disciplinary disapproval of the personal, and a more general cultural taboo against discussing (one's own) sexuality that constitute such silences. Referencing Newton's article, Kulick observes that not talking about the erotic subjectivity of fieldworkers operates on multiple levels: it makes invisible the norm(ality) of heterosexual male subjectivity (by cutting it off from the area of possible inquiry), and it works to silence women and gays for whom issues of gender and sexuality have never been easy. Besides performing within a register of sexism and homophobia, Kulick adds that "silence about the erotic subjectivity of fieldworkers also works to keep concealed the deeply racist and colonialist conditions that make possible our continuing unidirectional discourse about the sexuality of the people we study" (p. 4).

There is certainly a difference between doing the kind of fieldwork where staying in the field involves remaining in secluded places for long periods at a time, and the kind of fieldwork performed online from the comfort of your office, kitchen table, or favorite coffee shop. New media ethnography rarely puts the researcher in isolated and lonely situations (even if spending long hours at the computer sometimes feels that way), but it nonetheless involves closeness to the medium, and possibly to others through this medium and beyond. As with all fieldwork, it is about interacting with others, and about forming inter-personal relationships over time. Working with and through notions of desire in the field can be a powerful way of exploring the conditions of knowledge production in ethnographic work, of the very boundaries that constitute legitimate modes of knowing. Then again, there is an interesting discussion of the possible limits of self-reflexivity in an erotic vein. Kulick (1995, 5) makes clear that the chapters of *Taboo* aim at addressing issues of theoretical and methodological significance, not at providing "a catalogue of ethno-pornography". Critics of the reflexive turn point to the fine line between the personal and the self-indulgent, and to the risk of using experiential modes of working and writing as means of merely reflecting on oneself (see Probyn 1993). Michelle Kisliuk (1997, 39) suggests that in order to productively make use of our experiences in the field, we need to "ask ourselves whether an experience changed us in a way that significantly affected how we viewed, reacted to, or interpreted the ethnographic material".

For me, it was never a matter of uncovering the personal for the sake of disclosure in and of itself, of performing a textual striptease for the thrill of the act. Had this been the case, the text at hand would have been far steamier. In fact, I have been hesitant—and I still hesitate. "Epistemological uncertainty" forms part of the title of this section, and there are many things of which I am uncertain. Uncertainty, here, is meant to evoke a manner of not being sure of whether one's methodological strategies will work productively in an academic setting. Uncertainty points at how ways of knowing are shaky, partial, and always in the process of being proved otherwise. Uncertainty also signifies our positions as researchers of games in an emerging field where we are still attempting to find our footing. Uncertainty as concept is also central to game studies in its way of troubling the 'magic circle' and pointing at the embeddedness of games in everyday life. Uncertainty signals what Donna Haraway (1997, 190) calls a method of "being at risk", an ethnographic attitude in which something is *at stake* in the face of the practices and discourses into which the researcher inquires. It has become clear to me that the manner in which I began to learn about gaming and queerness carries far too much weight for my research project to be concealed. And if my story is a shameful one to tell within a research context, what would that tell us about this very context? What would it tell us about particular understandings of 'science' and the production of knowledge? As Probyn (2005, 75 ff.) has it, to feel shame speaks as much about the 'shamers' as it does of the person in shame.

## CRITICALLY CLOSE

Closeness is key in much ethnographic fieldwork. And yet, there is a longstanding discussion of what happens if you come too close, of 'going native' and no longer able to uphold the amount of distance required in the name of science. Even if self-reflexivity has been part of ethnographic work for decades, ideas and ideals of objectivity seem somehow to slip in through the back door. How close is too close—and why? What if a love affair—instead of blinding me—made me see particularly clearly? And what difference would it make if I dared be open about this shift in me? Does desire *per se* make you less critical? It is commonly understood that when 'in love' we experience, see, feel, taste, and smell things in a different way, and usually more *acutely*. Rather than dismissing such heightening of the senses as flawed in the sense that I may have 'lost my head' (an expression that points at the conventional opposition between to think and to feel), I would be more interested in investigating such intensity as something that could be an important part of criticality.

There are obvious questions of power and ethics at play in fieldwork. Commonly, the researcher is understood as not only having the right of interpretation, but also of inhabiting a more powerful position than the people being studied. Ethics in this context is about not misusing this power. The question of power in the field needs to be contextualized through the complex intersections of, for example, gender, sexuality, ethnicity, and in my case, technology and online game culture. As Newton (1993, 8) argues, "changing the gender and/or sexual orientation and probably the race of either fieldworker or informant modifies the terms of the erotic equation". Is the researcher perhaps a heterosexual, white, Western man with a Ph.D. and the informant/bed partner a prostitute from Morocco? Or, are the people involved two middle-class queer women from Scandinavia? In a reading sensible to colonial as well as patriarchal power, the 'erotic equation' figures differently in each situation.

In my case, there is also a need to contextualize power in terms of technological proficiency and knowledge of a particular game culture. Relations of power in the field have been anything but clear, and not always does the researcher have the upper hand. Initially, I was the one in need of introduction and protection. I have thought about the powerful draw in being guided and protected by a skilled player with a character on a much higher level. *World of Warcraft* has a lot to do with levels (at least during that part of the game when players are involved in the activity of 'leveling up') as well as with differences in knowledge of the game (cf. Sveningsson, Chapter 4, as well as her discussion of attraction in relation to levels in Chapter 3 of this book). When you let the cursor scan the landscape for friends and enemies, information about their levels are immediately available. This information tells you about your chances to defeat an enemy, or whether playing together with someone is mutually beneficial. When a high-level character plays alongside and helps a low-level character, the game benefits for the high-level are minimal. These are rather altruistic acts for the sheer pleasure of playing together. In my case, Bricka was the little one, and her admiration blended with my own for her protector and wild big sister.

Then again, to choose an unusually open way of writing about parts of the research process can be understood as an exercise of power. Therefore, it has been imperative to let the people involved in my study read and give me permission to move forward with my texts. For the present chapter, it was very important that I got permission and support from the woman I have met in multiple ways. On several occasions when playing, I hinted at my ways of writing about the game and about her, but it was not until I sent her a shorter draft of this text that she saw any of this in writing. I held my breath for a week, maybe more, without a word from her, which made me increasingly nervous. Had I violated our trust? Had I somehow betrayed her? If ethics, as Probyn (2005, 34) claims, is awareness of what one's actions might set in motion, was I no longer aware of what I may have stirred up? This surely was intense material in more ways than one, and I felt relief once I received the following email response from her: "Hi Jenny and Bricka! I smile. Slap grins. We flex our muscles. [ . . . ] This is hot, hot, hot". Not only did she give this part of my research project her blessing, she was also flattered. She even thought that bringing intimate issues out in the open was a vital part of the project, and one that could make an important difference.

Probyn (2005, 129 ff.) notes the importance of including the researching body in academic writing, of being attentive to how the body feels and reacts in the process as an important indicator of how you as a researcher relate to and understand that which you research. *World of Warcraft* has from the very beginning been a charged, social interface with obvious resonance in the body. The intensity of gameplay has involved everything from physical attraction to battle adrenaline and social complications. And as with most love stories, this one, too, had an ending. Or rather, our contact was over time transformed from having had a tangible erotic charge to instead be recharged and redefined. And at some point, in the midst of this process, I experienced a short, intense period of grief, which came to circulate in the most intricate ways throughout the game. If previously, I had held my breath when she logged on and felt my heart beat faster, I now experienced ambivalence. I simultaneously longed for and was unwilling to meet up. Her attitude towards me was different and more distanced, as was mine to her, I am sure. It is always a matter of survival. Not as much small talk. No superfluous gestures. Instances of co-play were few and far between.

I experienced this period of gameplay as quite lonely, no matter how many others were logged on at the same time. It is (perhaps not surprisingly) striking how lonely one might feel while playing solo in game interfaces that build on the social and on playing together with others. Bricka took on solo quests, but seemed to lack the necessary spark to stay alive and carry through. Moments of melancholia left marks in my field notes. Then again, even during this period of relative loneliness, playing was still more often than not a question of playing with others. Co-play while leveling up is often promiscuous and instrumental; it is about temporarily joining forces in PUGs (pick-up groups) to carry out a certain mission. I aligned Bricka with such temporary groups, but no one in these fleeting play situations made a lasting impression, no one was as charismatic as Slap used to be. Over time, my sense of play changed anew. Bricka grew stronger and became attractive for more complex missions. She formed a particular liaison with a female undead, who leveled up quickly to play with her as an equal. It still happens that I play alongside my initial contact, the orc woman, who is as vibrant as ever, but we now come together as friends with a particular history. And yet, sometimes when I ride my first rather slow Emerald Raptor mount (for purely nostalgic reasons) from the auction house in Orgrimmar, to the zeppelin tower in northern Durotar which connects the old world with that of the more recent continent Northrend, I can still feel the remains of an in-game as well as out-of-the-game love affair. What reminds me the most powerfully is the musicality and the feel of Durotar's burnt soil which provided a backdrop to first encounters, first impressions, first experiences (cf. Sveningsson, Chapter 3 of this book).

Kendall (2009a) asks the question of how an inclusion of the erotic potentials of fieldwork would change her analysis of embodiment and gender in a virtual world. In her case, it became clear that physical attractions belonged to the physical world. Even if occasional online flirts could make long sittings at the keyboard more interesting and tolerable, attractions were something that "began after meeting people in person. In short, they were physical attractions" (p. 106). Moreover, she argues that an inclusion of these feelings, of more information regarding her relationships with informants, "might well have made for a better ethnography" (p. 103). In my *World of Warcraft* ethnography, I believe including my particular introduction to the game in writing makes an important difference. Following Kisliuk, I ask myself whether this experience changed me in a way that significantly affected how I understood the field. It did. Not to address the ways in which I came to the game and was taken (in) by an alluring game world and an alluring woman alike, would be playing it safe, but would also downplay a potentially important source of knowledge. In studying *World of Warcraft*, motion and emotion, and then hiding my own experiences—which in significant ways have shaped my theoretical and methodological concerns—seems to me a mistake. My initial connection opened up to me a place and a culture that, in her words, could be "a sexy, organic, moving animation with a pulse". It provided me with an understanding up-close of how emotions may come to flow through the game, and of the potential queerness of it all. "Is this where you come to clean your dildos?" she asked Bricka (who happened to be fishing), immediately punctuated by brutal female orc laughter. Given that integrating discussions of queer theory and queer lives within the academic study of games is still something in the making, it seems valuable to contribute with a different story. There are other stories to be told, and telling mine might well be a risk worth taking.

## MACHINIC DESIRES

> Desire creates recognition (through identification and the gaze); it marks narrative; it highlights the moment when lovers' eyes meet; it affects the lives of characters; it marks their bodies; forces them to move; act or react differently; and it transforms people—radically alters their being-in-the-world. (Gorton 2008, 17)

The question is where an ethnographic project of writing about queer desire in the field—and of writing with passion—takes us. What does it tell us about an online game world, such as *World of Warcraft*? And what does it reveal about ethnographic methods and ethnographic writing? I believe that writing about desire in the field does at least two things. First, it helps challenge the modes and codes of hetero-normativity that efficiently, yet for the most part silently, underpin game studies and ethnographic fieldwork alike. Secondly, to make visible the ways in which desire and emotion may circulate through game spaces demands an articulation of desire as intimately related to technology, of desiring technology and of technological, or perhaps technologized desires. Kulick argues that questions of desire in the field are potentially useful sources of knowledge because desire does things, it puts things in motion (which previously were perhaps un-moving). Writing queer desire provides a critique of norms and normality in fieldwork. To bring to light that which is not fully of the norm, but which nonetheless is essential for the norm to work, is not merely writing from sexual margins. Rather, queer sexuality and queer theory speak volumes about the configuration of hetero-normal emotions, bodies, games, and ethnographies.

*World of Warcraft* is a place far from free of sexism and homophobia. The word 'gay' is used regularly as verbal abuse, as a way of reinforcing hegemonic heteronormativity (Pascoe 2007), and male blood elves with their relatively androgynous appearance and long hair are often classified as particularly 'gay'.[4] Then again, there are certain bodies, movements, and moments of play that could be termed 'queer'. Even if *World of Warcraft* culture rarely encourages non-normative or anti-normative ways of doing gender and sexuality, it is quite possible for, in my case, women to come together and play at least partly on their own terms. Those that I have met belong to guilds carrying names such as "bad girls". They introduce each other. They create groups to conquer the game world. They fight together and protect each other. They start guilds featuring the impersonation of male characters, such as the cross-dressing "Drag Kings of Azeroth". They play around with the in-game censorship of 'bad' words, such as the impossibility of naming certain female parts ("Yes, Priestess, I know where your ^&*!oris is, I just can't say the word"). They meet up, they flirt, and on occasion have hot play dates across candlelit kitchen tables. *World of Warcraft* becomes in such moments a space for sexual attraction and desire.

The question is, how did the specificity of *World of Warcraft* matter for the type of connection, emotions, and desires described in this chapter? And in which ways did the queerness of the relationship matter? Put differently, would it have made a difference if the love story had been of the heterosexual variety, and played out in, say, Linden Labs' *Second Life*? On a general level, there are probably many similarities, but I do believe that the particularities of the medium as well as of the sexual orientation in question made a difference. In their virtual ethnography of BDSM practices in *Second Life*, Shaowen Bardzell and Jeffrey Bardzell (2007) note that even if the interweaving of visual, literary and interaction aesthetics may make for powerful user experiences, there is a significant shift from the use of pain and domination in real-world BDSM cultures to the *representation* of pain and domination in the online context. In relation to *World of Warcraft*, there is a similar discussion about the lack of 'dramatic possibilities', in particular in role-playing player communities (cf. Mortensen 2008). The physical dimensions of intimate or romantic avatar play in *World of Warcraft* are limited, and yet such limitations may make the movements and gestures made possible full of meaning—and feeling. In my case, our coming together in the game did not play out in an explicitly sexual register, and yet it was densely sexually charged. This tension came into play through modes of non-verbal interaction, through a particular and to the point sense of rhythm and timing, through ways of moving and laughing together and responding to the other's movements. But perhaps more than anything else (and something that marks a difference between games and non-games), the most intense was the experience of questing and fighting together, and the ways in which weapons and armor—in particular guns, daggers and leather outfits—were fetishized. Reminiscent of erotic play with power and domination, the more violent the battle scene, the more the tension was building between us. In these instances, it became clear that the ways in which the game speed up the body in critical and violent moments of gameplay interlocked with how desire and attraction make the body go faster. These were also moments that echoed how power and violence itself can be a turn-on.

In terms of the particularities of 'queer', the type of femininities that *World of Warcraft* offers surely contributed to the quickening of our hearts. Discussed more at length in the chapter "A feel of play", a figure like the female orc with her distinctly 'butch' qualities, is likely to set things in motion for some female players. The same may go for the trolls and their laid-back, yet rough-around-the-edges femininity with rebellious undertones; their husky laughter, their grounded way of dancing from the hip, their bragging way of flirting. Moreover, besides having immense importance for those involved on a personal level, queer does make a difference in the larger scheme of *World of Warcraft* player cultures. The heterosexual, male bias and the ways in which words like 'gay' and 'rape' are routinely used as insults make queer connections between women in the game stand out. In a place where 'everybody' is assumed to be male (Yee 2008), as well as straight (and take part in or at least silently accept the never-ending gay-bashing in general chat), a connection between two queer, female players makes things shift in terms of providing a powerful counter narrative. The question is how such overlaying of desire—between women, and between women and technologies—could be understood and theorized. Put differently, in which ways could (lesbian) desire be conceptualized with or through technologies?

In her essay "Refiguring Lesbian Desire", Elizabeth Grosz (1995) formulates a critique of the conventional conceptualization of desire along the lines of a Freudian ontology of lack. According to this logic, desire is fleshed out as a heterosexualized binary arrangement of men as active, desiring subjects, and of women as passive objects of desire, rendering impossible the autonomy of subjects, particularly the autonomy of women. Desire as lack is desiring that which is unobtainable, since it can only function if it remains unfulfilled. And if desire, following Freud, can only be masculine in nature, this makes the notion of female (or rather feminine) desire a contradiction of terms. The only way in which 'she' can be positioned as a subject who desires is to abandon femininity, to instead desire "as a man" (p. 178). Grosz seeks to not only think women as desiring subjects, but also to find ways of thinking desire between women. She proposes a reconfiguration of desire, "not in terms of what is missing or absent, nor in terms of depth, latency, interiority, but in terms of surfaces and intensities" (p. 179). She draws on Spinoza's understanding of desire as a force of positive production, and on Deleuze and Guattari to envision desire as inventive, creative, as forms of contacts, intensities, and connections between bodily surfaces. She expounds, "the sites most intensely invested in desire occur at a conjunction, an interruption, a point of machinic connection [ . . . ] between one thing and another" (p. 182). For her, these 'things' in machinic connections (and disconnections) with one another are fragments, parts of bodies that never combine to integrated wholeness. They are points of contact between surfaces, "between a hand a breast, a mouth and a cunt" (p. 183), forging intensities for their own sake, always production, never reproduction.

For Grosz, the term lesbian does not disappear and become queer. Then again, lesbian is not being, but *becoming*, it enters into an assemblage of other (machine) parts, into a sequence of flows and disruptions, of varying speed and intensities. Lesbian is not an identity, it is not a position, but a mode of moving and changing, of always being in the process of becoming otherwise, always unstable, fleeting, provisional: "the question is not am I—or are you—a lesbian, but rather, what kinds of lesbian connections, what kinds of lesbian-machine, we invest our time, energy, and bodies in, what kinds of sexuality we invest ourselves in, with what other kinds of bodies, and to what effects?" (p. 184). Her imaginary lesbian is a lesbian-machine, a lesbian cyborg of sorts, which seems particularly apt to provide a conceptual framework—or a baseline—for queer, experiential, experimental techno-ethnographies. In parts and in interconnections, this lesbian machinery invests time and energy in her own body and in those of others, "eliminating the privilege of the human over the animal, the organic over the inorganic, the male over the female, the straight over the 'bent'" (p. 185). If there is something machinic at heart of lesbian (and other) becomings, there may also be something exceedingly queer, or 'bent', about intimate circuits of women and machines. It appears to me as if the lesbian-machine in Grosz's writing connects in interesting ways with affective encounters between women and technologies more generally. If women as desiring subjects border on the unthinkable, then how could women desiring technologies be understood (given that technologies much like desire have been aligned with masculinity)?

It seems to me that there are important ways in which female game bodies, even in the midst of heteronormative game interfaces, appear to be sexing these spaces in ways that are intriguingly queer. Even if the number of female players of online games is constantly growing, the ideas and ideals of normative straight femininity seems to collide frequently with how gaming as a technological practice is habitually coded as a masculine activity. Elsewhere, I have discussed and troubled the cultural paradox of female machines, of women's close relationships with technologies, since such alignments break with the tradition of the technological masculine, of men and machines, boys and their toys (Sundén 2007, 2008, 2010b). Wendy Faulkner (2000) discusses this paradox in women's passion for technologies, how for example female engineers need to downplay an interest in technologies to not be perceived as unfeminine, or, with Faulkner's terminology, 'gender inauthentic' (cf. Sveningsson, Chapter 4 of this book). At the point where that which is not feminine needs to be its opposite—as with the Freudian logic of desire as lack—is precisely where Grosz's lesbian-machine could prove useful. Even if it does not go by the name 'queer', queer is what it *does*. An alternative understanding of the seemingly unholy alliance between women and intense, passionate, violent gameplay could be to look at it as an instance of queer femininity. It is queer in the sense that female players are engaged in non-normative, or even anti-normative ways of doing femininity through their culturally illegitimate couplings with straight masculinity, technology, and power (cf. Kennedy 2006). It is neither a question of femininity as failure, nor as absence, but certainly of femininity gone wrong, and coming back with a vengeance.

By way of ending, and also as a way of pointing to questions for further discussion, I want to argue that writing with passion (as in writing passionately, and not only writing *about* passion, emotion, attraction) addresses the place of not only desire, but of sense-making through sensation more broadly in ethnographic work. The many connections between 'to sense' and 'to make sense' have long troubled ethnographic epistemologies. To take into account the full potential of knowing through the body and, in

Maya Unnithan-Kumar's (2006) words, "sensing the field", would demand a different set of ethnographic epistemologies. To recognize the critical potential of sensation demands a different understanding of the critical and the sensuous, as not in opposition, but rather deeply entangled with one another. For me, a step in this direction has been to recognize the significance of 'to fall' for someone, or something—a woman, an avatar, a game—and to trace this very falling as a way of thinking through the relations between desire, new media, and ethnography.

## NOTES

1. For exceptions, see for example Krzywinska (2006) and Linderoth (2008). See also Rettberg (2008), who explores with humorous self-reflexivity why *World of Warcraft* has managed to attract and immerse such a massive, highly devoted audience. The main reason, he argues, is because the game offers players a capitalist fairytale. It cleverly mirrors the logics of market capitalism (scoring and leveling) along the lines of protestant work ethics (grinding, play as work). As much as this line of reasoning captures some core issues of *World of Warcraft* practices, it leaves out the kinds of affects and experiences that the game may generate in playing bodies (excitement, calmness, anticipation, frustration, pleasure, joy, etc.)—including the body of the researcher—which might have an equally powerful impact.
2. The notion of emotions as something which moves between bodies, and consequently moves us, is informed by Sara Ahmed's (2004) *The Cultural Politics of Emotion*. Ahmed explores the ways in which emotions shape bodies and suggests that it is through emotions and how we relate to others that the very boundaries and surfaces of bodies take shape. This way of thinking contact, emotional intensity and the creation of bodies and boundaries have important consequences for her politics of emotion, and in particular for queer bodies and emotions. In online games, bodies of avatars and players alike can be understood similarly—as taking shape by ways of sensing and moving. Different(ly looking) bodies of avatars may generate different player experiences and affects. At the same time, there also seems to be a movement in reverse through which playing bodies take shape through gameplay, by the very contacts they have with others (objects as well as subjects). This discussion will continue in the following chapter, "A feel of play".
3. At the time, the upper limit for characters was level 70. However, at the time of writing (following the most recent expansion pack *Cataclysm* in December 2010), the highest level has been raised to 85.
4. Interestingly, male blood elves were initially slimmer, but Blizzard settled eventually for more muscles in an attempt to make the characters more 'masculine'. During the foreplay of the January 2007 release of *The Burning Crusade* expansion, the following post could be found in the *World of Warcraft* general discussion forum: "As many players have noticed, we have made a slight change to the male blood elf character models. In response to concerns that the blood elf male appeared to be too feminine, and after reviewing the model from a visual and conceptual standpoint, the decision was made to increase the body mass to give them a more substantial, masculine feel. It was also important that as members of the Horde that the blood elves gave the impression of strength and a more menacing presence". (http://forums.worldofwarcraft.com/thread.html?topicId=37185748&pageNo=12&sid=1).

The decision to change the original design of the male blood elves quickly became a hot topic within the gaming community. Gay-mers discussed the decision in terms of homophobia, and on more general forum pages players begged Blizzard to take back the model of the male blood elf, which was less pumped up with testosterone. Players had looked forward to play with a lighter, slimmer, less bulky male body, only to find themselves with yet another muscle package. (See for example, The Skinny Blood Elf Preservation Society at Livejournal: http://community.livejournal.com/bringingbesback/). Then again, even if the original design was changed and moved in a more 'safe' direction (along the lines of a heteronormal logic according to which body mass equals masculinity equals strength), the result is still routinely read as an instance of male femininity—and as such cherished among queer gamers.

# 6 A Feel of Play[1]

## *Jenny Sundén*

She is sitting on a slanting rooftop, sensing the sun-baked tiles burn through her sturdy leather pants. Her slow and steady breathing makes her protective shoulder pads move a little, up and down. Her knives are as sharp as ever, one in each side securely attached close to the hip bone, her impressive green mohawk adorned with two braids that come down on either side of her slender neck. She gazes at the horizon, at the glittery waves, the sea birds circling, and the big ships that land down at the pier like clockwork, letting off passengers with things to do and people to see in Booty Bay. The Bay of Booty, she thinks to herself, half giggling. A male low-level orc jumps into the water to go for a swim, his cloak floating behind him. "You are now AFK: Away from Keyboard", the dialogue box claims, and yet I am right here, attentive, my fingers persistently playing the computer. Booty Bay is right at the border of the jungle in Stranglethorn Vale (Eastern Kingdom, Azeroth, *World of Warcraft*), a small town, housing everything from Happy Bobber's fishing supplies to The Salty Sailor Tavern, as well as an important port for inter-continental traveling.

I write well on that rooftop, with the birds singing in my headphones, the sounds of waves, and a busy day at the harbor blending with the musicality of the jungle (mostly soft percussions). Up on that roof, my body is light and my head is clear. The jungle itself is inspiring as well, but far too distracting. Coming here is a way of reliving early in-game memories, when the Eastern Kingdom was replete with dangers and when my troll did not make it far into the woods. Here, in the midst of the steamy jungle, my writing energy used to be transformed into consecutive efforts to stay alive—to keep *her* live, and to have her sneak up on people and run her sharp blades deep into their backs before they know what hit them. It is a PvP-server after all.[2] Nowadays I come here for the slow pace and the nice view. She eats some local jungle-stew, based on tiger meat and apples, and drinks imported Dalaran Red. She feels tipsy and laughs her husky troll laughter. In the corner of her eye—actually she needs to turn her head ("You are no longer AFK")—she sees a fatally powerful, ridiculously well-geared human warrior woman approach her. Even if Stranglethorn Vale is an area with quests ranging from level 30 to 45, it is also notorious for gathering groups of level 80+ characters on spontaneous PvP-missions. The warrior looks pretty hot, she must admit, even if she is not really into humans. More importantly, at this moment, this warrior can easily take her out, there on the roof, in the stark light of day. It is too late for stealth. She gets to her feet, and leaps over the edge; I hold my breath for a fraction of a second, and she comes down on the landing with a thud and a sigh. She loses some health, but nothing to worry about. She still has some stew.

This chapter is an attempt to take a close look at the notion of 'close playing' as a critical strategy in understanding and analyzing *World of Warcraft*. Close playing is a medium-specific take on 'close reading'.[3] But in contrast to a tradition in which close playing is primarily understood to be rational, critical, and 'in control', this text attempts to recognize the critical potential of emotion and sensation, and the perhaps out-of-control element in gameplay. Working with this chapter has been a matter of playing closely and of listening to others' stories of play, of playing and writing, of writing from within the game, and, perhaps, of writing *as* play. The chapter develops queer feminist studies of online gaming by investigating embodied experiences, affective investments, and circulations within game spaces. It also explores the possibilities and limitations of a focus on games as 'text' by looking at the interplay between affect and meaning, corporeality and representation in acts of playing. Ultimately, this chapter asks what an online game like *World of Warcraft* puts in motion, and what consequences such stirring may have for ways of thinking—and feeling—games, critically, yet sensitively. What difference would it make if we were to theorize games from the playing bodies of researchers, as well as from those of other players?

As mentioned briefly in the previous chapter "Desires at Play", my ethnographic work in *World of Warcraft* went through two phases. The first phase, on which most of this chapter is based, was an affective investigation of queer potentials in mainstream *World of Warcraft* cultures. The focus of this initial one-year ethnography was on ways of exploring the game world and leveling up, on solo play, and play in pairs and smaller groups. The players I encountered and played with at this earlier stage had little interest in fast leveling, even if leveling up certainly was part of the draw. They took pleasure in explorative movements and detours through the gamescape. They took their time, and so did my ethnography. It was also during this earlier phase that I did a handful of in-depth, face to face interviews with female Swedish *World of Warcraft* players who identify as queer, or in other ways as non-straight. These women were between the age of 22 and 42 and all were dedicated, experienced players. My original plan was to carry out several more interviews than the six I managed to complete, but it turned out to be quite difficult to find non-straight female players to interview. Then again, my ethnographic online material from the game is rich (field notes, chat logs, screen shots, informal interviews), and the initial interviews became a valuable background material that allowed me to see more clearly certain phenomena in the in-game material.

The second phase was more explicitly focused on queer gamers—or gaymers—and consisted of play with a particular guild openly defined as LGBT (lesbian, gay, bisexual, transgender/transsexual), which in my writing is called *The Others*. The guild ethnography of *The Others* was different. Although there was a lot of room for casual play, questing, and leveling, this guild was more aimed at high-level content and experiences. For the present chapter, I will borrow a few examples from this second phase, but leave most of it to be fleshed out in more detail in the following two chapters. The two ethnographic phases were also marked and performed by different researcher characters, and on different (yet similar) servers. In following people onto their servers to be able to play together with them, on both accounts I found myself entering and playing on European PvP-servers. For the initial ethnography, I played the female green-haired rogue troll Bricka. For the second phase, I went more 'femme' and played the ebony-haired female blood elf death knight Lulu. All names of characters and of players have been changed throughout for the sake of anonymity.

## AFFECTIVE GAMING

As mentioned in the introductory chapter to this book, one way of understanding the formation of the field of game studies is to look at the initial friction between narratologists and ludologists. This tension no longer fuels much debate, in fact, narratologists and ludologists are becoming interestingly intimate in their ways of performing 'close playing'. The current split within game studies is rather disciplinary and methodological in nature, and runs between humanist approaches and those informed by the social sciences. Or perhaps, it was there all along. Game studies scholar Espen Aarseth (2007b) speaks of a friction within game studies that has to do with different ways of conceptualizing 'the player'. On the one hand, humanist approaches to games are consolidated through an interest in game aesthetics and player positioning, where the player is an implied player. Much like Foucault's (1969/1979) 'author function', the player exists only as a function of the game, as part of the game structure. Similar to psychoanalytic approaches in film studies, the viewer/player is conceptualized as firmly positioned by the 'text', a relationship in which the text plays the role of a dominant partner. The preferred method is self-play, or close playing. But as Aarseth points out, the fact that acts of close playing are prompted or shaped by a particular player, in ways not necessarily shared by other players, is rarely discussed. Her own part is unproblematic and "can be filled by any rational, critical, informed person" (Aarseth 2007b, 131). To this one might add that performances of close playing are certainly also *embodied* by the critical game theorist—in ways that may be everything but rational. Close playing builds on personal player experiences, but the theories emerging from ways of playing closely are often devoid of both the personal and the experiential.

On the other hand, social science-oriented perspectives concentrate on other, 'actual' players. The player is 'real', situated, flesh and blood, and the focus is on the social and cultural dimensions of play. This wider approach to games and gaming as social practice tends to employ an eclectic set of ethnographic methods, including observations, interviews, self-play, and social play. If the critical, aesthetic take on games makes the relationship between player and game primarily production-led, ethnographic approaches take into account a wide range of practices and strategies, allowing for player creativity and potentially subversive instances of play. Then again, the researcher—herself indeed a 'real' player—rarely writes herself into the analysis. Self-play may be used to better contextualize play by others, but rarely as a source of knowledge in its own right. Self-play may even be regarded as a shady activity (in being subjective, unrepresentative and utterly flawed). The players she observes and interviews may give passionate accounts of intense game sessions that made everything else fade into the background, or of long hours at the computer aiming for that next level, leaving their necks stiff and their eyes sore. But she herself is strangely dispassionate and utterly disembodied, leaving little evidence in the text of her own similar—or different—experiences of gameplay.

One strand of research that deserves closer attention—and which has an intriguing resonance within queer feminist theory—is the emerging discussion of games and affect (Carr 2006c; Colman 2008; Järvinen 2008; Lahti 2003; Shinkle 2005). Game researcher Diane Carr (2006c) has for example looked at how different ways of moving in games seem to support different affects in the player, more clearly linking issues of embodiment to the fields of game design and gameplay. A horror game, such as *Silent Hill*, may use a fairly strict, linear, labyrinthine mode of moving to create a claustrophobic feeling and frighten the player. The labyrinth as horror machinery is emphasized through dark yet creepily everyday-like surroundings. It is the ordinary and the everyday gone wrong that potentially creates fear or anxiety in playing bodies. A fantasy game (Carr uses *Planescape Torment*) may instead develop through a more open-ended, rhizomatic structure that encourages exploration and reflection.[4] The player's way of moving through the game is reflective, and the journey towards the solution is suspended by cyclic tours and detours in the landscape, through which particular places are not only discovered, but re-covered multiple times. The feeling becomes something entirely different. Fantastical monsters are quite evidently other than those belonging to the horror genre. They are schematic rather than realistic. They belong to worlds of fantasy and hence hardly make your skin crawl. Then again, even if Carr makes it clear that this is her own analysis and hence not necessarily valid for other players, she herself, her own body, is not part of the text on an explicit, epistemological level.

The disembodied, disinterested reader in textual analysis (broadly speaking) is an interesting figure. Lynne Pearce (1997) points out that reading, as professional practice, has been cerebral/cognitive rather than emotional/affective. Reading has been made respectable by figuring as an act of reason. The respectable reader (at least *symbolically* male) is educated, critical, disinterested, and fully in control over 'his' emotions. To master one's emotions is paralleled by a mastery of the text, a logic to which the seductive power of affect is a threat. Involvement indicates a lack of education, and display of emotion equals bad taste—in ways that have everything to do with class and gender. A disregard for emotions and desire in reading is secured through an understanding of texts as autonomous objects (as evident in structuralism, for example), which results in a blindness to dimensions of reading that move beyond questions of interpretation and meaning making. Isobel Armstrong (2000, 86–87, italics in original) argues similarly:

> A rationalist poetics, founded on the antithesis between thought and feeling which still goes largely uninvestigated in our culture, refusing the importunities of the desire of the text, acts as a screen for a more difficult and subtle problem. Sexuality, feeling and emotion are associated with a language of *affect* which is deemed to be non-cognitive and non-rational. Affect falls outside what is legitimately discussable.

To Armstrong, as a consequence of this resistance to the irrational and seductive power of affect, close reading has never been close enough. Based on one of the most deep-seated of Enlightenment binaries—thought/feeling—the text is viewed as something external, as 'other', as object, in ways that rather than creating closeness, mark a distance between text and reader. The challenge, then, is to define close reading anew, "to rethink the power of affect, feeling and emotion in a *cognitive* space" (p. 87, italics in original). If Pearce attempts to revalue affect and emotion in reading, to refocus the attention in textual analysis from the cognitive to the affective, Armstrong's project may be even more radical in the sense that she refuses the splitting off of feeling from thought in the first place. Do affect, emotion, and sensation *per se* make you less critical? Is admitting how we, as researchers, are moved by (and in turn move) what we study somehow incommensurable with critical thought? Or, could it be that such recognition would make for a richer, more interesting analysis?

The women in my study talk about first impressions and first experiences as some of the most intense moments of gameplay. For Jillian, it was her discovery of The Deeprun Tram:

> When I first discovered the subway from Stormwind to Ironforge, it was like . . . [holds her breath] wow! I didn't even know that it was there, and that it was a train, and that you could actually ride it. First, and I was perhaps a bit shy and didn't want to ask silly questions, so for the first time I *walked* on the tracks, and thought there was a monster flying over my head. And then [people] told me that it was a subway,

> and I was like really? And then I went for ride after ride after ride for hours! It was under the water and you could see fish and stuff, and I was like wohooo!

The Deeprun Tram, which connects Stormwind to the Dwarven capital of Ironforge, is a unique feature in *World of Warcraft*. While on the tram, the attentive player will glimpse underwater scenes, and even an elite sea monster called Nessie (with allusions to the Loch Ness Monster). The underwater scenery is there merely to create a particular feel. Other players talk about the first time on a flying mount, or the first time in the snow, with footprints lingering for a moment behind you as your avatar traverses the frosty landscape. Anna speaks of the soft, snow-swept landscape of Winterspring as one of the most beautiful places in the game, and emphasizes: "Oh how I love it when it snows ingame!" Situated in the midst of this snow-white, wintry gamescape is a goblin town named Everlook, enhanced by modern jazz tunes. Many refer to the first high end raid session, involving high-level characters in groups of ten or twenty-five players to carry out complex missions of defeating powerful monsters and bosses. The interviews and conversations show in these moments the difficulty to articulate that which at least partly escapes language. Attempts to put into words the bodily affects at play in instances of awe are punctuated with the illustrative and distinct taking in of air through the mouth and of holding one's breath for a moment. Armstrong (2000, 109) asks, "What could a [poetic] utterance and a burst of gunfire share? Most obviously, they temporarily alter breathing patterns, the gasp prompted by the assault of unexpected gunfire, the effort of responding to the aggressive speech patterns of the poem". Experiences of online gaming may share more with the affects here adjoined to the sharp sound of gunfire, than with the bewildering experience of a poetic encounter (Armstrong uses William Blake's *Infant Sorrow*), the point here being that these are moments that move the bodies of readers/viewers/players. These are experiences that make their rhythms shift and change, that temporarily alter breathing and pulse.

Brian Massumi (2002) speaks of affect and emotion as belonging to separate logics. Affect is about corporeal immediacy, but never coincides with the boundaries of the embodied subject. Affects are in excess, they are always something more and other than the ways in which they can be captured, made conscious and codified—by emotions. Emotions, on the other hand, are subjective. Emotions are semantic fixations of the affective and the immediate, those social and cultural conventions that transform corporeal intensity to linguistic categories and meaning. Affect in terms of intensity materializes directly on the skin, on the surface of the body, on its very interface to the world: "for the skin is faster than the word" (Massumi 2002, 25). The 'affective turn' is in many ways a critique of how cultural theory has been occupied with meanings and subject positions in ways that leave little room for movement, change, and that which is not easily captured in language. If 'the body' in cultural theory has been text, discourse, and sign system, which in various ways can be read and interpreted, affect theory addresses embodiment in more direct terms. In Massumi's understanding of affect, the *body as movement* is crucial: "When I think my body and ask what it does to earn that name, two things stand out. It *moves*. It *feels*. In fact, it does both at the same time. It moves as it feels and it feels itself moving" (Massumi 2002, 1, italics in original). Taking as a point of departure this intimate connection between movement and sensation, every move, every shift in the body, no matter how small, makes something change, and give rise to new modes of feeling. The body is here understood as neither mediated, nor discursive, but as something with a more immediate link between moving and feeling. This does not mean that the cultural meanings and determinations of, for example, gender, ethnicity, and sexuality are miraculously dissolved by the body in/as movement (even if such principles of difference are largely absent from Massumi's argument). Rather, such differences emerge through this very movement, and retroact on the process from which they emerged.

What happens, then, with the intimate connection between movement and sensation in a digital space where 'the body' is always more than one? (cf. Sundén 2003). What does it mean to sense, and to move, in situations when 'the skin' is no longer the only interface?

## MEDIATION, MOVEMENT, SENSATION

There are multiple connections between movement and sensation in *World of Warcraft*. The world of the game organizes the player's activities in particular zones and configures the movements between these zones. Georgia Leigh McGregor (2006) describes how the game world is divided into 'circulation space' and 'activity space', each with its particular feel, level of difficulty, groups of allies or enemies, and limited set of entrances and exits. The landscape makes possible certain movements and prevents others. Avatars cannot move through walls or other massive constructions, but they can move through each other (as well as through non-player characters). The objects of the game world are solid, but its subjects are permeable. And no matter how schematic the game design is when it comes to pre-programmed movements and emotional expressions, players develop highly personal ways of moving and interacting (cf. Colman 2008). Agnes says:

> When I picked my first character, which was a rogue, when I started to play, I felt that I picked that player class since it suited my personality. But in terms of looks, it wasn't me. I wouldn't say that I feel like my characters, because they are their own, but at the same time, I am the one who directs their actions, what they do. So in that sense it's me. And I think that if someone else played my character, others would notice that

> it wasn't me, since you act in particular ways. [ . . . ] In terms of actions, I'd say that it's me, because what comes through is my restlessness.

Agnes talks about how she felt a certain affinity with the light-footed, swift-bladed rogue, not because of the look of her character, but because of how playing a rogue resonated with her personality and a particular sense of restlessness. She talks about her characters as relatively independent, and yet she experiences certain connectedness since she is the one playing them and deciding on their actions. Moreover, it is quite evident that the play style of rogues, of constantly being on the move, silently sneaking up behind and surprising the enemy, may translate as or correspond with a feeling of restlessness.

Anna Munster (2006, 18) suggests that new media extends our bodies in ways that combine the capacities and sensations of different materialities (of the physical body and that of information flows):

> The doubling and extension of bodily capacities and sensations by digital means differs from the phenomenological experience of bodies in a world populated by subjects and objects. The interval between incorporeal and corporeal experience opened up by new media sets off the play of relays, deferrals, crossings and recuperation between them.

When I move around and play my green-haired female rogue troll Bricka, these movements and experiences do things to my body, to how I move and feel. When she jumps, something in me jumps with her. When she laughs her pre-programmed rough troll laughter, it resonates in me, in my body, in my own laughter. No matter how synthetic, it makes me warm and happy. Sometimes I make her laugh, only to laugh along with her. Sometimes I laugh first, and then immediately through her. But most often we laugh together, I in her, she in me. She laughs with me, and sometimes at me—or so it might feel. We laugh together and with those we encounter and play with. We laugh at the enemy, at dangers, at our own tricks and cunning acts. The laughter of other characters that I have become particularly fond of is a different story altogether. Female orcs may all laugh the same way, but the significance of this laughter is intimately tied to one female orc in particular, who has touched me in multiple ways. The laughter of female orcs has become entangled with the way she used to laugh and with how we used to laugh together.

When Bricka speeds up and works her way, methodically, through a group of monsters, timing her punches, building up her strategy, we feel in sync—she as an extension of me, but also as something distinctly her own. Playing with others takes on a whole other rhythm. There is a lot that must be timed well, and so much that may go wrong. But when you come together in a group with other players who play in a similar way as you do, who pick up on your rhythm, or you pick up on theirs, and your skills and abilities complement each other, it has a lot in common with playing music together—and of playing really well. Play has a lot to do with rhythm, of feeling a certain pace, on or off the beat, and also with the sense of being too fast or too slow, of losing track of timing, precision, and feeling. Critical player versus player situations can make my heart rush and my palms sweat. These are moments of swift improvisation, especially if you are the one under attack. It is the uncertain elements of this type of play, of never being able to fully know your enemy (compared to taking on groups of identical monsters) that make these moments particularly intense.

The question is whether it is viable to distinguish between affect and emotion—or between corporeality and representation—when ways of moving and sensing, most intimately, are connected with and circulate through screen-based images and imagery. Or, could it be that affect has been mediated all along? Sara Ahmed (2004) makes a different case from Massumi's by rendering problematic every splitting off of affect from emotion. Her critique of the discussion of affect as something other than emotion leads her to primarily focus on emotion, but in a more composite and elastic way. She also differs from Massumi when she argues that emotional reactions, no matter how immediate, are always, in some sense, mediated. Ahmed explores the ways in which emotions shape bodies by circulating between them, how they may stick to some, and slide over others. She suggests that it is through emotions and how we relate to others that bodies take shape, or materialize. Emotions are relational, she argues, "they involve (re)actions or relations of 'towardness' or 'awayness' in relation to [ . . . ] objects" (Ahmed 2004, 8).

Ahmed argues that affect and emotion can be separated analytically, but not as lived experience (which on the other hand may raise the question of whether the analytical in any meaningful way can be separated from the experiential). No matter how immediate sensations may be, there is always mediation in the sense that affects resonate in bodily remembrance and past experiences. What we feel is tied to what we already know. This mediation is a corporeal knowledge of sorts, transmitted by the skin. It does not need to be conscious, or articulated in language, but this does not necessarily mean that it is unmediated or in some sense *direct*. Ahmed does not deny that the experience of a sensation can be something other than the sensation itself—we may burn our skin before consciously registering that we have burned ourselves. Similarly, the experienced player may have nearly automatic reflexes in critical moments of play. Ahmed's main critique of Massumi is of how his thinking creates a divide between conscious recognition and directness, which undermines every line of reasoning regarding how experiences not (yet) conscious can still be mediated by previous experiences. I find with Ahmed an intriguing way of thinking emotions *more intensely*, by not separating the more immediately corporeal from experiences of or stories about emotions. I have come to think of emotions as movement between bodies, and online games as spaces where emotions may circulate, and bodies are shaped and reshaped. The discussion of mediation in the field of media studies is different and usually more literal (a medium is that which mediates). The question then becomes how emotion and/or affect figure in a context where digital media technologies are central.[5]

There are multiple ways in which the bodies of players and characters are set in motion in *World of Warcraft*. Key figures in the structuring of players' movements through game spaces are quest givers, around them spinning the mini-narratives of quests (cf. Walker Rettberg 2008). Many quest narratives may pass unnoticed if your mind is on the reward (gold, gear, or experience points) rather than on the underlying rationale as spelled out in the storyline of the quest. Yet once in a while, these tales may truly put things in motion, in particular if they hold dramatic twists. One of the more memorable quest encounters for me occurred one evening when Lulu found her way to the Horde outpost of Conquest Hold in the midst of the lovely and cheerful Grizzly Hills where Scandinavian folk song fiddles abound.[6] Early quests in the area involved helping Hidetrader Jun'ik, a troll NPC (non player character) trading in leather goods. Already on first contact with him, he talked of Conqueror Krenna—the violently brutal and tyrannical female orc leader of Conquest Hold—with great fear: "Conqueror Krenna, the she-wolf runnin' this place, she gave me a tight deadline. If I don't outfit her whole regiment by week's end she's gonna have me wrestling bears in the pit". Apparently, Krenna wanted 'worg' hides to equip her full army, but Jun'ik tried to substitute grizzly hides to prevent extinction of worgs in the region. For the quest "Delivery to Krenna", I was to present her with the Bundle of Hides from Jun'ik in the guise of my death knight. Off I went to the female conqueror, heart pounding as I stood before her, handing over hides smelling of flour that Jun'ik used in an attempt to get the right color of fur:

*Conqueror Krenna says:* That spineless troll has failed me for the last time. Anthis! Break his legs!
*Anthis says:* At once, my lady!
*Gorgonna says:* Let me take care of it, sister.
*Conqueror Krenna says:* I've never seen you so eager to cause harm to someone, sister. Such a pleasant development . . . very well, go!
*Gorgonna whispers:* What were you thinking, provoking her like that?
*Gorgonna walks outside to Hidetrader Jun'ik.*
*Gorgonna says:* You . . . half-idiot! You really did it this time. I'm going to have to make it look like your leg's broken.
*Hidetrader Jun'ik says:* No, please! Don't!
*Gorgonna says:* Now don't move if you ever want to walk again!

Here, Krenna's sister, the ever so clever and less violent Gorgonna, cuts in and makes it seem like she's following Krenna's order, but in reality merely kicks Jun'ik in the leg to make it look like his leg is broken. Ultimately, Krenna sees through Gorgonna's bluff and challenged her to a duel until death, along with the player(s) who aided her. Krenna made a lasting impression on me. With her broad, muscular shoulders, along with her sharp battleaxe and her signature black patch covering one eye like on a pirate, she came forth as one of the more powerful of female warlords of the game (and indeed, some of the biggest bosses in endgame instances and raids are female). This may partly have to do with her location in the narratives of quest-lines running through Grizzly Hills, firmly anchored in and twisted around her impressive figure. In these narratives, she is an instigator of conflict and drama, and as such memorable in an overall scheme of play experiences. But it may also have to do with the type of femininity at play. From the point of view of a feminist game scholar, powerful female game characters have a particular allure. After all, this woman has a group of big, buffed male orcs kneeling before her in terror. Even if Krenna is not a playable character, there is something quite tangible to this type of female badass power and its decidedly masculine qualities. Female orcs in the game perform what Judith Halberstam (1998) calls 'female masculinity'. Female masculinity is masculinity disconnected from a male body and read across a female body, primarily within a space of same-sex desires. In the context of game characters, female masculinity is rare, and it is precisely this quality that makes a character like Krenna stand out.

Although quest givers (quite literally) put the bodies of characters in motion, there are other ways in which bodies take shape through gameplay. The women in my study talk about gameplay as stress relief, as a way to unwind the body. Kari says that playing calms her nerves. She has two characters—one for in-game Battlegrounds (which is intense, action-packed team play between the two factions in the game), and one for regular play. It is primarily in Battleground that she unloads excessive energy. Maria, in turns, talks about how she used to cure adrenaline rushes with physical activity, and that *World of Warcraft* (much to her surprise) has the *effect* of physical movement. When she is angry or frustrated, Maria takes her character for a swim, or kills some monsters, which relaxes her. High paced battle scenes that require focus and coordination here become a way of cleansing the body from stress. She even recalls a situation when she started to feel cold—from playing:

> I started to feel cold late one night in, what's the name, Hillsbrad Foothills, is that the name? When it was raining [in the game]. It rained and it was dark and cold. It was dark in my kitchen too where I was sitting, playing. And then I noticed that my body was cold, and so I had to wrap myself up in a blanket. What connects me in reality with that which is me in WoW is some sort of shared soul. I get goose

bumps when it's raining in WoW. I feel calm from swimming in the ocean in WoW.

Game experiences are here stretched out in ways that include the body playing. Eventful battle scenes speed up playing bodies to the point where bodily energies appear to become external to the body, releasing anxiety and tension. The rain in the game, no matter how artificial, chills the playing body. The sound of waves, and of the body breaking the waves through swimming, is transposed, or translated into the body of the player as relaxing and soothing. Bodily states in the game here attain a capacity to retroact on playing bodies, to immerse them and perform a shift within them. Janet Murray (1997, 98) points out that immersion (as it is used in the study of digital media) is a metaphor "derived from the physical sensation of being submerged in water". Matt Barton (2008) elaborates this further, noting that the use of the term 'immersion' to describe a state of losing oneself in a game world is rather ironic, since water is notoriously difficult to design realistically in virtual environments. The use of water in *World of Warcraft* may not be 'realistic', because either swimming or moving through heavy rain make the bodies of characters wet. Nonetheless, the sensation of running, riding, or flying through the rain, or of swimming in the ocean, speaks a language recognizable by the body. As such, these moments of play make for different game experiences compared to days on dry land with bright, sunny skies.

## FEMME FIGURATIONS

The emerging field of game studies—even feminist game studies—is a rather straight enterprise. If a 'straight' gender analysis merely operates on a feminine/masculine scale, on which the former often maps pretty straightforwardly onto a biological female body and the latter onto a biological male body, that which is not feminine/female can then only be masculine/male. Even if a range of possible femininities and masculinities are considered, the foundational dichotomous figure remains. If gender is bi-polar, how can we then understand, for example, female masculinity? Or high femme? 'Femme' is queer femininity, an often parodic, exaggerated femininity of sorts performed primarily within a context of same-sex desires (cf. Dahl 2008). And what about the gendered positions of trans-women (and men)? Readings played out in a queer feminist framework may make the picture shift. At the point where the straight gender analysis tips femininity into masculinity, a queer reading sticks with the multiple and contradictory meanings of femininity (and masculinity) itself in ways that involve the sexual specificity and potential queerness of bodies and their relationships.

There is something exceedingly powerful about crossing femininity with violent game technologies, and providing such explosive, fierce femininity space for play in an area traditionally tied to 'the masculine'. Helen Kennedy (2006) has argued that such intersections of femininity, violence and game technology produce a range of 'inappropriate' femininities and pleasures in gaming, and T.L. Taylor (2006b) has pointed at the important connections between pleasure, game violence, and mastery. If the appropriate pleasures that games offer to female players are primarily based on the idea of quiet, thoughtful exploration with multi-layered game narratives, then a powerful, highly capable, and dangerously armed action game heroine challenges this understanding. She provides her female players with an unapologetic, illegitimate femininity, as well as a violently powerful vehicle for skillful uses of game technologies that is troubled by—but also in important ways troubling—the intimate connection between masculinity and machinery. Indeed, she is a troublemaker.

A note on femme orientations and desires may be in place, in particular as something 'to think with' in the realm of femininity as hyperbole in games. Femme as queer femininity and as a feminist project is highly skeptical of neat categorizations of gender, identity, and sexuality—and as such hard to define. In "A Fem(me)inist Manifesto" Lisa Duggan and Kathleen McHugh (2002, 165) write about femme as "not an identity, not a history, not a location on the map of desire", but rather an oppositional desiring subject on the move, always in the process of becoming different. Femme is an investment, not in femininity by nature, but in femininity by choice. It is a celebration of femininity as artifice, a critical exploration of femininity gone wrong. Brushwood Rose and Camilleri (2002, 12) understand femme as

> inherently 'queer'—in the broadest application of the word—as bent, unfixed, unhinged, and finally unhyphenated. Released from the strictures of binary models of sexual orientation and gender and sex. [ . . . ] Released from the 'object position' where femme is all too often situated.

Femmes have suffered from double marginalization in the history of feminist movements and lesbian communities alike. On the one hand, femme has been mistaken for, or conflated with, femininity as oppression and thus to be avoided for feminists; while on the other, femme has merely figured as the reverse side, or the 'other' of butch-femme constellations. Neither 'real' feminist, nor 'real' lesbian, the project of enhanced femininity as disruption and as something chosen is lost in translation (Harris and Crocker 1997). Then again, there is certainly a danger in thinking of femme as simply a matter of choice, or as inherently or automatically transgressive, since there is always a risk in playing with femininity to simultaneously be *played by* femininity.

The women in my study certainly pay attention to the process of crafting their characters, and the significance of these choices for their game experiences, although they are frustrated with the limited options of self-making.

It is not a coincidence that most of them play female characters. To play a female body seems to be a matter of identification, but also of *desire*. These are players who tend to think of gameplay as intensely physical, and of their characters as sexy heroines. They enjoy the feeling of playing beautiful, powerful, well-geared female bodies. They take pleasure in the contrasts between, for example, having a female shape and carrying heavy armor. Agnes told me about how she made her female blood elf a paladin, since paladins are strong in battle and may carry the most solid type of armor: "It was about that contrast between, having like a good, strong position and still showing some . . . That there was power or something in the fact that you could be a bit boyish, yet still be a girl". Female blood elves are small, delicate, yet voluptuous, and she enjoyed how her tiny blood elf was 'buffed up' through robust armor. No matter how 'femme' as a starting point, the body armor turned her elf into a tomboy of sorts. She recalls how powerful she felt in this guise, and how suddenly this feeling was significantly diminished when she found herself right next to a male blood elf with the same gear. Male characters of the same race are consistently larger, and in comparison, her elf woman seemed to almost disappear.

Ahmed (2004) describes the comfort of hetero-normative life for those who can live by its rules. She discusses how social spaces presume certain bodies, shapes, directions, desires and movements in ways that make the distinction between bodies and objects unclear. The relation between the two is one of comfort, and being comfortable is a state of not having to recognize what conditions the perfect fit. What happens, then, when bodies fail to fit, [ . . . ] "a failure that we can describe as a 'queering' of space?" (Ahmed 2004, 152). Discomfort—the feeling of being out of place, or of being in the wrong place—makes visible the premises and promises of hetero-normativity, and as such makes the safety of heterosexuality slightly less safe. Moving through the spaces of Azeroth is in many ways a journey through a heterosexual landscape (Corneliussen 2008). Even if Blizzard has made sure that male and female avatars are equally powerful as vehicles in the game world (i.e., male bodies are not stronger or better by default), female characters of popular races, such as humans and night elves, regularly become objects of sexual attention, whereas for example female orcs and the undead appear to move through the game with greater ease in ways that might suggest a 'queering' of space. Female orcs have a strong, muscular build and can have their heads shaven. Or, as Kari formulated this matter in relation to her female orc: "She's clearly not a babe". In not being a 'babe', the orc woman fails to fit the hetero-norm. But instead of primarily producing a disorienting feeling, this failure appears to generate a certain freedom of movement. Maria had a similar feeling for her undead (with its slouching posture and with the bones ripping through the skin) as an interesting alternative to more busty, hetero-normalized game bodies. Jillian tells me about how she often 'comes out' in the game, especially since the term 'gay' tends to be used as verbal abuse: "Then I tell them, 'I don't appreciate the language in this group right now. I am a lesbian, I am 40 years old and I live in Stockholm, Sweden. So shut up and do your work". To emphasize her lesbian in-game persona, she responds to flirtatious remarks from male players (or rather, characters) by flirting with nearby women (characters). And sometimes she plays a female hunter with a big, rare wolf named Butch at her side.

## ON THE VERGE OF REPRESENTATION

There are many ways in which *World of Warcraft* spaces may be queered, and several of these will be detailed more at length in the upcoming chapters. Even so, it makes sense within the context of games, affect, and emotion to expand some more on the relationship between players and their characters. In the world of game design, this bond is regarded as important due to the belief that without an emotional connection between the two, the player quickly loses interest in the game. This is not to say that the link between player and character needs to be one of identification, or of any psychological or emotional depth. Perhaps a conceptual move from emotion to affect would be helpful here. Many game characters are schematic rather than well-rounded, and playing them is less about getting to know their inner lives, and more about tuning in to their capabilities and ways of moving. In games if anywhere, a body is what a body does, what it is capable of doing. In my interview with Alex, who self-identifies as 'androgynous' (in this case, an in-between transgender position that is neither female nor male), s/he ponders the relation between gender and the feel of play:

> I have both male and female characters, but what really gets me hooked is rather the different talents that each character has. My first Alliance characters were actually female night elves, but they are a bit too feminine for my taste, I don't like that they bounce up and down in that silly way. I want more power! So, to a certain extent, looks matter. They should be powerful and muscular if they are melee, that gives me more of a battle sensation.[7]

The women in my study talk about 'clicking' with some characters and not with others, an affective response that has everything to do with the feel of play—and of comparing this feel across different playable bodies. Then again, such 'feel' embedded in the capacity of playable bodies is rarely disconnected from the 'look' of characters (cf. Tronstad 2008). In the example with Alex, a strong, muscular appearance was intimately connected with a powerful "battle sensation". In fact, when players talk about their characters, they constantly go back and forth between appearance, capacity, and affect.

| | |
|---|---|
| *Thehottie:* | keep forgetting i am not level 80 |
| *Lulu:* | :D |
| *Clym:* | lol |
| *Thehottie:* | keep going to lay into the yellow guys and have to pull myself back |
| *Lulu:* | you *could* move a main here . . . |
| *Thehottie:* | don't think a dwarf pally would last long |
| *Lulu:* | ah |
| *Thehottie:* | lol |
| *Lulu:* | no:) |
| *Thehottie whispers:* | *now she is butch lol* |
| *To Thehottie:* | *oh she is, is she* |
| *Thehottie whispers:* | *well, she's a little battleaxe, you know the type* |
| *To Thehottie:* | *i know it too well*[8] |

This conversation starts out with Thehottie observing how she forgets that the character she's playing is not high level, which results in her consistently withdrawing from the enemy. My suggestion is that she moves a high level main character to the server, but evidently her main is a dwarf paladin (and therefore of The Alliance), and hence would be impossible in a Horde guild. The interesting part of the conversation continues in whispers, with her claiming: "now she is butch lol". 'Butch' here is both a type of appearance and a sense of play. Female dwarfs have a sturdy, unapologetic build, drawing heavily on cultural references to 'Irishness'. They are heavy drinkers, use pick-up lines such as "I'll have you know I can flatten steel with my thighs", as well as being pre-programmed to do the River Dance. The paladin is a highly versatile player class, possible to use as tank, damage dealer, and healer, depending on the character build. Importantly, they can wear the heaviest type of armor and be used for tanking, which is one of the more powerful and masculine positions in battle (cf. Sveningsson, Chapter 2 of this book and the discussion of tanks in relation to femininity/masculinity). A tank is made to head first draw in the monsters to a group of players, as well as enduring the most crushing of blows, and as such it takes someone bold and fearless. The comment "she's a little battleaxe, you know the type" comes across as a bit flirtatious, or at least with an expectation of me knowing how to make sense of this particular double-bladed weapon wielder (my response being "I know it too well"). To be "a little battleaxe" reads as plenty of attitude and a cocky, bordering on careless, female masculinity that has everything to do with how 'she' is positioned in battle, how she can be played, and how it feels to tank.

Apart from playing with femininities across a range of female game bodies, there are other ways of queering a 'straight' game:

| | |
|---|---|
| *Thehottie whispers:* | *lol you a belf?* |
| *Lulu whispers to Thehottie:* | *hahaha i'm afraid so, yes* |

| | |
|---|---|
| *Thehottie whispers:* | *female?* |
| *Lulu whispers to Thehottie:* | *my first main was a troll* |
| *Lulu whispers to Thehottie:* | *always female* |
| *Thehottie whispers:* | *i can go either way* |
| *Thehottie whispers:* | *gotta nelf hunter called babemagnet* |
| *Lulu whispers to Thehottie:* | *male?* |
| *Thehottie whispers:* | *yep* |
| *Thehottie whispers:* | *well, when you're lesbian in a straight game you have to do something to be yourself* |
| *Lulu whispers to Thehottie:* | *of course* |

This passage starts out with Thehottie laughing about me being a blood elf, probably since female blood elves are the Paris Hiltons of the game. (There is even a female blood elf bag vendor in Shattrath City by the name Haris Pilton, from whom you may purchase outrageously expensive bags of epic quality). Blood elf is probably as femme as you can get in the game. Whereas I and many other female players tend to play female characters, Ellen who plays Thehottie "can go either way", and says that she has a male night elf hunter called babemagnet. She concludes: "well, when you're lesbian in a straight game you have to do something to be yourself". To play a male character as a lesbian woman, "to be yourself" in the game is an interesting strategy. If online 'cross-dressing' from male (the player) to female (in-game) is routine in cultures of online gaming, cross-dressers of the reverse order are less common and as such rarely discussed.[9] Nevertheless, to position oneself as a male character in a 'straight game' creates an opportunity for queer, female players to play with same-sex desire in ways that on the surface look nothing but straight. It simultaneously gives them the possibility of performing female masculinity by an overlaying of male and female bodies in the act of gameplay. (I will return to and develop the discussion about online cross-dressing in the chapter "A Queer Eye on Transgressive Play").

The study of digital games has long suggested the limits of textual analysis, or 'representation', as critical framework. Game interfaces are certainly representational, and the politics of images and imagery in games speak volumes about dominating values and worldviews in an ever more multifacetted, yet strikingly predictable game industry. However, to address play as an embodied, interactive practice, in which on-screen scenarios are continually altered through the material, physical process of gameplay, needs more of a somatic approach (Nielsen 2010). A critical approach to games as medium and as culture could fruitfully position itself in the intricate borderland between representation and corporeality, meaning and affect, to investigate the significance of how games are felt—through the bodies of (other) players as well as through the body of the player/researcher herself. In her study of (online) pornography, Susanna Paasonen (2007) speaks of the importance to take seriously the power of pornographic texts to move their readers/viewers, the bodies of scholars included. Similarly, it seems important to take seriously the ways in which digital games tend to set bodies in motion, including that of the researcher. Games could perhaps be understood in terms of what Linda Williams (1991) calls 'body genres', referring to 'low' genres such as melodrama, horror, and pornography—which seek to generate physical reactions in the viewer. If melodrama aims to make her cry, horror to frighten her, and pornography to arouse her, the question of interest here is the type of physical responses an online game like *World of Warcraft* may generate in playing bodies.

In this chapter, I have argued for an expansion of game studies along the lines of (at least) two key concepts: 'queer' and 'affect'. First, game studies are a relatively straight enterprise which could productively put to use 'bent' ways of thinking intersections of gender and sexuality, to further complicate the discussion of femininities and masculinities in games. Secondly, digital games as media genre tend to aim at and involve the bodies of players in multiple ways. This calls for an affective, experiential, passionate approach to games, theoretically as well as methodologically. This led me to an analysis of not only what a game like *World of Warcraft* might mean, but how it feels (and what that means). Ken Hillis (2009, 263) speaks of 'digital affectivity' as the emotional dimensions of the digital, and concludes "part of the seduction of the digital flows from the affective materiality of the digital sign/body". The particular feel, or affectivity of play is important to players. It matters for how they chose their characters, and for whether they stick with them and continue to enjoy playing them over time. It matters for the intensity of play sessions, for how *World of Warcraft* sometimes takes your breath away—be it the landscape, the atmosphere, particular encounters, or high end raid sessions. The feel of play also matters for the type of femininities and masculinities that are at play in the coming together of representation and sensation in the game. It matters for the affective potentials in the very contrasts between, for example, how something looks (a tiny, female character), and what 'she' may be capable of (acting as a slaying machine). The feel of play also has significance for how players and avatars take shape through each other. Celia Pearce (2009) speaks of avatar play as transformative social practices, as a 'social prosthetics' that operates as an extension of the player into the game world, and also as something that retroacts on and shapes the player. Players do not only shape the movements of their avatar through actions and reactions, but may have themselves, their bodies shaped in return. Play, in this sense, is transformative.

Armstrong (2000, 13) traces how "the constitutive nature of affect has been ignored or bracketed in contemporary theory because of its seeming resistance to analysis", and argues for an analytical poetics of emotion that includes, rather than falls outside of, the rational. Such a mixed approach to game analysis, both sensuous and clear-headed, seems like a path well worth exploring. In particular, Armstrong underlines how the tradition of reading for mastery, of controlling the text, inserts and confirms a distance between reader and text, subject and object, and as such fosters distance reading, not close reading. Masterly close readings, then, may have made use of the vocabulary of the erotic, of textual pleasures and pleasures in reading, only to sanction the power of the reader over the text. The distance between reader and text is to ensure that the boundaries between subject and object are intact, and ultimately to secure the boundaries of the subject 'himself', as a guarantee of 'his' autonomy, or as a resistance to the threat of disruption or dissolution of the subject. She concludes,

> I do believe that all reading that is not reading for mastery necessarily gets caught up with, imbricated in, the structure of the text's processes, and that this is where thought begins. The intensity of this experience can be renamed as affect and consigned to the non-rational, but this is impoverishment (p. 94–95).

It is precisely this getting intensely involved with, or 'imbricated in' the processes of gaming as analytical strategy that I have attempted to focus on in this chapter. The seductive power of games is multiple. There is certainly the draw of mastering the game, to control that which at times is uncontrollable, to outsmart the game and play for domination and mastery. At the same time, there is the desire to truly sense the game and its powerful machinery of enhancement and extension, the coming together of player and game that amplifies the senses and rushes the heart. Part of the enjoyment of play is bound up with the feel of games, with the very sense of play, in ways that are critical to understandings of games and gaming. A majority of close playing approaches to games, of up-close and careful analyses, has played for mastery and for control over the boundary between the player subject and the game object. Consequently, what is systematically left out of the picture, and quite violently so, is recognition of the critical potential of affect. To recognize how the boundary between subject and object in gameplay is constantly *at play* is to acknowledge the disorderly, unmanageable nature of playing (or reading, or analyzing). Playing for mastery is only one part of the story, but one that excludes or discriminates against other pleasures to be had in (research as) play, one of which is the analytical challenge of making sense through sensation, and perhaps of *the need to let go*.

## NOTES

1. A shorter version of this chapter was published as Sundén, Jenny. 2010a. "A Sense of Play: Affect, Emotion, and Embodiment in *World of Warcraft*." In *Working with Affect in Feminist Readings: Disturbing Differences*, edited by Marianne Liljeström and Susanna Paasonen. London: Routledge.
2. PvP stands for Player versus Player and indicates that battle between players is allowed/facilitated by the game interface.

3. The term close playing has consolidated efforts to close-read games within the humanist camp in game studies, and Aarseth (2007b) is one of few who explicitly map out the strategy in terms of research tradition and methodology.
4. Carr refers to Deleuze and Guattari (1980/1999) and their use of the concept 'rhizome' in *A Thousand Plateaus*. A rhizome within the field of botany, or plant biology, is a plant with a multitude of roots and shoots from its nodes, usually found underground (such as ginger). Deleuze and Guattari use the term to describe a theory with a large number of non-hierarchical points of entry and exit, which enables the connection between any point to any other point. Unlike the root structures of plants or trees, the lines and dimensions of the rhizome is far more complex, building on principles of multiplicity, difference, heterogeneity, and endless interconnectivity. Even if games rarely allow any one point be connected with any other point, the notion of the rhizome emphasizes the type of games that build on nomadic, exploratory modes of play.
5. If 'the digital' for Massumi (2002, 133–143) short-circuits his non-signifying philosophy of affect, then Eve Kosofsky Sedgwick and Adam Frank (1995) make a different case in their discussion of affect and cybernetics. In their reading of the American psychologist Silvan Tomkins, they point out how his theory of affect overlaps with perspectives in cybernetics in ways that result in an understanding of the human as a complex layering of biological and mechanical components in relation to which the digital (on/off) takes intimate turns with the analogue (the graduated or multiply differentiated). They resist every association of the machine or the computer with digital representations and the biological organism with analogue representations, which opens up for an understanding of affect as something that continuously moves back and forth between the digital and the analogue. For example, sexuality as a mechanism of desire can be a digitally on/off, whereas its link to motivation and action needs multiple and qualitatively different possibilities.
6. The music of Grizzly Hills and its Scandinavian folk music feel—including a Swedish 'nyckelharpa', sometimes called keyed fiddle in English—is quite distinct and has sparked numerous discussions in player communities. See for example: http://www.worldofwarcraftquesthelp.net/uncategorized/wow-wrath-of-the-lich-king-grizzly-hills-soundtrack;http://www.pinkpigtailinn.com/2010/01/tickled-pink-music-from-hearts-of.html; http://forums.worldofwarcraft.com/thread.html?topicId=13275279006&sid=1; http://multemusic.com/2008/12/16/swedish-nyckelharpa-world-warcraft/. Accessed: November 22, 2010.
7. A melee character belongs to a player class that fights well with hand-held weapons in close-range combat. Melee fighters do not have spells and ranged attacks to the extent that ranged classes do, and therefore must be in close proximity to the enemy in order to be successful. Examples of melee classes in *World of Warcraft* are warriors, rogues, and death knights.
8. Italics are added to clarify that this is a private conversation.
9. According to Nick Yee (2005a), about half of all female characters in *World of Warcraft* are played by male players, but only one in a hundred male characters are played by women.

# 7 Coming Home and Coming Out

*Jenny Sundén*

| | |
|---|---|
| *Lulu:* | could i ask you all a research related question? |
| *Cuddlybear:* | Shoot, jen-jen :D |
| *Lulu:* | when writing about the guild, what should i call it? |
| *Cuddlybear:* | "Bunch of weird guys who happens to like different things" |
| *Lulu:* | now . . . |
| *Lulu:* | something shorter? |
| *Cuddlybear:* | "The wrong people of the society" |
| *Dirt:* | "Fools"? |
| *Cuddlybear:* | "Tossers" |
| *Lulu:* | now we may be getting somewhere |
| *Cuddlybear:* | Or simply just "Those" |
| *Cuddlybear:* | As people tend to name us around here |
| | *[. . .]* |
| *Corky:* | or "The drama queens" |
| *Lulu:* | pretty good |
| *Twinkle:* | yeah appropriate |
| *Lulu:* | some would be offended though |
| *Corky:* | haha |
| | *[. . .]* |
| *Electromagnet whispers:* | *"the others"* |
| *Electromagnet whispers:* | *perhaps too boring* |
| *To Electromagnet:* | *it's actually very good* |
| *To Electromagnet:* | *i like it!* |
| *Electromagnet whispers:* | *i just thought that many view gays as that, or call us that . . .* |

It was a dusky evening in November, and I had anew grown tired of the pubescent quality in guild chat in my most recent guild. They claimed to have an age limit, but clearly such ways of speaking are not only related to age. I searched the web for an alternative, perhaps a group where it would not be necessary to remain in the closet, so to speak. Having a hard time convincing some of my previous co-players that I was 'truly' a woman (if we did not use voice chat), it became clear to me that being different in yet another way would be pushing it. I envisioned a group of people who instead would bring queer sensibilities to the game, and who would simultaneously infuse queer communities with a particular sense of play. Little did I know that this was precisely what I was about to find. Queer gamers or *gaymers* are an active, vocal part of game cultures, and it seemed plausible that the sheer market penetration of *World of Warcraft* would make the game a major hub of queer game communities. When searching online for a guild with non-straight players, there appeared to be quite a few options on US servers, but surprisingly less on European realms. In this sense, the guild that I found and made a connection with that November night was quite unique. In my work, I have come to call this group *The Others*. I needed a good cover name, and the suggestions from the members themselves as evident in the introductory quote were all playing with a sense of being other, strange, or odd, or with the imagery of queer communities as being densely dramatic ("the drama queens"). Eventually, I settled for the name *The Others* because of its clever way of playing with and at the same time taking questions of otherness and difference seriously.

*The Others* is explicitly defined as an LGBT (lesbian, gay, bisexual, transgender/transsexual) guild. The ethnography of this group was a ten-month project, starting in November 2008 and ending in September 2009. In the fall of 2009, the guild as I knew it began to slow down, diminish, and disintegrate. The group may be revived in other forms, it has happened before, but this was a point of transformation when previous key members moved on to other guilds, or to other activities in life. For this work, I leveled up and played the female blood elf death knight Lulu at level cap.[1] Lulu was my main character in the guild and came to work as my researcher alter ego. From time to time, I continued to play a couple of high-level characters elsewhere, as well as played a few low-levels for fun together with guild mates. My playtime varied, but the weekly average was about 15–20 hours. All names, of players and of their characters, have been changed throughout for the sake of anonymity. The ethnography is primarily an in-game ethnography, but it also includes the web forum belonging to the guild. More specifically, it consists of field notes from sessions of play, chat logs, screen shots, and informal interviews. As detailed in the chapters "Desires at Play" and "A Feel of Play", this ethnographic work was preceded by a one-year ethnography exploring queer moments and strategies in more mainstream *World of Warcraft* contexts. If the focus of the initial ethnography was on ways of exploring the game world and leveling up, the activities in *The Others* were more aimed at high-level content and endgame experiences.

During the time of my research, the guild was what Williams et al. (2006) terms medium-sized, with approximately 200 registered members, of which about thirty were active and visible. The number of people logged on at the same time varied, but it usually did not exceed twenty. The members came from all over Europe (Denmark, Serbia, Sweden, The Netherlands . . . ), but there was a clear dominance of members from the UK, as well as a clear dominance of men. The guild had an age limit of 16, but the typical player was in 'his' twenties and early thirties. Medium-sized guilds are often torn between different goals and ethics of play by potentially bringing together the tightly knit social bonds of smaller guilds with more large scale ambitions of raiding, advancements, and achievements usually characteristic of bigger guilds (Williams et al. 2006). The same can be said of *The Others*. Apart from providing a community in the game for non-straight players, the guild had a dual and sometimes divided focus on socializing and raiding. The ambition of *The Others* to advance together at level cap rarely went beyond five-man heroics and occasional ten-man raids. This discrepancy between ambition or goals and actual guild activities led to a series of disappointments in ways that reveal the social fragility of guilds, and which likely contributed to the gradual disintegration of the group.

This chapter is a home-coming story of sorts, of finding a home in the game for one's play, and of how players who orient themselves as non-straight make themselves 'at home' in a game culture infamous for its sexism and homophobia. Part of this story has to do with the potential differences between the 'straight' and the 'bent', between different contexts of play. As the chapter title also reveals, it is simultaneously a narrative of multiple (and continuous) acts of coming out in the game, as a researcher, but also as queer in particular ways. Through a series of playful performances of the roles of researcher, researched, players, and queers, the argument spins around ways of playing (and doing research) together. The chapter takes shape in the borderland between ethnography and play, and investigates the notion of participation in ethnographic work on online games. Sybille Lammes (2007) points out that game studies would benefit from more clearly spelling out methodological strategies grounded in play. She argues for the importance of reflexivity and situatedness in research on games, and uses as a point of departure Espen Aarseth's (2003) understanding of game studies as a field in need of including the position of the player/researcher in its methodology.[2] Nick Taylor (2008a), in turns, discusses the relative lack of attention in ethnographic research of MMOGs to how games are always situated in the everyday lives of players. To disregard the situatedness of play simultaneously makes invisible how the embodied subjectivities of participants are 'in play', including the play-based embodiment of the researcher herself. The politics of embodied situatedness matter in the coming together of online communities of play (cf. Taylor 2006a). Corporeal differences figure and are figured by play practices in ways that matter for who gets to play, and in which ways. They also matter for the researcher of games. In addition to working with and through notions of reflexivity and situatedness, this chapter is also an attempt to investigate the meaning of 'queer' for ethnographic work. What does it mean to perform a queer ethnography? Are queer ethnographies merely ethnographies of queer subject matters? Or, could queer be of use to unsettle or trouble the norms and conventions of ethnographic research itself?

## NEVER TRUST A ROGUE

Coming to *The Others*—with the previous experience of playing in more mainstream guilds—felt a bit like coming home, even if 'home' in queer circles may be ambivalent. Sexuality functioned as a tie that bound people together (people who may otherwise have had little in common). Sharing a passion for games, as well as sharing experiences of moving through life, and through the game as non-straight, formed a clear sense of togetherness and belonging. Finding the guild was similar to the feeling of traveling with your lover to places where public handholding and kissing is difficult, and of locating a gay/lesbian bar where you can relax and stop pretending. Moving through mainstream *World of Warcraft* culture as a sexual transgressor has a lot to do with acts of passing and blending in, or with public display, if you are willing to take the argument. The basic assumption in *The Others* is instead that you are *not* straight. Then again, this is not a separatist environment. Everybody is welcome, as long as they are aware of and respect the specificity of the guild. The borders of the guild are fluid. Yet, as will become clear, this fluidity is not without its own limitations and regulations.

Finding the guild was combined with a feeling of relief related to no longer having to worry about covering up bits of one's life that would not fit in, or would even be regarded as 'inappropriate' in the game environment. Entering the guild also came with a sense of happiness in experiencing the warmest of welcomes imaginable. As mentioned previously, the guild was clearly male dominated, but the handful of women that were active made up for in expressiveness what they lacked in numbers. Two women immediately took me under their wing, Anna and Sara. At the time, they were both part of the guild officers' group. I learned quickly that they were a couple, and that they were Swedish. Anna was the most verbal, charismatic, and curious of the two, and Sara the more low-voiced, yet noticeably outspoken. I immediately liked their dynamic. At this point, I was leveling up a new character as a member of the guild, and Sara offered to boost me (help with leveling) through low-level dungeons: "If you want a paladin Anna is your girl, and if you want a crazy hunter girl, I'm that girl". "Well, I like all kinds of girls", I had to admit. At this point in the conversation, a fourth person, Matt, spoke up in guild chat: "Omg, I log out for five sec, and when I log on the lesbians have taken over". "Get used to it Matt :-)", Anna replied. I was also informed that the first month as "Trainee Other" (before being promoted to the next step, "Other Soldier", and then possibly on to "Other Officer") was primarily "to see if you're gay enough". I was intrigued by this game within the game and wondered, indeed, if I was 'gay' enough. As a queer woman, the label 'gay' is one of slight discomfort. Or any label, really. Then again, I appreciated the humoristic, yet serious framing of a community that was clearly setting itself off in contrast to more mainstream cultures of play.[3]

I was 'out' in the game, and yet still closeted in other ways, having chosen to spend a week in the guild to cautiously feel my way in this new setting before asking permission to do research and declaring my identity as researcher. During that first week, I was home with a bad cold and a high temperature. I had a high-level character that I wanted to move, but the server was full to the point where you are not allowed to bring in characters from other servers, not even a paid transfer. This was the reason for my leveling a low-level character for the sake of the guild. I made her a female rogue and named her after one of my favorite single malt whiskies, a name packed with smoky flavors and with a strand of fantasy. I had tried out most classes, but had a soft spot for light-footed, agile, backstabbing rogues and their swift blades. I leveled her through the starting areas with feverish energy. After adventuring alone for a couple of days, and after complaining in guild chat that my daggers were dull ("I need sharper blades. These are useless"), I accepted the generous offer from Anna and Sara of a boost through Deadmines (which at the time was a low-level dungeon in Westfall). It was my first character-to-character encounter with these two women, and I was much impressed with their level 70+ gear (even if I myself had high level characters elsewhere). This was their first encounter with me, or with my level 10 rogue, and this at least initially came to define me as 'little' to them (cf. Sveningsson, Chapter 4 in this book).

After the run, and after having equipped new, sharp daggers along with a well-made pair of leather pants ("Jenny you are so pimped!"), Anna and I were making small talk. I decided to take my chances and come clean. This made me quite nervous, since LGBT guilds are rare, and I had high hopes for including *The Others* in my research. What if they did not accept me? Would a rejection mean a complete re-orientation of my research? Anna asked me what I did when I was not playing *World of Warcraft* ("look at me making conversation"). I told her truthfully that I was a teacher and a researcher, and that I did research on online communities and games, such as *World of Warcraft*. "Should I be careful?" she asked, "Am I like an animal in a cage?" "No, not at all" I assured her, "I would never allow that". "If the guinea pig wonders if she's part of an experiment, always say no", she concluded, and we laughed together. "No, but seriously", I continued, "that wouldn't be ethical at all". At the same time, I had to admit to her that my dream case would be a guild like *The Others*. She believed that the other guild members would approve of my research, and told me she would take a project description from me to present at the next meeting with the officers. I was relieved, and yet I still had to hold my breath.

During our conversation, Anna's girlfriend (and also the person she lives with) Sara interrupted me in whisper "you spy! I want gold:-)". Anna summarized the situation with the ever so fitting comment: "I say, never trust a rogue!" Rogues are notorious for their sly ways, their semi-transparent stealth mode, and for running their blades deep into the backs of others before they know what hit them. As such, rogues coincide with the idea of researchers performing their research in hidden manners, of working undercover to unobtrusively observe and get close to others. Then again, even the most skillful of rogues may have her cover blown at any point. Once detected, her stealth mode is interrupted, and she appears to her onlooker as sharp as ever. She may try to disappear and make herself blend with the shadows anew, but the attentive observer will notice that even the most subtle of stealths do not make her completely invisible. Once she has revealed herself, there is no going back to a more innocent or discrete manner of moving. And hence, this initial act of coming out as a researcher made my brief, introductory period of secrecy come to a full stop.

## COMING OUT

No sooner said than done. I sent a letter with Anna to the other officers, presenting myself and my research. The letter began:

> Dear fellow Others, This is a somewhat peculiar act of coming out . . . Certainly not as gay (yes, I am:-)), but as a researcher of games. Let me start from the beginning to get everything straight (oh wait).

'Gay' in this context is a simplification. It simplifies (and also displaces) my own position, and it simultaneously simplifies the positions of the other members of *The Others*. Yet, this was my initial contact, and I had noticed that 'gay' often functioned as shorthand to create a collaborative identity in the guild. Gay in this sense operates as a unifying way of marking oneself as well as the guild as 'not straight', or as 'not them'. Here, I use the term as an act of naming that makes possible recognition based on sameness. Then again, and as the analyses will make evident, gay may function as a starting point for understanding ways of playing together in *The Others*, but the story does not end there. In fact, there are competing and sometimes contradictory definitions and positions at play (gay versus gay and lesbian, the guild as LGBT, the guild as open to anyone who is respectful, etc.) which makes an analysis along the lines of 'queer' more interesting.

After sharing the letter with the group of officers, I was invited to a meeting and a voice chat interview. We talked about the process of making my case anonymous, how the names of individual players are easy enough to switch, but how it could be hard to make the guild itself completely anonymous. They expressed certain worries that my research would bring 'the wrong' (i.e., homophobic) people into the guild, but came to the conclusion that spreading the word among researchers of games would not be a greater risk than spreading the word among people in general. Overall, they seemed curious and very much liked the idea of having me around. They wondered whether I would keep my initial focus on women, or if I would include everybody. I told them that while I *do* have a particular interest in women (at which point they laughed), I would certainly look at the guild at large.

They also wondered what would happen if they did not like my writing, if they simply disagreed with my portrayal of them (Ehn 1996, see also Sveningsson, Chapter 1 in this book). This is a tricky question. On one hand, it evokes an ethnographic tradition that builds on how researchers often retain their 'right of interpretation', of always having the last word. On the other hand, there is a growing body of ethnographic work that instead dismantles the authority of the researcher, striving to develop ethnographic epistemologies of co-creation and collaboration (cf. Halberstam 2005; Dahl 2010). I may not think of the other members of the guild as co-creators of academic texts, such as this one, but I certainly think of them as important collaborators and co-producers in the field. The people who have populated my research are subjects of knowledge in their own right. Without their generosity, warmth, curiosity, and in-depth knowledge of the game, this project would never have happened. One concrete example of the collaborative dimension of my ethnography was the invitation to participants to share, read and comment on my texts before they were finalized and published. This invitation gave rise to a fair amount of interest in my writing, but then again, I got nothing but supportive responses. Obviously, it is more difficult to get people who may not be as thrilled with the project to speak up. Those who responded seemed to recognize and approve of my ways of making sense of guild activities, while at the same time admitting that my writing at times may be on the abstract side ("i read your stuff:D it was very good:P bit over my head at times tho:)"). This is the dilemma of writing for multiple audiences.

Efforts to trouble the division between researcher and researched may be particularly evident in queer studies. For example, Judith Halberstam (2005, 162) explores the relationship between subcultural producers and queer cultural theorists and argues for "the death of the expert" in that "queer subcultures encourage blurred boundaries between archivists and producers". The queer archivist/theorist and the cultural worker/producer (Halberstam draws primarily on examples of performative practices, such as performance art, drag, and music production) may work as 'coconspirators' in that they share theoretical references, networks of friends, and public spaces. Members of queer subcultures are not only providing material for queer cultural archives, but are often themselves active in archiving practices—no matter how ephemeral the archive itself may be in a time of digital media. If traditionally, cultural theorists have looked at groups of which they are not a part, "new queer cultural studies feed off of and back into subcultural production" (p. 163). The theorist then becomes a co-archivist, as well as a full-blown participant in those cultural spaces where she performs her research.

Within the bounds of my own fieldwork and its particular queer subculture, I recognize the blurring of boundaries in the field in terms of archiving practices. Players tend to keep private files with game memories, and the web forum of the guild is a continuous making of a collective archive of this group. The forum houses everything from screen shots of raids and social events, to guild applications, status updates, and lively discussion threads. Then again, even if I was far from the only archivist in the group, I may have been the only queer theorist. The performances in and around the *The Others* could fruitfully be understood as queer game theory in the making, but it takes certain tools and concepts to make such an analysis happen. No matter how political the mere presence of this guild and its ways of playing game may be, the tools and concepts of queer theory and queer studies were not something that I shared explicitly with them. Moreover, even if *World of Warcraft* has become my backyard of sorts, *The Others* does not overlap with my other more locally based queer circles in Stockholm. My *World of Warcraft*-life became an apparent part of my everyday queer circles, but like the other members of the guild, I operate in multiple, perhaps parallel queer communities.

I did get permission from the officers to perform my research, which was the first necessary step, but far from the last. I took their advice and posted a short note on the front page of the guild forum declaring "Jenny needs you!"—featuring a snapshot of my female blood elf death knight researcher character Lulu—as well as a longer note in the forum presenting my project and myself. A couple of players wanted to be left out of the study, but the majority welcomed me with open arms. Then again, as new players entered the guild, I had to ask in guild chat from time to time if they were aware of my project. Most of them were, but then again, some of them were not. The dilemma of getting 'informed consent' in semi-public online environments is well documented in the research on ethics in Internet research (Sveningsson 2001; 2003; 2009). One way of addressing the uncertainty of my status among new guild members was to post research updates in the guild forum, such as giving members access to texts that I was about to finish. These posts gave rise to enthusiastic responses from people wanting to read my texts ("^^ send some this way:P"; "Me wants to read Jenny hahaha I'll send you a PM"; "yay The Others research me 2"), and they simultaneously functioned as a reminder of my presence and my project.

As Eve Kosofsky Sedgwick (1990) argues in *Epistemology of the Closet* with regards to heterosexual/homosexual binaries, the closet is an impossibly contradictory place. It is neither possible to fully reside in the closet, nor is it possible to fully leave it behind. While 'in' the closet, you can never be certain of to what extent you have managed to keep your secret. Are people treating you as straight because they are deceived? Or, is it because they play along and are unwilling to give up the epistemological privilege you grant them by not telling? On the other hand, if the secrecy of the closet is "of and about the love that is famous for daring not speak its name", this is a secret that can never be completely and utterly exposed (p. 67). There will always be new social situations and new encounters, and there is always uncertainty in terms of who can be said to know. It also seems reasonable to say that the type of knowledge that the closet is supposed to hide is uncertain, for what exactly is it that is being revealed in acts of coming out? Sedgwick reads the epistemology of the closet as indicative of wider social and cultural mappings of secrecy and disclosure, as well as notions of private and public spaces. The ethnographic closet may not be a defining structure of oppression, but it is nonetheless a paradoxical space that makes ambiguous the question of who knows and who does not know. The members of *The Others* testify to how *World of Warcraft* cultures tend to operate along the lines of explicit homophobia, or by more implicit silencing mechanisms by making the sexual orientations of players irrelevant to gameplay. The guild, then, provides a place where players can be 'out' in the game (yet still closeted once outside of the guild), or where 'being out' is the community point of departure and something to be expected. In this sense, my second coming out process—as researcher—is more problematic, as it is completely unexpected. Hence, the act of coming out as researcher is something that you will have to do over and over again as new people enter the guild, much like in your everyday life when finding yourself in new social situations.

## QUEER ETHNOGRAPHY

With the purpose of bringing together queer studies and game ethnography, it is necessary to take a brief look at the place and function of 'queer' in ethnographic work more generally. Deborah Elliston (2002) notes that at the beginning of the new millennium, lesbian and gay studies—and its expansion in terms of LGBT studies—have increasingly become a legitimate field of inquiry within the discipline of anthropology.[4] Lesbian and gay studies have by no means been a unitary enterprise, or a 'happy marriage' (Lewin 2002), even if the commonality of the term may suggest otherwise. Their differences and tensions aside, the critics of lesbian and gay studies have pointed out that an area of research based on a sexed dualism excludes a whole range of other Others, such as bisexuals, transsexuals and transgender people (cf. Halberstam 2005; Kulick 1998; Shapiro 2005; Valentine 2002). As a consequence, the study of 'homosexuality' has been complicated and multiplied along the lines of 'bi-' and 'trans-', a call for both an inclusion and an expansion that resulted in acronyms such as LGBT. In a shift from lesbian and gay—via LGBT—to queer, there is a (somewhat paradoxical) proliferation of identities, positions, and orientations. Queer is often used as shorthand for multiple ways of positioning and orienting oneself as non-straight, and simultaneously as a way of rendering problematic every fixed definition. Queer ethnography takes up the challenge from queer theory to unsettle or trouble the seeming stability of categories, identities, and practices, while at the same time challenging the Eurocentrism in LGBT studies and queer theory alike.

Queer ethnographies are (usually) ethnographies of queer subject matters.[5] They provide stories of embodied experiences of what it is like to lead lives against the grain of the normal. They are performed and written along the striving within queer theory to not only emphasize that which is other, or strange, but to disrupt and dissect 'the normal', to ultimately reveal the constructedness of heterosexuality as well as of ethnography. I am interested in this doubleness at the heart of queer ethnography—as something that marks research of cultures that could be termed queer, and simultaneously as a possibility of queering ethnographic methods. More specifically, I am interested in exploring the radical potential in queering methodologies, rather than merely claiming that researching queer cultures in and of itself is a radical project. To think queer as disturbing, transgressive, or subversive *per se* neither gives insights into how queer communities are differentiated, regulated and, indeed, normative, nor does it readily address how for example heterosexual practices sometimes bend straight norms. Tom Boellstorff (2007b) speaks of this tendency as the self-congratulatory exercise in queer studies. If queer is rather used as a method and as a mode of writing, queer ethnography gets interestingly multi-layered. Alison Rooke (2009, 150, italics in original) argues:

> queer ethnography is not merely ethnography that focuses on researching queer lives; it is also a matter of taking queer theory seriously in order to question the conventions of ethnographic research, specifically the stability and coherence of the ethnographic self and the performativity of this self in writing and doing research. To *queer* ethnography then, is to bend the established orientation of ethnography in its method, ethics, and reflexive philosophical principles.

To Rooke, there is an important dual emphasis on queer subject matters and queer as a method of bending the dominant rules of ethnography itself.[6] Then again, given that ethnographers have been pushing up against different ethnographic traditions for decades, it is not self-evident which rules queer ethnography aims to bend. If, for example, bending the established orientation of ethnography means questioning the authority and coherence of the researching 'I', then the reflexive turn (as discussed in the chapter "Desires at Play"), as well as the 'turn' to auto-ethnography, is a way of queering ethnography. If ethnography as messy, corporeal, and partial is always already part of an ethnographic tradition, then it would be reasonable to say that ethnography has been queer for quite some time. Rooke speaks of the queer ethnographer as someone working with and through an ethic of involvement and vulnerability in the field, as someone who acknowledges that ethnographies are based on emotional investments and embodied experiences (cf. Behar 1996). In particular, she points out that queering ethnography demands that we, as researchers, make visible the 'normative logics' of ethnographic practices that tend to construct the gendered and sexual subjectivity of the researcher as uncomplicated and stable (or irrelevant and invisible). While we are busy analyzing or deconstructing the positions of others in the field, "we might ask ourselves [ . . . ] to what extent are we willing to be 'pulled apart' or undone?" (p. 153).[7] My ethnographic work is an attempt to explore what it would mean to 'come undone' as a researcher, to make emotion, desire, and vulnerability an intimate part of ethnographic epistemologies.

## RESEARCH AT PLAY

| | |
|---|---|
| *Honey:* | Lulu, what's your irl name? |
| *Lulu:* | Jenny |
| *Andromeda:* | oo sparkly jenny with the guns! |
| *Honey:* | ah! you're the one doing research? :D |
| *Lulu:* | yes! |
| *Andromeda:* | ^ ^ |
| *Honey:* | way to go! :D |
| *Andromeda:* | I like being watched o.0 |
| *Lulu:* | so be careful |
| *Honey:* | hihihi |
| *Lulu:* | just kidding! |
| *Lulu:* | good for you |
| *Lulu:* | i'm very kind, as far as researchers go :D |
| *Andromeda:* | ^ ^ |
| *Whishie:* | I was never asked anything :( |
| *Whishie:* | :p |
| *Lulu:* | you will |
| *Honey:* | haha |
| *Lulu:* | :) |
| *Andromeda:* | what's the term for people who stay with their subjects too long . . . gone native? |
| *Lulu:* | yes |
| *Andromeda:* | woo, get me =P |
| *Andromeda:* | I think you have to get into deeper corners |
| *Lulu:* | exactly |

In this passage, I got the question from Honey "what's your irl name?" and after clarifying that my name is Jenny, I was immediately recognized as "the one doing research". Andromeda's comment "oo sparkly jenny with the guns!" refers back to a picture of me that I had posted in the guild forum in a 'real life picture thread'. The real life picture thread was an interesting space where the fantastical bodies in-game get company of the real life faces and bodies of players. The thread was a wild mix of vacation snap-shots, everyday pictures, portraits in front of the computer, and pictures of people all dressed up or (partly) undressed. It was a space that invited complements and flirts, such as a male member in uniform saying "Okay everybody get in line, so I can perform full frisk for all of you", who immediately got the response "*Pushes to the front of the queue*". Interestingly, several players seemed pleasantly surprised by how the guild had so many 'good looking' people, evoking the culturally dominant image of gamers as not particularly attractive.

The example reads as a playful yet serious way of relating to me as a researcher and to the process of doing research in terms of fieldwork. On the one hand, I am positioned as the one who's doing the watching, and they the ones being watched. They recognize me as someone there to learn by 'looking' at them, and they come forth as curious and excited. They even strike poses to ask for my attention ("woo, get me =P"), and ask of me to see them ("I was never asked anything"). In this sense, I am not the only one who's watching, but they also clearly watch me, and keep track of whether I seem to include them in my research by asking them questions. On the other hand, they are also showing certain awareness of ethnographic practices and acknowledge the doubleness of my position. I am not only an observer, but also a participant of the group. Parallel to the activity of watching and being watched is the activity of participation and co-play. My taking part in the guild in this sense even leads them to wonder "what's the term for people who stay with their subjects too long . . . gone native?" Significantly, this more intense way of taking part in or being part of the group as a valuable research strategy is reflected in Andromeda's comment "I think you have to get into deeper corners", pointing at the idea that to truly understand a phenomenon, there is a need for deep, intense engagement.

The guild members' ways of relating to me were indicative of how they related to the whole process of being involved in research. Many were intrigued and enjoyed posing for me, teasing me, or play around with the idea of my research. At one point, I was invited to go to Manchester to give a seminar on my ongoing research, and Anna was curious about my trip:

*Corky whispers:* *what is it that you'll do in Manchester?*
*To Corky:* *talk about my research!*
*To Corky:* *for 30 minutes*
*Corky whispers:* *oh!*
*Corky whispers:* *but 30 minutes is not enough! you won't have enough time to tell them about how imba i am when healing and tanking . . . hm hm . . .*
*To Corky:* *no i KNOW*
*To Corky:* *so little time!*
*Corky whispers:* *in that case, i would prefer if you talked about my healing*
*To Corky:* *ok! if i have to chose then :D*
*Corky whispers:* *yea, if there's so little time . . .*

This is an example of how members playfully positioned themselves in relation to me and my project, and also an expression of curiosity of how she (in this case) figures in my work. 'Imba' is short for imbalanced, and means that a character manages to take on enemies well above its expected level of performance. Thus, this passage reads as an instance of a tongue-in-cheek brag for me as researcher and friend, and simultaneously a wish to be portrayed in a certain way—as a competent, powerful, fabulous player. The question at stake is how can I possibly use my time wisely when there is so much to say about her talents? If half an hour is all I have, then she recommends me to wisely focus on one aspect of her talent, in this case her ability to play healer.

Guild members were not only striking poses for me, but they did also from time to time check up on me, wondering if I was making any progress:

*Dorian:* Jenny can I ask you a question?
*Lulu:* yes of course
*Dorian:* have you been able to get any research done? it seems like the guild has gone more and more quiet lately
*Lulu:* i think a little bit yes
*Dorian:* that's good :)
*Lulu:* and yes, sometimes a bit quiet, more so than before perhaps
*Dorian:* yeah it's a bit unusual i think
*Lulu:* i think it may change though, since a lot of new ppl keep applying
*Dorian:* yeah after Sunday we'll be full of drama again haha
*Lulu:* i don't worry, i have time:)

This is an interesting episode in the sense that there is not only a question of whether my work is moving forward, but also a concern that perhaps I am not able to get as much material as I need, or the kind of material that I am interested in. The guild had been slower than usual for some time, people were busy with exams, or busy at work, and the guild chat had fallen unusually silent. I was fully occupied with leveling and learning new tricks, so I did not worry, but could not help smiling at Dorian's "yeah after Sunday we'll be full of drama again haha". This comment points at the idea of me as a researcher of a queer guild having a prime interest in 'drama', and that there might be reason to worry when such social density could not be provided. Certainly, *The Others* is a place that at times became dense with emotion. Members made dramatic exits based on, for example, disappointments of failed raid-sessions, only to re-enter a couple of days later to give the guild another go. Alongside these dramatic exits were often humorous, self-ironic remarks that played with the idea of the guild as 'gay'—and as such housing a bunch of 'drama queens'. This witty, self-reflexive use of the term 'queen' performs a double gesture in that it seems to simultaneously criticize and proudly appropriate the camp figure of the overly emotional, effeminate gay man:

| | |
|---|---|
| *Teleopat:* | btw, has The Others imploded yet? |
| *Corky:* | I felt that one coming lol |
| *Blackpriest:* | not sure lol |
| *Corky:* | it seems to implode every 3 months or so =) |
| *Blackpriest:* | they're all gays i hear lol |
| *Teleopat:* | I've said it once, I'll say it again |
| *Corky:* | omg rly? |
| *Teleopat:* | you get too many gays in one place and it distorts the fabric of reality |
| *Corky:* | lol |
| *Blackpriest:* | lol |
| *Corky:* | I blame the dramaqueening men |
| *Violet:* | oooh aaaah *grabbin drink and watching drama* |

## ETHNOGRAPHIC VULNERABILITY

> Playfulness is, in part, an openness to being a fool, which is a combination of not worrying about competence, not being self-important, not taking norms as sacred and finding ambiguity and double edges a source of wisdom and delight. (Lugones 1987, 19)

If the term 'gay' in *World of Warcraft* in general is routinely used as an insult, as a reinforcement of hegemonic heteronormativity (Pascoe 2007), it is given a very different spin in a guild where 'gay' serves as the point of departure. As a queer woman, the label 'gay' is one of slight discomfort and ambivalence, even if it simultaneously operates as a comforting marker of belonging and community. Importantly, 'gay' pushes at my own uncertainty regarding ways of living and defining myself, something that was brought to the fore a couple of times during fieldwork.

| | |
|---|---|
| *Thehottie whispers:* | *so which side of the fence do you stand on?* |
| *To Thehottie:* | *do i need to pick?* |
| *Thehottie whispers:* | *lol Bi answer lol* |
| *To Thehottie:* | *well* |
| *Thehottie whispers:* | *well it doesn't really matter either way I'm just nosey* |
| *To Thehottie:* | *i'm leaning to the ladies in the sense that i don't think i'll ever be turned on by a man again . . .* |
| *Thehottie whispers:* | *:D* |
| *Thehottie whispers:* | *men make great friends but that's about the closest i get* |
| *To Thehottie:* | *to me . . . what you do is more important than labels, which may be another bi answer, not sure* |
| *To Thehottie:* | *got you* |

| | |
|---|---|
| *Thehottie whispers:* | *it's like ex bi or bi active . . . lol . . . personally i have always said i am attracted to women but couldn't rule out that my soulmate could be a man* |
| *To Thehottie:* | *right* |
| *To Thehottie:* | *i'm ex bi then:D* |
| *Thehottie whispers:* | *hehe* |
| *Thehottie whispers:* | *i only ask cause it's hard enough finding a girl in wow, think i was the only non straight one lol* |

My inclination since I was quite young could perhaps be called bisexual, but I have always found it hard in practice to operate along parallel corporeal registers. And sometimes, to follow one's passions is to end up somewhere fairly different, such as when I noticed some years ago that I had completely fallen out of the habit of seeing men's bodies sexually, my eyes kept sliding, as if there was no longer anything for them to 'stick' to. Instead, my senses were heightened in ways that turned me, my body, again and again towards women. My body had been turned before, but it had also had its other turns. Then again, sometimes you need to be recognized and recognizable. In the guild, when introducing myself as part of the community, recognition was more important than elaborative identity disclaimers. At first glance, these personal reflections may appear as an autobiographical side-note, and as such stealing focus from what is actually at stake. What I am hoping to show is how this seeming detour is rather aimed straight at questions that are vital for queer ethnographies. It is a way of raising questions about the researcher as queer, and how such queerness comes to matter in particular ways in fieldwork.

In *Communities of Play*, Celia Pearce (2009) includes a careful exploration of researcher vulnerability in her multi-sited game ethnography of the Uru diaspora. Due to a crisis halfway through fieldwork related to her legitimacy in the group she studied, Pearce was forced to change her methodological approach: from the position of a relatively low-key, modest observer to that of a more active, engaged participant. In my own fieldwork, when thinking with and working through notions of researcher vulnerability as a potentially queer epistemological strategy, several moments and experiences come to mind. Some of these have to do with desire in the field and were detailed in the chapter "Desires at Play". Other moments were rather tied to inquiries regarding my sexual orientation ("so which side of the fence do you stand on?"). Yet other experiences of vulnerability as player and as researcher were moments of failure and embarrassment. To address failures of play speaks to mundane player experiences (cf. Juul 2009). Failure is simultaneously at heart of ethnographic fieldwork, or with Boellstorff's (2006, 32) words: "It is a method based on failure, on learning from mistakes to develop a theory for how a culture is lived—for its norms and its 'feel'". To play games is to make mistakes, to fail, again and again, and to slowly learn how to get it right, how to improve and advance.

And even then you will keep making mistakes, and sometimes stupid ones because you did not pay attention, even if you should have known better. Such moments may throw even the most skilled players and researchers, and as such they are significant.

*Lulu:* word of advice . . .
*Lulu:* never do hc's while drinking wine
*Bakerman:* lol
*Lulu:* i'm serious
*Vaniel:* lol go jenny
*Bakerman:* what happened jenny?
*Lulu:* i've equipped really really bad pants
*Lulu:* with intellect!
*Lulu:* for a dk!
*Bakerman:* OMG! Lol
*Lulu:* oh dear
*Zara:* to make u smarter now :P
*Lulu:* yes!
*Lulu:* LOL
*Lulu:* so bad
*Lulu:* and apparently i've sold my old ones
*Lulu:* *giggles*
*Zara:* haha
*Lulu:* have to go to ah—so embarrassing
*[. . .]*
*Bakerman:* I've seen you and dodgy pants jenny!!
*Lulu:* hahaha!
*Bakerman:* granny pants ftw
*Lulu:* LOL
*Lulu:* that's what they are
*Bakerman:* mine are furry . . . Barbaric Loincloth
*Bearme:* I got Cabalist Leggings of the Monkey
*Viljhalm:* heya!
*Vaniel:* sexy!
*Lulu:* hey!
*Bearme:* We were showing our sexy pants
*Bearme:* And hey Neal
*Bakerman:* show us your pants Neal
*Viljhalm:* oh! Hahaha
*Viljhalm:* i don't have pants on atm :P
*Bakerman:* oh my. . . .
*Bakerman:* *faint*

This was not a moment of pride. In fact, I'm blushing as I incorporate the example in this text. But to include it is to acknowledge the meaning of failure, not only for (other) players in general, but for the researcher of play herself. It is, indeed, an eventful example, starting out with me advising my co-players to never engage in guild runs on heroic mode (a heightened level of difficulty) while having wine. Then I admit to my beginner's mistake of equipping pants that were not made for my class: the death knight. Death knights are slaying machines and use the heaviest of armor, high on 'strength'. Death knights have little use for armor with 'intellect', and the comment from Zara was dead on: "to make u smarter now :P". The problem was not only that I had equipped lousy pants, apparently I had also managed to sell my old ones right before logging off (which then becomes a non-reversible act). This gave me the option of running around in my everything but flattering pants, or to sport no pants at all. It was a long, awkward walk to the auction house to purchase something I could actually wear. On my way there, I evidently ran into a guild-mate, even if I pretended not to see him. But he saw me: "I've seen you and dodgy pants jenny!! [ . . . ] granny pants ftw".[8] This was an excellent way of describing the situation I had put myself in: a young hot female knight in granny pants. The whole story of my pants came to feed into a more flirtatious comparison of the kinds of pants the others had on for the moment ("mine are furry . . . Barbaric Loincloth" and "I got Cabalist Leggings of the Monkey") up until the point when Neal entered guild chat and was challenged to show his pants. He admitted to not having any pants on at all at the moment (in real life, one must assume), which caused one of his interlocutors to 'faint'. Such playful flirtatious remarks between the male members were part of the everyday fabric of the guild, and came to operate as a bonding activity in ways that made the roles of female players rather unclear. For, who does she become within this game in the game of imagining one's co-players pantless? I will return to this point shortly.

## QUEER FRIENDSHIP

This chapter has been played out in the borderland between ethnography and play. The discussion covered ways of playing together, and also ways of doing and playing research together. At the very heart of the argument were a series of performances of shifting roles, positions, orientations (as researcher, researched, player, queer), of a playful turn-taking in which I tried to make sense of them, and them of me. Ethnography and play share many traits, which points at the interconnectedness between the playlike, performative elements of ethnography (Denzin 2003), and the ethnographic qualities in coming to, learning and trying to understand a play-based culture like that of *World of Warcraft* (see Boellstorff 2008). Importantly, play and performance are brought to the fore even more clearly in games, since games need to be performed, or played, to exist. New media scholars have discussed the dramaturgical dimensions of computing in general (Laurel

1991; Murray 1997), and with the growth of text-based virtual worlds and communities like IRC, MUD, and MOO, discussions of the performative and playful dimensions of online textuality proliferated (Danet 1998, 2001; Danet, Ruedenberg and Rosenbaum-Tamari 1998; Sundén 2003; Sveningsson 2001). In a culture where text is all there is, where everything and *everyone* needs to be typed into being in order to exist, a particular way of using the keyboard does not only set the limits for what you can do, but ultimately for who you can be (Sundén 2003). In a game like *World of Warcraft*, there is a similar need to perform—to play—in order to be someone in the game, as well as to make sense of play.

In this chapter, my aim was to open up for a discussion of participation in ethnographic work on online games by a playful engagement with reflexivity, situatedness, and co-performance. It started out with an account of how I came to find a home away from home in *World of Warcraft*, and of how the members of the guild *The Others* have made themselves 'at home' by creating a free zone of sorts in the game. Parallel to the story of homemaking was the trope of multiple acts of coming out in this particular context of play—as a researcher of games as well as a non-straight player. If in general, acts of coming out are entwined with questions of sexual orientation and sexual practices, in the context of a queer guild, it is rather the practice of doing research that needs to be declared. By drawing on Sedgwick's (1990) discussion of the epistemology of the closet, it was revealed that the ethnographic closet is a similarly contradictory place in the sense that there is always uncertainty in terms of who knows and who does not know (that you are a researcher).

What difference, then, does it make to play with a queer guild, in comparison with more mainstream contexts of play? The simple answer to this question is that it may well make all the difference in the world. *The Others* provides a warm, witty, somewhat kinky space for play. It is a place where the sexual and the playful coexist and intermingle in ways that may make more interesting even the most repetitive acts of gaming. This is not to say that sexuality and sexual orientation is always in the foreground (or that sexuality would not be part of other gaming contexts, which is evident in Sveningsson's chapters in this book). Sometimes it rather works as a back-grounding of the everyday ups and downs of gameplay, but still as something that binds people together. Guild members have told me about the reactions from random players that they have come across who do not understand the point with a guild for non-straight players. Isn't the purpose to just play the game? Implicit in this question is another question: What does sexuality have to do with playing the game? At first glance, it may seem to have limited importance in relation to gear scores and achievements, with excellent raiding skills and strategic timing. Then again, it has everything to do with all of these things and more, since *World of Warcraft* is an intensely social game (in particular at level cap). It is a game that fosters coalitions between players, that demands of them to spend long hours together online. If many people tend to play with people they already know, people with whom they are close, such as family, friends, and partners (Nardi and Harris 2006; Peterson 2007; Yee 2003; 2008), a group like *The Others* is no exception. But one important difference between the 'straight' and the 'bent' in relation to notions of closeness and letting gameplay stay 'close to home' is bound to the very understanding of what counts as home, and what counts as family. In a context where the question of family and kinship is not primarily based on blood-ties or marriage legislation, but rather on choice (Weeks, Heaphy, and Donovan 2001; Weston 1991) and a set of different belongings, affiliations, connections (Freeman 2007), the value of choosing a group like *The Others* for one's play is significant. Put simply, they become your family in the game. They are home.

If *The Others* provides a home and a family of sorts in the game for players who orient themselves as non-straight, the question then becomes: what kind of home? And what kind of family? Do the members feel equally at home? Or is it the case that some feel more at home than others? In a discussion of the particular type of playfulness characteristic of the guild, what are the rules, limits, and conditions of such playfulness? In other words, who gets to be playful, in what way, and with what consequences? I will return to and discuss these questions more at length in the next chapter on the transgressive potentials and limitations of playfulness, but it makes sense within the context of alternate intimacies to foreground that discussion already here. As mentioned earlier, the guild had a clear male domination, and there were certainly moments when you—as a woman—became somewhat superfluous in relation to the men's ways of flirting and showing interest in one another. One example discussed in this chapter is the flirtatious comparison of pants (in the game), which got more heated when Neal confessed to not having any pants on at the moment (in real life), which caused one of the other male members to 'faint'. In this moment, I was the only female guild member logged on, and I think that it is safe to say that nobody would have 'fainted' had I admitted to be playing the game pantless. In a context of same-sex desire, flirtatious remarks are not equally accessible to everybody, and cannot be used in the same way.

Who, then, does the female player become as a member of a male dominated queer guild? If a woman in straight contexts becomes a mediator of male desire and a guarantee of the framework being properly heterosexual (cf. Sveningsson, Chapter 3 of this book), who does she become when such assurance is no longer needed, when she finds herself in the midst of a story about desire between men? The one position that was largely available and possible for female players to inhabit in relation to the male players of *The Others* was that of a friend. These cross-gender friendships, while lacking the promise of erotic fulfillment, did not necessarily lack a flirtatious feel. In fact, there were plenty of lighthearted, playful female-on-male flirts, but without the suggestion of such flirts ever 'going somewhere'. One example was a standing joke between Anna and one of the guys, Brian, about being 'married' to one another in the game (which in and of itself is rather queer, given that same-sex desire was the ground rule). Since Anna had a girlfriend in the guild, there would be occasional bursts of pretend jealousy on the part of Brian, and threats of breaking into the two women's wedding in the style of the vicar from the BBC series "The Vicar of Dibley" performing Yvonne Fair's "It Should Have Been Me". At first look, such female-on-male flirtations may seem nothing but straight, but in the context of the guild they meant something different altogether. The basic understanding was that these flirts had little bearing on 'reality', and it was precisely this loose connection with the 'real' that made such moments safe in a way they would not have been otherwise.

Interestingly, the orientation of female players as friends with men within an overall homosexual framework is an orientation that an emphasis on male homosexual *desire* disguises, or even makes invisible. Put differently, the perpetual focus on sexuality in queer communities and queer theory alike discriminates against other meaningful social forms (cf. Roseneil and Budgeon 2004). Several of the examples in this chapter point in the direction of a shaping and making of a particular form of friendly, flirty intimacy that operates across gender on a sliding scale between the sexual and the non-sexual. Jennifer Doyle (2007) discusses such unexpected and queer belongings in terms of the intimacies and friendships that bind men and women together in ways that are otherwise invisible or culturally unintelligible. They are invisible within a heterosexual framework, in which, as Doyle has it, "sex is often built up as intimacy's destination, and, at the same time, friendship's obstacle" (p. 332). They are equally invisible in a homosexual framework dominated by gay men in the sense that these spaces are assumed to be built on and around sex (between men). Put differently, if sex is all there is, friendship simply becomes pointless. This is not to say that such unexpected friendship relations are not there, or that they would not be real. The importance of cross-gender friendship as a way of organizing guild relations testifies to the opposite. But what this analysis implies is that such an investment of time and energy in friendship for its own sake, within a queer space dominated by gay men, is not commonly understood as a culturally viable social practice.

This invisibility of mixed-gender friendship in queer spaces is noticeable on, for example, the level of language. Even if the importance of friendship practices within queer communities is well documented (see, for example, Berlant and Warner 2000; Weeks et. al 2001; Weston 1991), the language for describing the role of, in this case, women in spaces largely populated by gay men is rather limited. Doyle performs a careful interrogation of the one term that comes to mind, namely that of the 'fag hag':

> As a stereotype (the insecure straight woman who retreats into asexual friendships with similarly stunted homosexual men) the fag hag obscures the full range of relationships between women and gay men

> and, indeed, the complexity of queerness itself. She serves as a symbolic distraction—a flattened out caricature who stands in for all women, including lesbians, in queer bohemia (p. 332).

There were moments during fieldwork when I was momentarily read as 'straight' by male newcomers to the guild, an orientation along the lines of 'fag hag' that simultaneously downplays the importance of close bonds across gender in queer spaces. Understood as straight, the potential queerness of the relations between men and women in these spaces, along with queer as a way of orienting oneself, becomes nothing but an appendix to the main story, "a story about the men in the scene and their relationships to each other, in which she figures merely as part of a sham romance" (Doyle 2007, 332). Understood as straight, 'she' is devoid of sexuality, or at least of a kind of sexuality that counts and that makes sense within this particular context. She is reduced to the role of an audience member, or an unthreatening admirer of the ongoing social 'drama', and her presence helps clarify the limits of a desire between men and for men. Such straightening of the queer woman does not only desexualize her, but also diminish the value of those friendships and relations that may lack a clear erotic charge or destination.

Then again, in describing the feel of the guild as a continuous making of a particular form of friendly, flirty intimacy, such atmosphere did not only work along the lines of male domination. As has been shown, sometimes this story was challenged by, or turned on its head, by the female players and their ways of actively and vocally making the game into a space in which women come together and play. Even if there was merely a handful of female members, through their ways of appropriating the technologies involved, as well as appropriating the tools of interaction, they showed how a space for the boys and for significant cross-gender friendship was simultaneously a space for girls who like other girls. In this sense, they managed to create a powerful platform for female players to come together, serve as mentors for one another, and play the game together. No longer merely reduced to the roles of witty sidekicks, such interventions made room for women as subjects (and objects) of desire in their own right, but also in important ways for powerful friendships between women. Such women-only breathing spaces within the framework of gay male domination (within the overall framework of straight male domination in *World of Warcraft*) proved as vital to recruiting new female members as they were to keeping those already onboard.

## NOTES

1. Level cap is the highest level a character can reach in the game, which at this point was level 80.

2. For reflexive accounts in game studies of play-based research, see for example the co-authors of the collection of essays *Digital Culture, Play and Identity* (Corneliussen and Walker Rettberg 2008b), the work of T.L. Taylor (for example *Play Between Worlds*, 2006b), as well as Celia Pearce and Artemesia's (2009) *Communities of Play*, which is a careful, innovative ethnographic account across online play communities building on a collaborative authorship between Pearce and her intra-game character Artemesia.
3. A shorter version of the story of my coming to the guild was previously published as part of Sundén, Jenny. 2009b. "Play as Transgression: An Ethnographic Approach to Queer Game Cultures." Proceedings of DiGRA 2009 Breaking New Ground: Innovation in Games, Play, Practice and Theory, London, UK, September 1–4.
4. Kath Weston's (1993) essay "Lesbian/Gay Studies in the House of Anthropology", as well as Tom Boellstorff's (2007a) "Queer Studies in the House of Anthropology", mark significant moments in the intersection of queer studies and anthropology.
5. For central queer ethnographies, see, for example, Boellstorff (2007b), Manalansan (2003), Rofel (2007), Sinnot (2004), and Valentine (2007).
6. For a later version of this article, see Rooke (2010).
7. Suzanne de Castell and Mary Bryson (1998b) similarly argue that queer ethnographies seek to lay bare the mechanisms of the normal, making evident the very constructedness of ethnography 'proper'. As such, they seek to subvert—or invert—ethnography by an im-proper questioning of the foundations of ethnographic authority. They point out that telling queer stories has the potential to not only situate and position the ethnographer, but to reposition the readers, "not to ethnography's other but to themselves, so that they cannot fail to see themselves" (p. 109). Similarly to the discussion by Rooke, this argument emphasizes how queer ethnography is not merely about inclusion and visibility, but about inversion and about making unsafe both writers and readers of ethnographic texts.
8. 'ftw' meant originally 'for the win', but has come to be used as a rally cry in games such as *World of Warcraft*, or as a more general, yet noticeably geeky way of expressing enthusiasm.

# 8 A Queer Eye on Transgressive Play

*Jenny Sundén*

| | |
|---|---|
| *[Party] Dragonred:* | yack, 3 belf males, how gay :S |
| *[Party] Viljhalm:* | uhm |
| *[Party] Lulu:* | :) |
| *[Party] Viljhalm:* | :P |
| *[Party] Lulu:* | well you have no idea . . . |
| | *Dragonred is now the group leader.* |
| *[Party] Lulu:* | how gay this truly is |
| *[Guild] Ebon:* | hahaha nice said |
| *[Party] Viljhalm:* | hehe |
| *[Party] Lulu:* | lol |
| *[Guild] Ebon:* | he doesn't know that bears are even gay-er |

This conversation took place late one evening when a group of *World of Warcraft* players from across Europe got together to defeat monsters and loot treasures in a high-level dungeon in Northrend. This land of the north was at the time of playing the most recent of continents, a snow-clad, frost-bitten landscape that draws heavily on Norse mythology, swept in musical references to, for example, the classical composer Arvo Pärt. Lulu is my researcher character, but certainly also a co-player, as well as a member of the guild *The Others*.[1] Viljhalm and Ebon are both male blood elves, as well as members of *The Others*. Dragonred, together with another random player (who was also a male blood elf), were picked up along the way. One of the first things Dragonred, a male tauren druid, said upon greeting us at the summoning stone was "yack, 3 belf males, how gay", finished off with a confused smiley ":S". With their relatively androgynous, slim appearance, male blood elves are routinely read along the lines of male femininity—or 'gay'—and as such cherished among queer gamers. This utterance gave rise to both slight hesitation, but mostly amusement, since it unwittingly with absolute pitch stroke the very chord that functions as the prime baseline for this particular guild. There is nothing innocent about the comment itself in its characteristic bordering on compulsory way of expressing homophobia in the game (cf. Nardi 2010, 152–157). The comedy of the situation sparks from the fact that the player of Dragonred has no clue that 'gay' is what binds these particular players together. Furthermore, it is unclear if s/he figures it out along the way, since my remark "well you have no idea . . . how gay this truly is" was left without comments. I got a supportive "hahaha nice said" from Ebon in guild chat (not shared by the full party), as well as the killer finale "he doesn't know that bears are even gay-er". 'Bears' have a double function in this quote, both alluding to the bear shape which druids may shape-shift into, and simultaneously evoking gay male bear culture.[2]

Later on in the dungeon run, the 'gayness' of the group was made more explicit, and there was even a sign of possible recognition in the appreciative comment from Dragonred on healing being well performed:

*[Party] Ebon:* the gays are doing pretty good huh?
*[Party] Lulu:* lol
*[Party] Viljhalm:* hehe
*[Party] Dragonred:* good healing there

Like the previous chapter, this chapter builds on the guild ethnography of *The Others*, and continues the discussion of the ways in which sexuality is 'at play' in the game for players who orients themselves as non-straight.[3] The chapter focuses in particular on the role of sexuality in 'transgressive play'—or what I would like to call 'queer play'.[4] There is a tendency within game studies and queer theory alike to favor a player/subject who is active, creative, unruly, transgressive—be it in relation to the game as norm or to heteronormativity. While this chapter certainly invests in the promises of transgression, it simultaneously explores its limits. The term 'queer' is used as a way of making strange and of making visible how sexuality shapes practices of play. It signals an affinity with queer theory and ways of unsettling or troubling the stability of norms and normality. Then again, there is always a risk with queer. While offering a critique of how straight norms produce a whole range of deviant sexual practices and oppositional others, these others may have little else in common, indeed their various ways of being other may make queer communities dense with tension. Elizabeth Grosz (1995) discusses the usefulness "to talk about queerness, or even gayness when theorizing sexed bodies and their sexual relations" and argues for ways of "specifying at least broadly the kinds of bodies and desires in question" (p. 219). It is thus my intent to make explicit some of the differences, specificities, and contradictions in relation to queer as analytical strategy.

Sexuality, here, is understood as forms of action that shape and direct bodies toward certain objects (and not others), informed by Sara Ahmed's (2006) 'queer phenomenology'. Ahmed asks what it means to be 'oriented'—to be directed toward or away from objects in the world—for queer subjects and queer lives: "If orientation is a matter of how we reside in space, then sexual orientation might also be a matter of residence; of how we inhabit spaces as well as 'who' or 'what' we inhabit spaces with" (p. 1). She takes up the question of 'orientation' in 'sexual orientation' and articulates how bodies are turned toward the objects around them, and how this (sense of) direction matters in understanding orientation. Our actions create lines of direction that shape our perception and how we orient ourselves. Different objects create different lines of direction. Lines of direction are neither neutral nor originary, and yet heterosexual orientation creates 'straight lines' of direction as if this process was nothing but natural. Ahmed speaks of this naturalization in terms of 'straightening devices', which comes close to Adrienne Rich's (1980) 'compulsory heterosexuality', and Judith Butler's (1990) 'heterosexual matrix'. What happens, then, if our orientation turns our bodies in ways they are not supposed to be turned, toward the objects that are not supposed to be there? What happens when our bodies are not in line with the dominant lines of direction—when they wander off line, as it were? The straightening devices of heterosexuality sometimes fail to regulate bodies. New lines of direction are formed when bodies make contact with objects that are not supposed be there—such as (other) queer bodies. Pulled by desire, and through their contacts with other objects, the orientations of bodies shift. As such, queer bodies and queer sexualities are re-orientations that shape and direct bodies differently.

Looking at the history of *World of Warcraft*, there have been several events that in interesting ways tie in with queer orientations and sexualities in player communities. The one that stands out the most is the Sara Andrews case in early 2006, which gained a fair amount of media coverage (Krotoski 2006). In brief, the player Sara Andrews made an announcement in the public chat channel that her guild was 'LGBT-friendly', which rendered her a warning by an in-game administrator. The reason for this (or so she was told) was a violation of Blizzard's harassment policy, which among other things aims to protect players from harassment due to sexual orientation. Blizzard's harassment policy (2010), under the heading 'sexual orientation', reads: "This category includes both clear and masked language which insultingly refers to any aspect of sexual orientation pertaining to themselves or other players".[5] Quite paradoxically, the mere mentioning of the term 'LGBT-friendly' was regarded a violation of the harassment policy. Such moderating and silencing of LGBT-players is a powerful straightening device. Andrews pointed out that many players use homophobic language in the game, without this being acknowledged, and she received massive support from fellow gamers. Andrews also requested help from Lambda Legal (the largest legal organization in the US working for the civil rights of LGBT people), and in an official letter to the President of Blizzard Mike Morhaime, Lambda Legal argued: "Although Blizzard is well within its rights to insist that players avoid referring to other gamers in an 'insulting manner', Blizzard cannot issue a blanket ban on any mention of sexual orientation or gender identity" (Kotaku, February 6, 2006). Eventually Blizzard apologized, removed the warning from Andrews' account, and referred to the whole incident as "an unfortunate mistake" (Kotaku, March 9, 2006). In a discussion of otherness in online worlds, Brian Jennings (2008, 105) aptly sums up,

> Blizzard's acknowledgement and mea culpa has probably done little to curb the rampant homophobia and gay bashing present in general chat [ . . . ], but Andrews was able to score something of an ideological victory for gay rights in the game.

Well aware of this game cultural pre-history, I was curious about the status of queer orientations and desires in an LGBT guild in *World of Warcraft* a few years later.

## BENDING PLAY

There is a range of concepts at use by game scholars aimed at disobedient play against the rules, norms, and ideologies of the game: critical play (Flanagan 2009), deviant play (Mortensen 2008), subversive play (Sutton-Smith 1997), transgressive play (Aarseth 2007b), transformative play (Salen and Zimmerman 2004), and probably several others.[6] These concepts are usually taken to mean play against the 'ideal' or 'implied' player of the game (cf. Aarseth 2007b), of playing the game and bending the rules in ways not anticipated by design. These are concepts that point at play as innovation and, possibly, subversion, of finding, exploring, and exploiting loopholes in the game fabric.

Espen Aarseth (2007b) uses the notion of 'transgressive play' to address the tension within game studies between a critical humanities approach to the player as implied in or as a function of game aesthetics, and a social sciences' interest in the social practices of (potentially disobedient) 'real' players. The tension between these two directions in game studies, between games as social practices, and games as mechanical-aesthetic objects, echoes the kind of friction between 'playing the game' and 'being played *by* the game' characteristic of any act of gameplay. While statistically unrepresentative, moments of transgressive play are crucial to understand game culture, Aarseth argues, since they challenge the kind of player always already inscribed in the game: "Transgressive play is a symbolic gesture of rebellion against the tyranny of the game, a (perhaps illusory) way for the played subject to regain their sense of identity and uniqueness through the mechanisms of the game itself" (p. 132). Aarseth models his idea of the implied player on Wolfgang Iser's (1974) notion of the implied reader of reader-response criticism in literary theory. To Iser, literature is not so much an object as a set of effects controlled by the text, and the implied reader is the kind of reader that the text calls for. 'He' is a hypothetical, presupposed figuration, representing a set of cultural norms and expectations that the text needs to achieve its full potential.

In this chapter, I use the notion of 'queer play' similarly but not identically to how Aarseth uses transgression, by departing from a slightly different understanding of what constitutes the ideal player. In Aarseth's line of reasoning, there is a clear difference between games as aesthetic objects and games as social practices, even if he concludes that the study of games needs both perspectives, since "games are both aesthetic and social phenomena" (p. 130). In online games, aesthetic and social dimensions are certainly integral to an understanding of the phenomenon. The question is if these two dimensions can be distinguished from one another in a meaningful way. I would rather argue that online games like *World of Warcraft* consist of a certain type of 'social aesthetics' (see Kücklich 2008) in the sense that meeting other players and playing together is part of the very backbone of the game. The game world as always already social renders unstable the distinction between the 'implied player' and 'actual players'. To think of the game 'itself' as social makes it hard to talk about the implied player without taking into account the kinds of social positions, norms, and expectations that are continuously shaped and reshaped by practices of play. As a player of *World of Warcraft*, you are certainly positioned in particular ways by the game. But being positioned by the game does not only entail positioning in relation to game mechanics and game aesthetics in a more narrow sense, but also by a wider game culture in ways that play with, for example, gender and sexuality in certain ways. The design of avatars—how they look, move, feel, fight, jump, speak, laugh, flirt, dance, etc.—speaks volumes about social and cultural perceptions of sexed bodies (Corneliussen 2008, see also Sveningsson, Chapter 3, and Sundén, Chapter 6 of this book). But equally important are the ways in which designers and players are collectively imagining who 'the player' is. The player required by the game, a player who embodies the cultural norms necessary for the game to achieve its full potential, does not necessarily involve 'actual' players. Nonetheless, this ideal or implied player is in important ways socially and culturally informed, and as such housing expectations and preconceptions dominating the game industry and player cultures alike.

In *World of Warcraft*, gender and sexuality come into play in ways that make visible the cultural norms of the 'ideal player'—*a player who is at least symbolically male and straight*. Even if the group of female players of online games is significant, the ideas and ideals of (straight) femininity seem to collide frequently with the ways in which gaming is habitually coded as a masculine activity. In her interview, Agnes argues:

> It's not always that you play in groups with the people in voice chat. You jump around and join groups here and there, and then it's often like 'hey mate' and all kinds of things. Yea, but I have noticed that they kind of take things for granted. I don't usually tell them my gender, but they take things for granted, and then if they happen to write something like 'yea, we're waiting for the tank, he's late' and then I write 'hey, it's actually a she'. But then they give you a hard time if you're a girl tanking and if you do it badly. Then it's like 'what are you doing?!' And then if you have happened to mention your gender and do a good job, you get perhaps too much praise.

Female players testify to frequent situations of fleeting play where they are assumed to be male by their co-players (cf. Yee 2008). As long as the fantasy of 'the player' is intact, the game works smoothly. But once a player is unwilling or simply unable to embody 'his' position, the fantasy cracks. And once revealed a female player, 'she' can no longer merely play along and be a player among other players, but will have her performance measured in gendered terms (cf. Sveningsson, Chapter 4 in this book). Similarly, even if queer players have a vivid presence in online communities, to 'come out' in the game, or simply express an inclusive attitude in terms of sexual orientations, has proved to sit uneasy with the 'don't ask, don't tell'-policy of the game. Furthermore, the recurring use of the word 'gay' in derogatory ways is a clear sign for gaymers that players are assumed to be straight. Thus, another potentially transgressive, disobedient, unsettling figure is the non-straight player—male, female or in-between—who makes explicit how sexuality comes to matter in online game cultures.

In *The Others*, sexuality as a matter of orientation is entwined with gaming and with community in several ways. There is a broad range of sexual practices and desires that in various ways entered play sessions, stretching from 'vanilla' (sex without twists or kinks, a definition that is definitely fluid) to SM. One way in which sexuality entered play was through word play. SM in this context stands for Sadism and Masochism. Then of course, in *World of Warcraft* terminology, SM is the abbreviation for the dungeon Scarlet Monastery, which could be a subject for endless amusement. The same goes for the achievement "Going Down" (which means falling sixty-five yards without dying, and nothing else), armor such as Ceremonial Leather Harness and Deadly Gladiator's Cuffs of Dominance, and everything with a twist on 'bear', such as the quest "Going Bearback".[7] On the one hand, *The Others* is a guild like any other moderately ambitious guild, a place where players strive to advance together while having a blast. On the other hand, it is a guild like few others in its ways of bringing together the modes and codes of a queer community with the rules of the game, which makes game-related terms intermingle with queer sexualities (e.g., "What do you call a player who plays both Horde and Alliance? Bifactional"). What was perhaps most striking when entering the guild, after having played elsewhere, is how queer sexualities operate as an explicit, humoristic, sometimes flirty resource in guild chat as part of instances of co-play.

*Dorian:* Anna do you use Bartender
*Corky:* no I drink from the bottle
*Dorian:* haha funny
*Corky:* I did, but didn't like it
*Corky:* you?
*Dorian:* did it screw with the key bindings in the wow menu?
*Corky:* can't remember what it screwed and how, it got me drunk

*Lulu:* that's a good addon
*Slap:* lol
*Corky:* lol
*Dorian:* I use it and never had any problems with bindings
*Corky:* what kinda ropes do you use?
*Dorian:* omg, someone needs to get laid
*Corky:* yeah I know lol
*Ilshenar:* go watch some Nigella!
*Corky:* ok ok I will lol
*Corky:* she'll marry me one of these days I tell ya
*Lulu:* . o O (you plus a chocolate fudge cake)
*Dorian:* =P
*Corky:* that works for me lol

To the question of whether she uses the addon Bartender, Corky plays on its literal meaning, "no I drink from the bottle".[8] Dorian says that he "never had any problems with bindings" (bindings are keyboard shortcuts, or hot keys), which Corky counters with "what kinda ropes do you use?", moving the conversation from technical terminology to SM practices. This move from the technical to the sexual becomes evident in Dorian's comment "omg, someone needs to get laid", which prompts a third character Ilshenar exclaim "go watch some Nigella!", throwing the queen of gastro-porn—Nigella Lawson—into the mix. Corky (a female player) flips the argument by claiming "she'll marry me one of these days I tell ya". What this excerpt captures, apart from its clever twists and turns between technology and sexuality, is the type of atmosphere typical of the guild. Sexual connotations were foundational, as was pace, timing, playfulness, and wit. Lauren Berlant (2010) speaks of the joke as a most intimate sexual genre, an 'economy of surprise' that is both affective and social—when it works. Part of the comedy in this exchange has to do with how Nigella is positioned as something of a gay icon among the British men (in particular) of the guild. Nigella is a phenomenon of the British TV world of cooking—a saucy, beautiful, ironic 'domestic goddess'—with a sensual relationship to cooking and eating, as well as a flirtatious rapport with the camera. The draw for a gay audience may be femininity as excess, bordering on drag. But it may also be her quite vulnerable, human side and way of being nothing but a 'real' woman, coupled with a shameless pleasure in outrageously rich, creamy, buttery food. The amount of fat in her food is in and of itself a clear break with health norms and as such bound to appeal to other norm breakers.

## I'M A SHE

*The Others* is in many ways a safe haven of sorts, a home away from home in *World of Warcraft*, a place with warm hearts and sharp tongues. It is a place with plenty of room for queerly playing up against, or transgressing the implied or ideal player. Then again, queer runs the risk of loosing its critical potential if no distinctions are made between different ways of embodying—or playing—queer. Within the guild, sexuality as orientation device is a playful point of connection between players. At the same time, sexuality operates as a community border practice, as continuous negotiations of belonging, and of not belonging. No matter how LGBT-inclusive, this place is not without its own norms, regulations, and expectations. As a female player of *World of Warcraft*, you quickly get used to being mistaken for a 'dude' in random play situations. The situation in *The Others* is quite different, and yet in terms of gender, there is an interesting similarity. As a queer woman, it becomes evident that you do not embody the imagined *gay*mer:

| | |
|---|---|
| *Lulu:* | how do you like your warrior? |
| *Beastlord:* | who? Lol |
| *Lulu:* | Foliage, sorry |
| *Beastlord:* | he is a rogue |
| *Foliage:* | I'm a she and a rogue |

This scene could have taken place just about anywhere in the game, and it is indicative of the default mode in terms of gender. If in mainstream *World of Warcraft* culture, the ideal or implied player is a player who is male and straight, in *The Others*, you are often assumed to be a gay man, until proved differently. Or, you run the risk of being referred to as 'one of the boys':

| | |
|---|---|
| *Brazil:* | the shaman in my group whispered me "is your guild nice? can i join" and I'm like "it's kinda a special guild" "whaddya mean?" "let's just say unless you've searched precisely for it, you don't wanna join" |
| *Ilshenar:* | =P |
| *Shylanderan:* | want me to make it clear to him what kinda guild it is brazil :P |
| *Brazil:* | he was so shocked that someone actually came to help out |
| *Fudgefatale:* | normally when someone asks me, i just ask them "you like to kiss other boys too?" |
| *Lulu:* | or girls! geeeeeeeee |

This is a rather sweet story about an encounter in a temporary group of players. By being kind and helping out, Brazil apparently made an impression on a particular player in this group, which gave rise to the question "is your guild nice? can i join". Brazil answered in a rather veiled manner "it's kinda a special guild [ . . . ] let's just say unless you've searched precisely for it, you don't wanna join", which made Shylanderan wonder if he should "make it clear to him what kinda guild it is". This, in turns, prompted

Fudgefatale to speak up about his own strategy "normally when someone asks me, i just ask them 'you like to kiss other boys too?'", at which point I could no longer stay quiet: "or girls! geeeeeeeee". In this exchange, not only are every other player assumed to be male, but the guild itself is defined as a place for boys who like to kiss other boys. Female players—along with girls who like to kiss other girls, as well as bisexual and trans-players with whatever inclination—are not even on the map. It is important to point out that *The Others* is not an environment that is hostile toward women or trans people. For example, queer women will most likely feel welcome, even wanted. There was also a certain amount of pride in having a few powerful female players. But it is equally important to point out that gender makes a difference to queer cultures, desires, and orientations. Not everything is fluid. In the previous example, male players are oriented toward each other, drawn to each other, desiring each other. As a woman, you are automatically less interesting (and yet interesting, since you are different). A woman does not enter the picture as love interest, neither as sex object, but perhaps as friend. She is one of the boys—yet different from the boys.[9] The objects of our orientations matter to how we turn and to whom, they matter to how we move through and inhabit the (game) world.

Coming to *The Others* as a female player marks you as belonging to the minority of this group. Then again, the group of women in the guild tended to be highly active and vocal. In the hands of these players, some places, dungeons, characters, and quest lines were more readily open to 'lesbian' play than others.[10] The shield maidens of Northrend were favorites ("such big, buffed, butch Viking women!"). But perhaps the most beloved of places, creatures, and narratives in the game for the women of *The Others* were the Hyldnir—a small faction of female frost vrykuls who live in Brunnhildar Village in The Storm Peaks. The vrykuls of *World of Warcraft* draw on Norse mythology and are a race of half-giant warriors. The Hyldnir wage a war against the Sons of Hodir, a faction of ice giants, as well as battle amongst themselves in order to rule by the side of Thorim, one of the titan watchers. The Hyldnir are the Amazons of Northrend, a group of powerful, blue-skinned warrior women who imprison and kill men, or use them as slaves in the mines near the village.

*Electromagnet:* should we start the quest line that leads to the infamous dyke village?
*Lulu:* of course!
*Electromagnet:* :)
*Quest accepted:* They Took Our Men!
*Electromagnet:* They Took Our Men!
*Lulu:* lol

"They Took Our Men" is the opening quest of a long, fun, and winding quest line in The Storm Peaks which eventually lets the character gain reputation with Sons of Hodir.[11] After running in and out of the Forlorn Mine on different missions, including helping Mildred the Cruel to slay Garhal in the quest "Examples to be made", Lulu was ready to enter Brunnhildar Village (with a little help from a buff that automatically disguised her as a Hyldnir). "Examples to be made" is typical of the jargon surrounding the Hyldnir warrior women:

> For every action there is an opposite reaction, sister. In the case of us applying pressure on the males, this has meant newly spread rumors of insurrection. The bearded pig behind this rabble-rousing is called Garhal. Put an end to him . . . and make sure the other males see his demise. They must learn that insubordination will not be tolerated.

Once in Brunnhildar, cleverly disguised as a big, blue warrior woman, Lulu rode polar bears into battle ("Do you have the heart of a warrior queen? Or that of a sniveling seamstress?"), fought other Hyldnir in Hyldsmeet (a woman-to-woman competition to determine who will get to rule with Thorim), and had Astrid Bjornrittar fashion a powerful leather harness out of yeti hides. After having done the regular quests in the area, a player may later on return to Brunnhildar and the Hyldnir for their dailies.[12]

| | |
|---|---|
| *Corky:* | if Gretta doesn't give me the polarbear today I'll frakking kill her |
| *Elphlaba:* | what polarbear :S |
| *Corky:* | the polarbear mount that I have grinded for every day for like 2 months |
| *Elphlaba:* | what!? from where? |
| *Corky:* | is a daily for the blue lesbians |
| *Corky:* | in brunnhildar village |
| *Corky:* | this was news to you I reckon? |
| *Elphlaba:* | yah |
| *Elphlaba:* | i knew about them just didn't know they gave that |
| *Corky:* | the big blue women who look angry |
| *Lulu:* | they are fab |
| *Corky:* | they are like "Lets do this sister" and I'm like "Hell yeah lets do it!" |
| *Lulu:* | haha |

Here, the Hyldnir of Brunnhildar are referred to as "the blue lesbians". One of these, Gretta the Arbiter, may give you a white polar bear mount upon completing one of her daily quests, if you are lucky. Corky expresses fondness of the Hyldnir and their argot ("they are like 'Lets do this sister' and I'm like 'Hell yeah lets do it!'"), and they surely stand out as a tribe of powerful, violent, and capable women in the game, populating and defending a world without men. The association between 'Amazon' and 'lesbian' is not coincidental. The Amazons as a matriarchal tribe of warrior women were first represented in ancient Greek myth, as border figures of sorts between patriarchal civilization and fiendish savagery, and later re-imagined in the 20th century by lesbian/feminist writers and thinkers as an oppositional identity and as an original lesbian separatist society. But it was not until the 20th century that the link between the mythic Amazons and lesbians was made explicit. Bonnie Zimmerman (1990) notes that the first explicit literary connection between Amazons and lesbians was made by the lesbian writer Natalie Clifford Barney in the 1920s, but the literary trope of the lesbian Amazon did not come into its own until the 1960s and the 1970s. Monique Wittig's (1969) *Les Guérillères* is a milestone in lesbian feminism, and an epic story of a conflict between Amazon and patriarchal warriors set in an Amazonian utopia. In the field of feminist science fiction, Joanna Russ's (1975) *The Female Man* uses Amazon imagery to contrast a sexist world with a lesbian-only universe. On a pop-cultural note, the Hyldnir of *World of Warcraft* also appear to flirt with the animated science fiction sitcom *Futurama*, and the episode "Amazon Women in the Mood". As such, the manners in which the women of *The Others* are drawn to the Hyldnir as the 'blue lesbians' with their mighty, no-nonsense ways of speaking of violently fierce sisterhood has a multi-layered pre-history in the cultural imaginary of women-only societies.

## OF BEARS, TWINKS AND CROSS-DRESSERS

As mentioned previously, the term 'gay' housed a multiplicity of meanings within the context of *The Others*.[13] Sometimes it functioned as a unifying way of erasing differences. Sometimes it was rather used as an abbreviated identity that brought together but also highlighted multiple ways of defining and positioning oneself as non-straight. Most of the time, it was used self-reflexively and with humorous self-distance ("getting a couple of gays together for a HC is not easy")[14]. Then again, 'gay' was often put to use in reference to gay *men* (as is commonly the case in compositions such as 'gay and lesbian'), as something that played with and fed off of particular gay male bodies and orientations; the twink, the bear, the queen, the stud, etc. The frequent allusions to gay male bear culture in the guild—often drawing on the animal race tauren as well as the class of druids with their abilities to shape-shift into bear form—came to form something of a subculture of its own:

| | |
|---|---|
| | *Cuddlybear has joined the guild.* |
| *Atezcatentli:* | Welcome mate |
| *Cuddlybear:* | Hi! |
| *Dirt:* | Welcome! |
| *Erin:* | cuddly ^^ |

| | |
|---|---|
| *Clym:* | hello |
| *Lulu:* | welcome:) |
| *Cuddlybear:* | Thank you :) |
| *Dirt:* | Looks like another bear addition |
| *Ricky:* | hello! great name :D |
| *Quin:* | hellooo |
| *Dirt:* | Are you a bear or is it cause you're a druid? |
| *Cuddlybear:* | Well, mainly because I'm a druid :) |
| *Dirt:* | pfft. was hoping for a real bear :) |
| *Cuddlybear:* | Sorry to disappoint you :P |
| *Ricky:* | hehe leave him alone :) |
| *Dirt:* | Booo! Atez, revoke the invite! |
| *Ricky:* | lol |
| *Cuddlybear:* | :o |
| *Atezcatentli:* | hahahahahaha |
| *Atezcatentli:* | It's ok not to be a bear |
| *Cuddlybear:* | Are you sure? :P |
| *Ydeath:* | xD |
| *Atezcatentli:* | Sure sure mate . . . we love you /hug |
| | *[. . .]* |
| *Dirt:* | WHERE HAVE ALL THE BEAR MEN GONE?! |
| *Atezcatentli:* | Ah, no . . . they were kicked hahahahaah I'll send them emails so they bring their hairy ass back |
| *Dirt:* | Who kicked them! And why?! Bet it some jealous twink skinny screaming blood elf queens :o |
| *Atezcatentli:* | No no, it was a sexy man: me lol |

The question "Are you a bear or is it cause you're a druid?" draws attention to the possibility of how someone playing druid, and even using the word bear as part of a character's name, may simultaneously express a belonging to gay bear culture. The answer "Well, mainly because I'm a druid :)" disappoints Dirt and makes him wonder where all the bear men have gone. When realizing that a couple of bears have been kicked from the guild, he exclaims, "Who kicked them! And why?! Bet it some jealous twink skinny screaming blood elf queens :o". The term 'twink' takes on an interesting double meaning in this context. If (straight) masculinity in games and elsewhere sets itself off from femininity as well as gayness, the dominant ideal of gay masculinity is "the feminized, hairless, and gym-toned body [or] 'the twink', as he is dismissively known in Bear culture" (Hennen 2008, 117). A twink, then, in the context of gay culture refers to the young, slender, hairless, clean-shaven gay male body, and as such evoking certain characteristics of the male blood elf. On the other hand, a twink—or the activity of twinking—in the world of games describes a style of play that aims to maximize a player's performance. In MMOGs, twinking references the activity of power-leveling characters by using superior gear for their level—often with considerable help from high-level characters—basing play on the accumulation of resources rather than on skills. Twinking is often regarded as anti-social within player communities, as a kind of play that disrupts the social fabric of online gaming, and even as cheating. Then again, the idea of twinking or 'power gaming' as anti-social and spoiling the fun for everyone else builds on a particular view of what constitutes 'the social' as well as what constitutes pleasures in play (cf. Taylor 2003c). Twinking is not prohibited by design, but could rather be seen as a way of challenging or bending game design, and is as such a form of transgressive play (Glas 2007).

The preceding conversation works with and through a juxtaposition of the bear and the twink (the hairy and the hairless, the fat and the slender, the older and the younger, the down to earth and the extravagant, the 'natural' and the artificial), both on a general level of gay culture, but also on a more game specific level. Twinks of both gay cultures and game cultures can be understood as flamboyant figures that take pleasure in showing off luxurious outfits, and who delight in artifice and technological enhancement (be it gym technologies or power gaming technologies). But if the gay twink is considered the homo-norm, or the ideal gay masculinity, the game twink rather moves through the game as an outsider and a transgressor. In *The Others*, the bear was a more common point of reference than the twink—a possibly oppositional gay masculinity in its celebration of 'fat male embodiment' (Monaghan 2005). In sharp contrast to the showy, colorful, relatively feminine/twink blood elf, the tauren race and the bear shape of druids are the big, cuddly, furry in-game options that offer a counter-cultural masculinity of sorts. Bear masculinities tend to build on an affirmative attitude to the fat, ageing, 'natural' male body, along with a set of negations, such as 'not feminine' and 'not straight'. To Les Wright (1997, 9), "When a Bear makes such a counter-statement, that he is not a 'woman', not a 'twink', not a 'heterosexual', he is using his body to participate in changing social practice and challenging hegemonic power". But as Peter Hennen (2005, 34) points out, this statement obscures the fact that bear masculinities not only challenge but also reproduce hegemonic masculinity through their refusal of femininity: "In their virulent rejection of the effeminate stereotype and female drag, Bears certainly wish to convey that they are 'not women', but in practice, this is accomplished indirectly, through an attack on the feminized, narcissistic body of the twink".

If bear masculinities are oriented away from 'the feminine', there were other types of play in *The Others* that rather used femininity as a point of departure:

*Numero:* hey Cole
*Yasashisa:* hi
*Nosenose:* Colette :D
*Yasashisa:* hush :P

| | |
|---|---|
| *Lulu:* | Colette?! Haha |
| *Nosenose:* | yeps |
| *Lulu:* | very cute |
| *Nosenose:* | i've seen him with a wig and purse in Murder's Row in Silvermoon |
| *Yasashisa:* | -_- |
| *Steve:* | wb cole |
| *Lulu:* | perfect:D |

Here, the real name of Yasashisa's player 'Cole' has his name transformed into 'Colette', by Nosenose. Yasashisa/Cole tries to silence Nosenose, only to have more information leaked: "i've seen him with a wig and purse in Murder's Row in Silvermoon". Silvermoon is the capital of the blood elves, and the Murder Row a surprisingly seedy part of a city that elsewhere soaks in light and technicolor. If the rest of the city bathes in sunshine and enjoys the sights of dancing brooms, Murder Row with its eternal night, broken bottles on the ground, even drunks sleeping in the gutter, is a place where it would be more likely to spot a male character "with a wig and a purse". It should be made clear that sporting wigs and purses are not explicitly part of the game, but something that nonetheless could be part of a character's imaginary life. Even if *The Others* was not a role-playing guild, it was not uncommon that participants played around with the idea of their characters having distinct personalities and leading something of a life of their own. Moreover, it was not unusual that players flirted with references to cross-dressing practices, such as hunky male characters sporting a "Simple Black Dress", or took pleasure in other gender-bending potentials of the game. One day, one of the more recent additions to the guild, Ellen (here playing the male character Magiataur), got the question if 'she' was a trans-woman (female-to-male):

| | |
|---|---|
| *Magiataur:* | well lesbian so close enough lol |
| *Lulu:* | she kinda is;) |
| *Magiataur:* | hey my voice ain't that deep |
| *Magiataur:* | :D |
| *Lulu:* | i only meant it in the best of ways |
| *Magiataur whispers:* | *well magiataur is my hunky male tauren :)* |
| *Fafnir:* | so long as it doesn't involve strap-ons |
| *To Magiataur:* | *hahaha! Great* |
| *Magiataur whispers:* | *i feel more like a male tauren but would like to date a female belf . . . what does that say about me lol*[15] |

The question of whether Ellen identifies as 'trans' here becomes a matter of linking her female, lesbian body with that of Magiataur, "her hunky male tauren", to arrive at: "i feel more like a male tauren but would like to date a female belf . . . what does that say about me". To feel like a male tauren with the desire to date a femme female blood elf expresses a trans-orientation of sorts, or at least an orientation in terms of female masculinity of a body turned toward, and turned on by femininity. In real life, she refers to herself as 'soft butch', as a masculine woman a bit soft around the edges. The game, then, seems to operate as an amplifier, as a way of reinforcing her masculinity by the use of male characters. Then again, the masculinity of male taurens is as soft, kind and cuddly as they come, which perhaps not so much reinforces her masculinity as working well within the bounds of 'soft butch'.

Christian Schmieder (2009) discusses modes of communication and the meaning of 'gender-bending' in *World of Warcraft*. He argues that the act of playing characters of the opposite sex (he is primarily referring to male players playing female characters) has little to do with sexuality:

> Being male and female at the same time does not imply (at least not in the situation of playing) sexual preferences, nor does it suggest either trans-sexuality or androgyny. It does not provoke questioning or the problematization of sex and gender. It is simply *unproblematic* that someone has a female name and appearance, but speaks with a male voice. (p. 16, italics in original)

"Being male and female at the same time" refers to someone who looks like a woman in the game, but has a voice of a man (in voice chat), with the result that the gendered pronouns in reference to the player/character may shuttle back and forth between masculine and feminine determinants in both written and spoken communication. But rather than emphasizing or challenging the links between sex, gender, and sexual orientation, this gender doubling or blending of genders is understood as a consequence of the game itself, and as such unproblematic: "The 'queerness' in playing *World of Warcraft* [ . . . ] is more of a side effect of the game, which evolves from the co-existence of the different layers of communication" (p. 18).

Without doubt, there is something very mundane and also pragmatic about the use of mixed genders and pronouns in online games like *World of Warcraft*, even in a guild like *The Others*. This situation is interestingly different from the discussion in the 1990s of the promises and anxieties related to what Amy Bruckman (1993) termed 'gender-swapping' online. If for Bruckman, online performances of the reverse gender order held plenty of transformative potential (see also Turkle 1995) others were more cautious in their readings of gender transgressions online (Kendall 1998; O'Brian 1999; Sundén 2003). The question "Are you male or female?" became something of a cliché in the text-based worlds of IRC, MUDs and MOOs (Kendall 1998), pointing at the underlying anxiety around not being able to securely anchor 'the other' in a gender-specific body.[16] Such policing of the boundaries around credible gender performances in online venues, which had everything to do with questions of trust and deception, made the room for experimentation seriously circumscribed. The fact that a creation of an online character of the opposite gender (or rather, sex) was only a few keystrokes away did not automatically normalize online cross-dressing.

In *World of Warcraft*, there appears to be less anxiety around gender inconsistencies of the kind that permeated early cyberculture, possibly due to the fact that many play together with people they already know (cf. Svengingsson, Chapter 3 in this book), or at least know the voice of. People who play together may pay little attention to the potential mismatch between players and characters. According to Nick Yee (2005a), 50% of all female characters in MMOs are in reality played by men. To return to Schmieder, the sheer volume of male-to-female 'cross-dressers' suggests that a majority has less to do with sexual orientation, and more with for example preferences in game mechanics and game aesthetics (cf. MacCallum-Stewart 2008). On the other hand, the potential queerness of it all should not be underestimated, even in more mainstream contexts of play. The fact that something is mundane does not automatically exclude it from having critical or political implications. Gender bending is un-problematic up until the point where something interrupts the flow, and turns the discontinuity between player and character into a point of discussion. Such as when players get caught up in forum discussions about what is the most 'gay' for a male player, to play 'as a woman', or to play a male character from behind, staring at his behind for hours on end. There seems to be no way out of that 'gay' paradox, which ties back to the anxiety of the early Web. Another example of when the potential mismatch between player and avatar is of relevance is tied to the activity of cybersex and the fear of (straight) male players to engage in sexual fantasies and acts with other male players (Valkyrie 2011). Last but not least, even if the 'queer' elements of play in *World of Warcraft* is understood as "more of a side effect of the game", this does not rule out the possibility of such queerness being given a very different spin in player communities where queer is everything but a side effect.

## THE TRANSGRESSIVE POTENTIAL OF PLAYFULNESS

In this chapter, I have looked into various strategies of bending play, of playing the game queerly, and how different types of queer play create a sense of belonging to an LGBT community of play like *The Others*. Some of the examples I have brought forth—such as word play, community border work, lesbian sensibilities in play, and gender bending—might at first glance seem marginal to what is often perceived as core activities in a game like *World of Warcraft*. As Bonnie Nardi (2010, 55) recalls, "When I first started giving talks about WoW, I emphasized community and collaboration. An audience member who played the game said, 'Well, that's interesting, but you've left out the most important thing—mastery of the game.'" In her interviews, the constant references to leveling, as well as the continuous mentions in guild chat of advancement, achievements, and improved equipment initiated a discussion of the critical importance of skill and performance for player experiences (Nardi 2010, 52–93). It is obvious that playing the game for advancement and improvement, to for example 'gear up' to be able to experience endgame instances and raids, is a powerful part of the draw of the game. To play for mastery was also a powerful pull for the players of *The Others*, as it was for my own play. The guild was certainly a platform for playing the game in this sense and advancing together. Then again, the ways in which this group of players came together, and the role of sexuality, desire, and playfulness for this very formation, had everything to do with ways of playing the game together. In other words, there was a dual emphasis on raiding/gear progression and sociality/sexuality.[17]

Perhaps a turn to the play theorist Roger Caillois (1961/2001, 27, italics in original) and his understanding of forms of play as ranging from imaginative, improvisational play ('paidia') to structured, rule-bound games ('ludus') is instructive here:

> Such a primary power of improvisation and joy, which I call *paidia*, is allied to the taste for gratuitous difficulty that I propose to call *ludus*, in order to encompass the various games to which, without exaggeration, a civilizing quality can be attributed. In fact, they reflect the moral and intellectual values of a culture, as well as contribute to their refinement and development.

Paidia is about playfulness, improvisation, and imagination, it describes free-form play that is unscripted and open-ended. Ludus, on the other hand, refers to formal play that is rule-bound and rule-driven. If paidia describes an unleashing of fantasies and of disorder, ludus is a way of tempering, disciplining, and transforming this energy, or with Caillois' words, ludus operates as "complementary to and a refinement of paidia, which it disciplines and enriches" (p. 29). The move from paidia to ludus simultaneously describes an evolution of play into increasingly rational and civilized forms of activity. As (Western) societies are modernized and civilized, free-form improvisational play came to operate as a subordinate function to the rationality of ludus, mirroring the tendency in modern cultures to privilege the rational structures of ludus over the "frolicsome and impulsive exuberance" that is paidia (p. 13). Similarly, ludus has received more attention within game studies. Celia Pearce (2009, 28) argues, "The game bias is deeply embedded in the discourses of technoculture and digital media, as epitomized by the very naming of the discipline 'game studies'". Even if this is changing, there still seems to be a tendency to regard ludus-like games as the proper objects of study (as having a higher degree of 'gameness'), or to focus almost exclusively on ludus in games that are played across a range of play styles. In Caillois' thinking, paidia and ludus operate on a continuum, which allows for interplay and intermingling between forms of play. Rules may develop out of free play (in fact, it is hard to imagine play that completely lacks rules). Conversely, rule-bound play may be challenged by, and partly dissolve into imaginative play. The going back and forth between paidia and ludus parallels the activity of 'playing with' versus 'being played by' a game at heart of any act of gameplay.

Digital games may support both ludus and paidia, they can be strictly rule-bound or more open-ended and lacking a clear-cut victory condition (Frasca 2001). The type of game world set the tone for specific types of play, but players are free to engage in opposing play styles within the overall framework. Online games like *World of Warcraft* are heavy on ludus in the sense that the world and its rules are pre-given, but they are simultaneously hybrids that allow for a range of different forms of play that sometimes intermingle unexpectedly; play for mastery, social play, exploratory play, experimental play, etc. Pearce (2009: 29) contends, "MMOG players often engage in paidiaic play alongside, around, or in some cases, against the prescribed rules of the game". If pleasure in the form of play that is ludus is about the joy in skills and mastery, in overcoming arbitrary obstacles, then the pleasure in paidia is the joy of playfulness. In a return to Nardi's discussion of performance, this is doubtlessly a potent concept to account for ludus and the desire to strive for mastery of a game, to address play that aims to advance player performances as well as for acts of playing by the rules. But if the notion of performance captures the strive for mastery of the game, it is simultaneously geared toward play that is seemingly (straight)forward and rational. Ahmed speaks of the etymology of direction, as in to 'be straight' or to 'go straight to the point': "To go directly is to follow a line without a detour, without mediation. Within the concept of direction is a concept of 'straightness'. To follow a line might be a way of becoming straight, by not deviating at any point" (p. 16). *World of Warcraft* evidently supports and rewards goal-oriented, 'straight' play aimed at measurable advancement and performances (to level up, to excel at endgame, etc.). Other more paidiaic game pleasures—such as play that makes detours, takes time, and invests in playfulness and sociality for their own sake—are not prohibited by design, but are neither as clearly rewarded. The game allows for disorientation (and sometimes players are indeed disorientated against their will), but more clearly supports straight, measurable, rational play.

This chapter has called attention to the transgressive potentials of playfulness, to alternative ways of moving and taking pleasure in play. Transgressive play is crucial to understand game culture, Aarseth argues, since it is "a symbolic gesture of rebellion against the tyranny of the game, a (perhaps illusory) way for the played subject to regain their sense of identity and uniqueness" (p. 132). In a similar way, I would like to argue that queer play is critical to understand how sexuality comes to matter in online game cultures. Queer play is a symbolic act of rebellion, of disobedience, of deviance from dominating ways of inscribing and imagining 'the player'.

Queer play is a (perhaps illusory) way for players that are 'out of line' to regain a sense of identity and belonging. Queer play is evidence of how the straightening devices of online games, such as *World of Warcraft*, sometimes fail to regulate playing bodies. As such, queer play reorients players, desires, and shapes the bodies at play differently. Then again, there is doubtlessly a danger in being seduced by transgression. At the end of her essay "Is Transgression Transgressive?" Elizabeth Wilson (1993, 116) concludes: "We transgress in order to insist that we are there, that we exist, and to place a distance between ourselves and the dominant culture. But we have to go further—we have to have an idea of how things could be different, otherwise transgression is mere posturing". Wilson argues for political strategies that not only aim to transgress rules and norms, but to *transform* them. Queer play in guilds such as *The Others* may not profoundly transform the game world. On the other hand, *The Others* is not a self-contained universe. There will always be 'queer leakages' (Rosenberg 2002) into more mainstream game contexts ("when someone asks me [about what kind of a guild this is], i just ask them 'you like to kiss other boys too?'"). As such, queer play has the potential of shifting and changing the idea of who it is, more precisely, that plays online games. What my ethnographic work suggests is that there are queer uses of game spaces that in significant ways make visible—and play around with—norms and expectations that are shaping what online game communities are, and what they could be.

## NOTES

1. As detailed in the chapter "Coming Home and Coming Out", *The Others* is an LGBT (lesbian, gay, bisexual, transgender/transsexual) community of players in the game, and also the home of my guild ethnography in *World of Warcraft*.
2. In Michael B. Cornelius (2000, 80) encyclopedic treatment of bear culture, he describes it as "A subculture within the gay male cultural strata that rose to prominence in the late 1980s" which "defies a strict definition of both its ideals and members. Although most bears share certain physical characteristics, among them a hirsute appearance, a stocky build, and facial hair [ . . . ], 'bear' is often a self-applied label and defies a precise meaning". See also Wright (1997).
3. This is not to suggest that sexuality would not come into play in supposedly straight game spaces (which for example Sveningsson's ethnography in this book makes clear). Rather, the chapter is an attempt to explore the role of sexuality in a gaming community that uses sexual orientation as a point of departure, and how this very foundation shapes notions and experiences of play.
4. This chapter builds on, but also significantly develops Sundén, Jenny. 2009b. "Play as Transgression: An Ethnographic Approach to Queer Game Cultures." *Proceedings of DiGRA 2009 Breaking New Ground: Innovation in Games, Play, Practice and Theory*, London, UK, September 1–4.
5. See http://us.blizzard.com/support/article.xml?locale=en_US&articleId=20455, and in particular http://us.blizzard.com/support/article.xml?locale=en_US&articleId=20226. (This is the same wording as in the 2006 harassment policy).

6. There is also a more general discussion of player creativity and game altering activities, including, for example, cheating (Consalvo 2007; Kücklich 2008), modding (Sihvonen 2009; Sotamaa 2007; 2010), skinning (Kennedy 2006; Wirman 2008), the making of machinima (Lowood 2006), and player protesting (Castronova 2005; Taylor 2006c).
7. "Going Bearback" brings together 'bear' with 'barebacking', which apart from referring to the quest of riding a bear without any equipment is a term for unprotected sex, mainly between gay men.
8. An addon is a user interface modification to enhance gameplay. The addon Bartender relates to the player's action bars, which are command shortcuts linked to abilities and spells.
9. Becoming 'one of the boys' in terms of being friends with the boys in the context of a queer guild is quite different from Sveningsson's discussion in Chapter 4 of being 'one of the boys' by downplaying one's femininity in straight contexts of play. For a comparison across these two contexts, see the closing chapter of this book.
10. See also the intriguing "A Guide to Gay Characters in World of Warcraft" at the Border House blog: http://borderhouseblog.com/?p=2896. Accessed October 20, 2010.
11. Reputation is quite similar to how experience functions in the game. By completing quests for a quest giver belonging to a certain faction in the game, the reputation with this faction increases. This gives advantages, such as unlocking rewards and new quests, discounts at vendors belonging to this faction, etc. But unlike the system of experience points, which can never be subtracted, reputation with one faction may decrease, if you for example increase your reputation with a rival faction.
12. Daily quests (often called dailies) are quests possible to repeat that can be obtained and completed once per day. These quests have considerably better rewards than other repeatable quests. Daily quests come in many different shapes and guises, and many are for reputation, instances, professions, and battlegrounds. It is possible to complete up to twenty-five daily quests per day per character. For many dailies, a certain quest line needs to be accomplished to unlock the quest.
13. In the field of 'lavender linguistics' (Leap 1995), the term 'gay' moves between the use of "*Gay* as a superordinate term, including both women and men, [and] *gay* as either subordinate term, taking in men only, or as an ambiguous term (like *animal*, with a superordinate sense that include human beings and a subordinate sense in which it is opposed to *human being*). [ . . . ] *Gay* as a superordinate term, including both homosexual (in some sense!) and bisexual people in opposition to *straight*, versus *gay* as a subordinate term, in a ternary opposition with *(bi)sexual* and *straight*". (Zwicky 1997, 23, italics in original).
14. HC stands for heroic mode, which refers to the setting of a dungeon difficulty. Heroic is a heightened level of difficulty compared to the default setting 'normal'.
15. Italics are added to clarify that this is a private conversation.
16. The frequency of the question "Are you male of female?" even turned in into an acronym: RUMORF.
17. Torill Elvira Mortensen (2008) makes a similar point in discussing role-playing in *World of Warcraft* as a form of what she calls 'deviant play'. Role-playing may not be the kind of 'straight play' that the rule-driven part of the game calls for, but this does not stop players from identifying with something more than raids and gear progression. Then again, role-play is a sanctioned form of play on a more formal level, since there are RP-servers devoted to this particular combinatory play of advancing together while 'in character'.

# Closing Chapter
## Writing a Twin Ethnography

*Malin Sveningsson and Jenny Sundén*

In this book, we have been following two separate trajectories. They take place in the same game world and have the same focus—to study how gender and sexuality come into play in online game cultures. However, the settings of the two studies are different, as are our points of view and perspectives. From this follows that the experiences we have had, and the stories that we tell throughout the book, are similar yet different from one another.

When terming this ethnography a 'twin ethnography', we were not picturing a pair of identical twins, but rather of dizygotic, or so called fraternal twins. Then again, the term fraternal does not take us far in a critique of male domination. Instead, we have rather imagined our twins to be sisterly—or even sororal—as is sometimes the term put to use when the naming of dissimilar twins puts a feminine spin on notions of fraternity and brotherhood. Sororal twins, like our ethnographies, are born at the same time, but unlike identical twins they may differ both physically and genetically. Born practically simultaneously, but no more alike than two sisters would be, they move through the world differently, developing distinct lives. And yet, there is the possibility of a special bond being developed, a bond that may stem from the similarity in age and the particular closeness such similarity creates.

Our twin ethnography provides a framework of disorderly twin-sisterhood for this book, consisting of two parallel stories that are as distinctively different as they are intimately linked. Looking more closely, one of our twins came to orient herself as 'straight', the other as 'queer'. These labels have functioned as orientation devices in the field and in our writing. However, they are in no sense stable definitions or identifications. Although they provide the means of orientation, such ways of finding one's bearing are rarely more than provisional. Rather than providing a straightforward model of the 'straight' versus the 'not straight' for the structure of this book, we have instead come to think of our different parts, perspectives, and ways of looking as existing on a continuum in ways that complicate binary modes of understanding sexuality, as well as gender.

In this chapter, we will start out with a discussion of the specificity of play by a comparison between our two case studies. Secondly, we will move on to a summary of some of the key points in our respective cases. Thirdly, we will complicate the structure of the book and its division in a 'straight' versus a 'queer' ethnography by a closer look at Sedgwick's (1985) notion of homosociality. Finally, our aim is to clarify what the study of online games may bring to feminist theory and feminist studies.

## THE SPECIFICITY OF PLAY

One of the aspects that separate the two case studies is that we played on different servers, each with its own distinct focus and character. Sundén studied player cultures on PvP (Player versus Player) servers, while Sveningsson's case study took place on a Normal or PvE/RP (Player versus Environment and Role-Play) server. Our choice of servers had certain repercussions on what kind of ambiance and atmosphere we met and what kind of experiences we had, since player cultures, core activities, and playing styles often differ between server types. Despite taking place in worlds that *look* identical, the game that is being played can vary considerably depending on the setting.

PvP is generally a more aggressive gaming context than PvE, and it is competitive in the sense that players fight against each other, apart from also battling computer-generated enemies. Fighting against other players is sometimes even apprehended as the main allure of the game, while the computer generated challenges, such as instances and raids, may be perceived as secondary. The focus on combat between players affects many aspects of the game. For example, leveling up is generally more time consuming on PvP than on PvE servers, since players in addition to the ordinary game content also have to be on their guard against other players.[1] The same can be said about other everyday routine tasks, such as gathering material needed for crafting items (such as herbs, leather and ore) or even traveling between places. PvP requires concentration and fast reactions from the players, as well as flexibility, since one can never foresee the actions and reactions of other players in the way that one might with NPCs (non player characters). The PvP environment clearly opens up for a discussion of 'affect' in gaming, since critical player versus player situations are moments in gameplay that are decidedly physical. This is not to say that gameplay, overall, is not an embodied experience (raiding would be a prime example of powerful adrenaline rushes). But in talking to, and playing with PvP players, Sundén found that combat between players of opposing factions are particularly intense situations of play in ways that call for a discussion of such corporeal intensity. PvP is not only about swift improvisation, but also about a particular sense of uncertainty or undecidability, since these are situations in which you can never fully know your enemy (see also Sundén, Chapter

6 of this book). In a survey on the demographics of MMO players, Yee (2005b) found that of the players who preferred PvP servers, males were in a clear majority (even with respect taken to the actual gender distribution of the game). There was also a substantial correlation with age: above all the younger players preferred PvP servers.

PvE servers, on the other hand, put more focus on the built in content of the game. Here, players focus on overcoming the obstacles that the computer generated enemies constitute, in quests, instances and raids. Especially the latter two requires a fair amount of coordination between players who gather in groups to complete their missions. Hence, the relation between players in PvE is characterized by cooperation rather than competition (even though PvE is competitive too, in that players in the same group often rival each other in skill and performance). Although PvE is male-dominated, too, it is popular across gendered lines, and women are overrepresented in relation to their numbers (meaning that a majority of the actual female players choose PvE over PvP; Yee 2005b).

Finally, RP servers are dedicated to role-play (although, as was discussed in Sveningsson, Chapter 3 of this book, far from all players on RP servers actually take part in role-play practices). Those who do role-play generally put much focus on the narrative aspects of the game, sometimes at the cost of its ludic content (cf. Mortensen 2008). They may take part in both PvP and PvE activities, and as a matter of fact, there are both PvP and PvE servers that are dedicated to role-play. Role-players sometimes create their own role-play events, with independent storylines and plots, but more often they try to anchor their activities in game lore and make them consistent with the already existing game world and its history. According to Yee (2005b), male and female players are just as likely to prefer RP servers.

The server types as just described focus on various playing styles along with associated activities. However, there are no sharp dividing lines between them, as players' preferences may intertwine in various ways. For instance, some will probably be surprised at finding Sundén's queer guild on a PvP server, and not an RP server, since role-playing environments more clearly leave room for the kind of playfulness characteristic of a group like *The Others*. Then again, it was a conscious decision on the part of this group to play on a PvP server, since the desire for action in the game was as strong (if not stronger) as the desire to be queer in the game in particular ways. Similarly, the goal-oriented character and high raiding ambitions of Sveningsson's guild is not specific for RP servers. The guild was first created on a regular PvE server, but decided to move to an RP server for reasons related to the ambiance, since RP servers were claimed to host more mature and civilized players than the other server types. This illustrates that even though the server types as previously described can be used for a rough classification of playing styles and ambiance, there are still overlaps. All types of playing styles and activities—PvP, role-play, high end raiding and socializing—exist on all types of servers, although their extent may vary.

Our choice of servers meant that the environments that Sundén studied were probably somewhat rougher around the edges, and with a more aggressive ambiance than those that Sveningsson studied. When comparing our gaming experiences, it was also clear that our styles of play and how we perceived the goals of the game differed. Sveningsson's gaming was high on ludus: goal-oriented, straight-forward, and aimed at leveling up to be able to take part in endgame content, such as heroic instances and raids. Sundén's trajectory, on the other hand, was more winding. For her, playing for mastery was certainly a powerful part of the draw, but following the play styles of her fellow gamers, there was also a clear emphasis on sociality and playfulness (in ways that sometimes stole focus from the 'straight' story of measurable advancement and gear progression).

Admittedly, regardless of what type of server players are on, the orientation of particular guilds is very important for what type of activities they take part in, as some guilds are oriented towards leveling, while others focus on raiding or PvP. The guilds that we belonged to and played with were also built up in different ways. Sveningsson's guild was largely anchored in a local community geographically speaking, and consisted of networks of friends who knew each other and had IRL connections to at least some of the other players. The guild was all-Swedish, as was the language used in guild chat and on the voice chat Ventrilo. One of the prerequisites for joining the guild was even fluency in Swedish. Moreover, the age limit was 18, albeit with exceptions for the children and nephews of the players. Even if sexual orientation was rarely discussed in explicit terms, the overall ambiance and the taken for granted perspective was a straight one. Sundén's guild, on the other hand, consisted of players from all over Europe, and some but far from all players knew each other outside of the game. The guild had an age limit of 16, but the typical player was in 'his' twenties and early thirties.

Within the context of *The Others*, nationality, or national belonging, was important in a realm of play where the only common denominator was 'Europe'. Nationality often entered the picture as a wish of locating the bodies of co-players geographically and culturally ("where are you from?"), but sometimes it took more of a distinct shape in terms of the importance of location for queer lives. Even if at first look, *The Others* may read as a privileged, trans-national, out and proud queer community, the presence of members from, for example, Serbia and Poland works as reminders of how 'Europe' as a location and as a set of ideas incorporates multiple contradictions and tensions. In Serbia, for example, homosexuality is far from accepted. The gay scene is underground, and discrimination and violence targeting homosexuals is part of the everyday fabric.[2] This is certainly not to say that a country like Sweden is not homophobic, but to put forth that location matters for queer lives. It is also to point out the value of spaces provided by an online game like *World of Warcraft*. Even if geographically spread out, the coming together of this group as a queer community within the game created a sense of cultural closeness, across national borders.

In addition to playing on different server types and in player constellations with different goals and constitution, we also belonged to different factions. Sveningsson played as Alliance and Sundén as Horde. The difference between the two factions has been described as that between the familiar and the foreign along the lines of race—from a white, Western perspective (Langer 2008). As discussed in the introductory chapter, the distinction between the familiar and the foreign can also be extended to norms of gender and sexuality. In other words, the races of the Alliance are in general more 'civilized' and proper, at times even goody two-shoes. In comparison with Horde races, they are strikingly light skinned and heteronormal (even if the introduction of *Cataclysm* puts a spin on this analysis in introducing an animal race in the midst of the Alliance), staying close to the ideas and ideals of beauty and appropriate femininities and masculinities permeating mainstream Western cultures. The Horde races, on the other hand, carry more potentials for transgression of such norms—both concerning appearance and preprogrammed behaviors (cf. Sveningsson, Chapter 3 in this book). In Chapter 6, Sundén shows how her informants think about their choices of Horde characters in relation to sexual orientation. By suggesting options of being 'other' or strange, they find an affinity with what the Horde races can offer; how they look, move, and feel. Thus, even if it may be premature to state that the Horde faction hosts more players who deviate from mainstream ideals of gender and sexuality, it seems reasonable to suspect that players' attitudes to such ideals may influence their choice of race, and thus of faction.

Taken together, our choices of servers, guilds and factions contextualize our ethnographic experiences in particular ways. On the normal server, Sveningsson found what at first sight may look like rather 'ordinary' or 'normal' situations, seen from a white, Western, and straight perspective. Her ethnography does not reveal the obviously dramatic or spectacular, the focus is rather on the ordinary scenarios of everyday life in and outside of the guild. Even though it might have been exciting to look at more extraordinary gaming environments, for example strongly misogynous ones, the ordinary or (apparently) normal is by no means unproblematic or innocent. In the midst of the seemingly mundane, there are important patterns and structures to expose, in particular in terms of hegemony and power. Once the ideological dimensions of the ordinary are uncovered, it becomes possible to show how the perspective of the dominant group becomes internalized by players to the point where they no longer discern the underlying power structures that guide their interactions. In other words, the presence of an ordinary or normal gaming environment depends on its suppressing of the deviant.

Sundén, on the other hand, looked for gaming environments that can be described as more unusual, or even deviant, from mainstream gaming culture. She wanted to bring to light that which is not fully of the norm, but which nonetheless is essential for the norm to work. Constituting a contrast to and a transgression of the normal, queer sexuality and queer theory has a lot to say about the configuration of hetero-normal gaming culture. Still, despite existing at the margin of what is constructed as 'normal', a queer gaming community is not without its own norms, conventions, and regulations. These norms will sometimes turn the regulatory power of 'ordinary' gaming communities on their head, but sometimes also repeat major ideas and fantasies within game cultures at large (such as implying the ideal or default player to be male).

Our choice of servers and factions was not a conscious one, since in the beginning of our studies, we did not know much about the game and its player cultures. In both cases, our choice was governed by the contacts we had that led us into the game. To some extent, one could say that what we got was to be expected, given our different ways into the game. Sveningsson followed a white Swedish middle class guy to a guild where he played with his friends and their networks. It was strongly dominated by other middle class men, of which many worked in technology related white-collar occupations. Sundén, on the other hand, followed a white, Norwegian, middle-class lesbian woman to her worlds of play, and came through that experience to seek out game environments that gathered non-straight players. For the introductory ethnography, this meant playing with women in smaller groups, while searching for a fun, warm, welcoming guild where deviations from the default player would not be a problem. The LGBT guild *The Others* came to provide such an environment—or 'home'—in the game. Besides from being oriented toward non-straight players, this group, too, was clearly male-dominated, as well as housing a large portion of players from the UK.

The environments of play that we experienced in our studies are specific, and exact equivalents cannot be found anywhere. The group cultures and the ambiance that we met in our respective settings depend to a large extent on the specific players of the guilds and groups we played in. Still, much of what we have experienced throughout our fieldwork seems to be typical for *World of Warcraft* culture as the whole, an assumption that is supported by the fact that many of our observations are similar, despite deriving from such diverse settings.

## SIMILAR, YET DIFFERENT

In the first case study, the 'straight' ethnography, Sveningsson observed that women are often met by a warm welcoming, but that this has its prize. There is quite a lot of goodwill, however, the men's rationales for welcoming the women often lead to a continued suppression of women in the hierarchies of players. Women are expected to take on the responsibility for relationship work, create a nice atmosphere and mitigate the aggressive ambiance that results from when men perform a hegemonic masculinity. By constituting targets for the men's helpfulness, women can also be used to strengthen the men's position as skilled and competent players. Finally, female players constitute romantic objects that the men can act towards in their demonstrations of heterosexuality. Thus, female players are an important resource in the men's masculinity work.

One theme that permeates the first ethnography is the experience of how difficult it can be for a woman to be fully admitted into the gaming communities, and be seen as an authentic and adequate member. It is true that most of the male players appeared to enjoy the company of female players and acted nice towards them. However, many of them seemed to not see women as players on the same level, but as something else: as mascots or as fineries on the side, something that brightened up the gaming environment and added a touch of color to it. What, then, happens when women are not happy with the positions they are offered? What happens when they strive to get a position other than being props in the men's performances, stagehands that do the job behind the scene, or admiring spectators of the show?

There are several strategies that can be employed for a female player who wants to be accepted and admitted into the group, however, all have their downsides. The most efficient strategy was found to be to voluntarily enter a subordinate position. However, this means that the player sacrifices her value and status as a player. The strategy of trying to become 'one of the boys' may benefit the individual player, but at the cost of women as a collective. Furthermore, that position depends on renouncing one's identification as a woman and one's affinity with other women. It is also a position that is contested and has to be defended. For many women, the best solution is instead to become 'one of the girls', by joining female-dominated or even all-women gaming communities. Here, female players can play and have fun, no matter if they are newbies or excel in skills, without having to defend their rights to play. However, this relative freedom is connected to the secluded character of the gaming communities in question. In these 'sanctuaries', or even 'reservations', women are largely rendered invisible, thus, their actions do not threaten the men's hegemony or affect the larger power structures of the gaming culture.

Within the bounds of the second, 'queer' ethnography, Sundén discusses (among other things) the specificity of lesbian desire in the game; the importance of the feel of play for particular ways of connecting in and with the game; the game as home and as a family of sorts; and the queer potential of playfulness. A point of departure is the story of falling for someone or something—an avatar, a woman, a game—as a way of discussing desire between women, and between women and game technologies. As it turned out, such desires were shaped in particular ways due to the specificity of *World of Warcraft*. The lack of dramatic possibilities for intimate avatar play in the game made the movements and gestures that were possible all the more sexually charged. Desire and emotions were circulated through soundscapes and landscapes, through modes of nonverbal communication, and through an almost musical sense of rhythm and timing. In particular, such desires at the interface became even more explicit through the power of violence and the experiences of fighting together. The ways in which desire makes the body go faster here came to be intimately entwined with how the game speeds up the body in critical and violent moments of gameplay.

Central questions for the second ethnography concern the difference that 'queer' may make, and the particularities of a non-straight orientation for gameplay. A violent coming together of women and games was discussed as a case of 'queering' femininity, through its unexpected connections between femininity and technology. The type of femininities that *World of Warcraft* provides may surely contribute to a quickening of the heart for some female players. A figure like the female orc and her unapologetic female masculinity is likely to set things in motion, but so may also a figure like the high-femme female blood elf. In their efforts to find ways of combining masculinity and femininity, to get a powerful battle sensation yet still being 'girls', a range of well-geared, buffed-up feminine game characters came to express something of a tomboy position for the players (through the contrasts between powerful armor and an unmistakably feminine shape). Moreover, the game certainly also provides options for queer masculinities, such as the twink, the bear, and the stud. The recurrent allusions to gay male bear culture in the queer guild formed something of a subculture of its own. In contrast to the flamboyant relatively feminine/twink blood elf, the tauren race and the bear shape of druids are the big, cuddly, furry in-game options that offer a counter-cultural masculinity of sorts.

Moreover, queer connections between players may well make a difference in the larger framework of *World of Warcraft* player cultures. In a place where 'everybody' is assumed to be male and straight, powerful liaisons between queer players may make things shift in terms of providing a significant counter narrative to the main story. On the one hand, queer play in guilds such as *The Others* may not change the game world in any fundamental way. But then again, *The Others* is not an independent, isolated universe. There is always the possibility of queer play to seep, or leak into other, more mainstream contexts of play. As such, queer play has the potential of performing a shift in the idea of the default, implied, ideal player. Far from being devoid of its own sets of inclusions and exclusions, norms and regulations (such as the player still being assumed to be a man, if yet gay), what this ethnographic work suggests is that there are ways of appropriating game spaces that make visible certain norms that are shaping online game communities. In doing so, this work also evokes alternative ways of making sense of play, and as such showing how things could be different.

## FROM STRAIGHT TO QUEER AND BACK

One of the most central points of both our ethnographies, and the key to explain much of what we have seen, can be summarized in the concept of homosociality. In her classic introduction to *Between Men*, Eve Kosofsky Sedgwick (1985) defines male homosociality as describing the basic structures of patriarchy: men who are promoting each others' interests through the medium of women. Homosociality as a form of male bonding is formed through an asymmetrical triangular structure. Such triangles take shape between two men who are competing for the same woman, and where the bond forming between the men is as potent and powerful, if not more powerful, as their individual links to the woman. This desire of men for other men, secured by the presence of the woman within a properly heterosexual framework, serves as an affective social force, or glue, that holds patriarchal societies together: "in any male-dominated society, there is a special relationship between male homosocial (including *homosexual*) desire and the structures for maintaining and transmitting patriarchal power" (p. 25). Importantly, Sedgwick speaks of 'male homosocial desire' as a somewhat paradoxical continuum between the homosocial and the homosexual in ways that challenges hetero-homo binaries. It is paradoxical, since male homosociality is often clearly distinguished from homosexuality. Thus, to align the homosocial with notions of desire is to suggest a possible continuity between 'men promoting the interests of men' and 'men loving men', "a continuum whose visibility, for men, in our society, is radically disrupted" (pp. 1–2). Such a continuum between the homosocial and the homosexual becomes particularly interesting in relation to the structure of this book, since it problematizes every clear distinction between the straight and the non-straight. To think desire between men along such a continuum also makes explicit the relationship between gendered politics and sexual politics. In other words, it links together the seemingly disparate practices of male bonding as power play within straight game spaces on the one hand, with the types of erotic intimacy between men in queer game spaces on the other. To speak of a continuum between the homosocial and the homosexual is to acknowledge that homosociality has everything to do with men's desires for one another (even if this desire is not spelled out, as Sedgwick has it, in a genital sense, and even if properly heterosexualized through the presence of women). Moreover, to speak of this continuum is to recognize how male homosexual desire, just as homosociality, has everything to do with power exchange between men, and with men's power over women.

We have written about who the female player becomes in male-dominated game contexts, be they straight or bent. We have both experienced being positioned as default male players, a positioning to which we have strongly objected. But we have also both made efforts to blend in, and in different ways 'become one of the boys'. The question is, one of *which* boys more precisely? Sveningsson has written extensively on this topic (see Chapter 4 in this book), and it became clear that the straight men in her guild were quite unwilling to let her give up her position as 'woman'. To become one of the boys would mean making a claim to power, and it would mean leaving the position as a mediator or facilitator *of* power. Here, 'the boys' represented a straight hegemonic masculinity. To become one of them, as a woman, meant to try to appear more masculine, and perform values that are associated with masculinity. At the same time, being a woman made it next to impossible to leave behind the position of love interest or romantic object, which turned every attempt at performing a (technological) masculinity into a delicate, contradictory balancing act.

If thinking with and through Sedgwick's continuum, male desire written in a homosexual framework is far from separate from the gendered politics of men's power over women. The history of gay and lesbian politics gives evidence of the many tensions within the movement in the sense that women have often suffered from a double marginalization—as women in society at large, and as lesbians within LGBT communities. Who, then, is the female player of a male-dominated queer guild? If the woman in straight contexts becomes the mediator of male desire and the guarantor of heterosexuality, who does she then become when such guarantee is no longer needed, when the desire between the men in question is explicitly homosexual? Put differently, if women as love interest are the weaker link in a heterosexual triangle of male rivalry and desire, what becomes of her when she is no longer even an object of love and desire?

Sundén discusses this topic in Chapter 8, and notices how "as a woman, you are automatically less interesting (and yet interesting, since you are different). A woman does not enter the picture as love interest, neither as sex object, but perhaps as friend. She is one of the boys—yet different from the boys" (p. 179 of this book). On the one hand, she becomes fairly superfluous in relation to the boys' interest in and attraction to one another. On the other hand, she has the possibility of entering the position of a friend. But, as discussed in Chapter 7, the position as friend is one that an emphasis on male homosexual desire disguises, or even makes invisible. As a friend, there is also the risk of her being understood as 'straight', a straightening that desexualizes her and simultaneously diminish the value of cross-gender friendships in queer spaces.

In a sense, the role of the woman in gay spaces that denies her queerness is quite similar to the one she has in straight settings. In the straight context, the women's roles may be more salient in that they provide the links between the men at the same time as they act as chaperons. Their principal raison d´être is to serve as the props, or maybe as stagehands in the men's performances of hegemonic masculinity. In queer contexts, the role of women can rather be compared to that of an extra, or even to serve as a backdrop to the primacy of intimacy and desire between men. Then again, as has become clear in this book, sometimes such roles and positions are questioned and negotiated in ways that emphasize the volatile nature of gendered and sexual relatedness.

## LESSONS FROM THE STUDY OF GAMES

Throughout this book, we have made explicit what the field of game studies can learn from queer and feminist theory. Using feminist theory as well as feminist ethnography as points of departures has helped us to spell out the political implications of, for example, inclusion, exclusion, transgression and playfulness. More generally, feminist and queer perspectives make explicit the role of embodied situatedness within player cultures of an online game like *World of Warcraft*.

However, one can turn the question the other way, and ask what feminist theory and feminist studies can learn from a study of game cultures. Put differently, what is it that the study of online games can teach feminist theories and methodologies? We will attempt to give two answers to this question. The first one is methodological in nature and develops an argument about the ways in which game ethnographies may provide queer and feminist ethnography with important tools for reworking questions of intimacy and closeness in fieldwork in new ways. The second answer is more theoretical and circles around notions of gender and how game cultures provide an intriguing platform for rethinking femininity (and masculinity).

Within our ethnographies, we have worked along a queer, feminist ethics of closeness, involvement and vulnerability, acknowledging that ethnographies are based on affective attachments and embodied experiences (cf. Rooke 2010). Feminist and queer ethnographies are not merely ethnographies researching the lives of women and queers, but a mode of critical inquiry that simultaneously holds the power of critiquing the normative logics of ethnographic research itself. Such normative logics involve ideas of clear distinctions between the 'here' (at home) and the 'there' (the field), subject and object, self and Other, inside and outside, insiders and outsiders, closeness and distance, the sensuous and the sensible, the passionate and the rational. Then again, as has been discussed (Sundén, in Chapter 5 and Chapter 7 in this book), this is not to say that other ethnographic traditions have not been self-reflexive or self-critical for quite some time—a process in relation to which a feminist and queer critique has been crucial. But it seems safe to say that such rewriting of a tradition is a continuous, on-going effort, and one that has not yet managed to once and for all destabilize the norms, logics, and academic heritage of ethnography. This seems particularly true outside of the (mother) discipline of anthropology, in those instances when ethnography as a method and mode of writing has travelled to other disciplines, such as sociology, but also more recently to game studies.

Queer and feminist ethnographers have done a lot of work in terms of questioning the possibility of there being a stable, coherent, ethnographic field that is easy to locate and delineate. They have also questioned the idea of a field that once located actually stays put, a field that does not move, and thus safely can be distinguished from the everyday, academic life of the researcher. In a recent edited collection entitled *Queer Methods and Methodologies* (Browne and Nash 2010), the authors call attention to the exceeding instability of boundaries in and around 'the field' in fieldwork. They underline that fields and ethnographies are messy in ways that fundamentally destabilize the binaries of here/there, field/academy, home/away, insider/outsider, researcher/researched (Boellstorff 2010; Dahl 2010; Jackman 2010; Nash 2010). Concerned with the uncertainty of time, space, and subjectivity, this border instability calls for an ethnographic ethics, not of distance (from the field, from those 'we' research, and in writing), but of closeness and complicity. Such questions of closeness become perhaps even more critical in feminist and queer studies of communities to which the researcher already belongs. To this we would like to add that this kind of boundary confusion also becomes particularly clear in the study of online games, for similar reasons due to community, belonging, and intense participation, but also due to the particular types of technologies involved. This book has kept pushing up against the limits of feminist modes of inquiry by, for example, interrogating the role of closeness, emotion and desire within knowledge production in fieldwork. In doing so, we have also come to examine what the ethnographic study of online games has to offer, more specifically, to the current discussion of feminist and queer ethnography.

It seems to us that there are important lessons to learn from the study of online games when it comes to what role digital technologies and game worlds play in the construction of contemporary forms of intimacy and closeness. It is not only our archives that are becoming all the more digital, so do our ways of socializing, getting close, hooking up, and falling in and out of love. In Dominic Pettman's (2006) tracing of Eros in the information age, love is articulated as a technology of belonging in ways that are becoming increasingly mediated over a range of media platforms. For sure, it can easily be argued that passion and matters of the heart have always been dependent on various technologies, tools, and devices: from the classic love letter written by hand to cell phone text messages and the 'ambient intimacy' (Reichelt 2007) of social networking sites. The question that interests us more is what difference particular technologies play in the construction of, not only love and passion, but a range of intimacies and forms of belonging in the field. As opposed to the kind of fieldwork where you need to leave your country, or at least your house, ethnographies of online game worlds bring with them the possibility of having the field at your fingertips, so to speak, no further away than a computer hooked-up to the Internet and having the right kind of software installed. As Sundén discusses in Chapter 5 in this book, this provides a particular type of closeness to the field that has resonance in the body in the sense that the game/field never quite leaves the body. The pace of the game becomes part of the pace of ourselves, our own bodies, and our technologies of field-working are the same as those for writing the field. Such *technological intimacy* in the field of online games is of a particular kind, and one that has resonance in the type of knowledge we can form in online field sites.

If online games provide important tools for rewriting queer and feminist ethnography, they also provide a powerful platform for rethinking gender. A recurrent theme of this book is an idea that seems to permeate *World of Warcraft* player cultures, namely the notion of the default gamer as white, heterosexual and above all, male. This implies that as a woman (of whatever racial and sexual variety), one's gaming interest and skills may at any moment be called into question, or simply rendered invisible. What appears to be at stake in these moments is a repetition of the age-old story of the extraordinary cultural closeness between masculinity and technology (Wajcman 1991, 2004). This close relation between men and machines, boys and their toys, has primarily come to signify culture, power, civilization, virility, as well as a mastery over or a taming of 'nature', which according to a reverse logic is associated with women, and with femininity. This, in turns, leads to an understanding of intimate connections between women and technology as virtually impossible, as a cultural paradox as it were. Within this book, this paradox has often been expressed as an inability to recognize female gamers (to recognize them as women, and once recognized as women, to recognize them as gamers). The fact that this closeness between women and technologies is paradoxical, bordering on the unthinkable, certainly does not mean that such intimacy does not exist. But what it does suggest is that close attachments between women and machines holds an explosive force, since their mere existence poses a threat to the technologically masculine. Technological femininity, then, becomes something that threatens to overthrow the order in relation to which men are in control (of machines, of masculinity, of women and of other Others).

It is important to notice that regarding the dominant cultural script of technological masculinity, there is no real distinction between men and masculinity on the one hand, and between women and femininity on the other. In other words, it is a heteronormative, binary logic that binds masculinity to men and femininity to women. In relation to this logic, the only way for a woman to become culturally intelligible within technological domains is, as we have discussed in this book, to abandon femininity and instead appropriate and use masculinity, to relate to technologies 'as a man', and to become 'one of the boys'. Then again, by doing so, the script is broken, since this very move of course challenges heteronormativity. Not surprisingly, both our studies were populated with a certain number of tomboys, with women having appropriated both masculinity and technology in particular ways. In Swedish, the word for tomboy is *pojkflicka*, which literally translates as 'boygirl'—a boyish girl while still possibly inhabiting the group 'girls' does so in ways that make her close to 'the boys'. In her study of female 'geeks', Rhiannon Bury (2011) describes a similar situation to the ones that we have discussed in the sense that her informants had to negotiate gender and technological skills in particular ways. Many of them described themselves as tomboys and consciously adopted masculine attributes in clothes and behavior. What the figure of the tech-savvy tomboy questions, then, is perhaps not so much the close affinity between masculinity and technology, but certainly the assumption that this affinity would be a male-only affair. In doing so, she also questions the stability of gender itself, by emphasizing the flexibility of masculinity. She calls attention to masculinity as a cultural repertoire that may travel, to the fact that masculinity, in essence, is *playable.*

What about femininity then? Where does the notion of a seemingly impossible alliance between women and technology leave questions of femininity in the world of gaming? Femininity is certainly a problematic concept, linked to a range of heteronormative associations and characteristics, such as being pleasing, sociable, nurturing, and beautiful (see, for example, Skeggs 1997). When such meanings of femininity are faced with the content of many computer games (and their emphasis on violence and competition), it becomes clear why computer games and femininity are seen as incompatible. Furthermore, in the discussion in Chapter 5 of desiring technology, it becomes evident that desire, much like technology, has been aligned with masculinity. The argument makes use of Elizabeth Grosz' (1995) way of challenging the Freudian understanding of desire as lack (along the lines of a heterosexualized binary composition of men as active, desiring subjects, and of women as passive objects of desire). In contrast to such understandings, Grosz attempts to think women as desiring subjects, and also to find ways of thinking desire between women. In a similar vein, in this book, we have tried to find ways of thinking women as *technological* subjects, to find ways of articulating women desiring technologies, and of women having intense connections with technologies in the company of, not only men, but of other women.

The many skilled, passionate female gamers out there are living proof of the possibility of other relations to be had and other meanings to be associated with technology, and with femininity. We have been trying to show that in the midst of the cultural imperative of technological masculinity, there is always the possibility of breaking the script, of putting a spin not only on masculinity, but on femininity itself. If masculinity is playable, the same can certainly be said about femininity. The script breaks when women claim technology for themselves, and when they do so unapologetically. Claiming technology in this sense rewrites femininity in specific ways, and in our case along the lines of a *gamer femininity.* As we state in the introduction: if passion for technology is closely associated with men and masculinity, then to claim close links between femininity, passion and games works by necessity to *queer* femininity. What this means is that the culturally improper, unbecoming, unacceptable attachment of femininity to the technological (guilty by association) makes the meanings of the term femininity shift. It is queer in the sense that female players (of whatever orientation) are involved in non-normative, or even anti-normative ways of performing femininity. This is neither the breakdown of femininity, nor its abandoning, but rather a head-on reworking of the concept in ways that suggests technological femininity as not merely a paradox, but a potent, dangerously explosive possibility.

## NOTES

1. Experience points used to be given to players when they did quests and/or killed monsters. However, in addition to this, since the release of the expansion *Cataclysm* in December 2010, experience points are also given for a range of other activities, such as practicing professions or taking part in PvP.
2. A fairly recent example, which attracted a lot of media attention, was the cancellation of the gay parade that was planned to take place in Belgrade in September 2009. The decision was based on a fear of violence manifested in an upsurge of homophobic graffiti across the city, as well as a fear of a repeat performance of the 2001 parade, which had to be abandoned half-way through due to a violent group of protesters.

# Authors

**Jenny Sundén** is Associate Professor at the School of Gender, Culture, and History, Södertörn University, Sweden. Her research interests are primarily in new media studies, cultural studies, science and technology studies, queer feminist theory, ethnography, and games. She is the author of *Material Virtualities: Approaching Online Textual Embodiment* (Peter Lang, 2003), and a co-author of *Digital Borderlands: Cultural Studies of Identity and Interactivity on the Internet* (Peter Lang, 2002), *Cyberfeminism in Northern Lights: Gender and Digital Media in a Nordic Context* (Cambridge Scholars Publishing, 2007), and *Second Nature: Origins and Originality in Art, Science and New Media* (Axl Books, 2011, with Rolf Hughes).

**Malin Sveningsson** is Associate Professor at the Department of Journalism, Media, and Communication, Gothenburg University, Sweden. Her research interests include Internet culture, computer game culture, computer-mediated communication, social interaction, gender and identity. She is the author *of Creating a Sense of Community: Experiences from a Swedish Web Chat* (Linköping Studies in Art and Science, 2001), a co-author of *Digital Borderlands: Cultural Studies of Identity and Interactivity on the Internet* (Peter Lang, 2002) and *Cyberfeminism in Northern Lights: Gender and Digital Media in a Nordic Context* (Cambridge Scholars Publishing, 2007).

# References


Aarseth, Espen. 2003. "Playing Research: Methodological Approaches to Game Analysis." Paper presented at *Digital Arts and Culture* (DAC), Melbourne, Australia, May 19–23.

———. 2007a. "Forskning på spel: Metodologiska ansatser till spelanalys." In *Datorspelandets dynamik. Lekar och roller i en digital kultur*, edited by Jonas Linderoth, 209–230. Lund: Studentlitteratur.

———. 2007b. I Fought the Law: Transgressive Play and the Implied Player. *Situated Play, Proceedings of DiGRA 2007 Conference.* http://www.digra.org/dl/db/07313.03489.pdf. Date accessed: June 11, 2011.

Adams, Ernest, and Andrew Rollings. 2007. *Fundamentals of Game Design.* Upper Saddle River, NJ: Pearson/Prentice Hall.

Adamse, Michael, and Sheree .D. Motta. 1996. *Online Friendship, Chat Room Romance and Cybersex: Your Guide to Affairs of the Net.* Deerfield Beach: Health Communications.

Adelswärd, Viveka. 1991. *Prat, skratt, skvaller, gräl och annat vi gör när vi samtalar.* Stockholm: Brombergs.

Ahmed, Sara. 2004. *The Cultural Politics of Emotion.* Edinburgh: Edinburgh University Press.

———. 2006. *Queer Phenomenology: Orientations, Objects, Others.* Durham, NC and London: Duke University Press.

Altork, Kate. 1995. "Walking the Fire Line." In *Taboo: Sex, Identity and Erotic Subjectivity in Anthropological Fieldwork*, edited by Don Kulick and Margaret Willson, 107–139. London: Routledge.

Ambjörnsson, Fanny. 2004. *I en klass för sig. Genus och sexualitet bland gymnasietjejer.* Stockholm: Ordfront.

Andreasson, Jesper. 2003. "Brudar, bärs och bögar—maskulinitet och sexualitet i en enkönad miljö." In *Sexualitetens omvandlingar. Politisk lesbiskhet, unga kristna och machokulturer*, edited by Thomas Johansson and Philip Lalander, 25–46. Göteborg: Daidalos.

Armstrong, Isobel. 2000. *The Radical Aesthetic.* Oxford: Blackwell.

Asad, Talal. 1973. *Anthropology & the Colonial Encounter.* London: Ithaca Press.

Åsberg, Cecilia, and Bodil Axelsson. 2007. "Digital Performances of Gendered Past." In *Cyberfeminism in Northern Lights. Digital Media and Gender in a Nordic Context*, edited by Malin Sveningsson Elm and Jenny Sundén, 152—181. Cambridge: Cambridge Scholars Publishing.

Baker, Andrea. 1998. "Cyberspace Couples Finding Love Online Then Meeting for the First Time in Real Life." *CMC Magazine* 5(7). http://www.december.com/cmc/mag/1998/jul/baker.html Date accessed: June 11, 2011.

Balsamo, Anne. 1995. "Forms of Technological Embodiment: Reading the Body in Contemporary Culture." In *Cyberspace, Cyberbodies, Cyberpunk: Cultures of*

*Technological Embodiment*, edited by Mike Featherstone and Roger Burrows, 215–238. London: Sage.

———. 2000. "The Virtual Body in Cyberspace." In *The Cybercultures Reader*, edited by David Bell and Barbara M. Kennedy, 489–503. London: Routledge.

Barad, Karen. 2009, *Meeting the universe halfway: Quantum physics and the entanglement of matter and meaning*. Durham, NC: Duke University Press.

Bardzell, Shaowen and Jeffrey S. Bardzell. (2007). "Docile Avatars: Aesthetics, Experience, and Sexual Interaction in Second Life." *Proceedings of HCI 2007*, Lancaster, UK, September, 3–7.

Bartle, Richard. 1996. Hearts, Clubs, Diamonds, Spades: Players Who Suit MUDs. . http://www.mud.co.uk/richard/hcds.htm. Date accessed: June 11, 2011.

———. 2004. *Designing Virtual Worlds*. Indianapolis: New Riders Pub.

Barton, Matt. 2008. "How's the Weather: Simulating Weather in Virtual Environments." *Game Studies* 8(1). http://gamestudies.org/0801/articles/barton. Date accessed: June 11, 2011.

Baym, Nancy. 2000. *Tune in, Log on: Soaps, Fandom, and Online Community*. Thousand Oaks, CA: Sage.

Behm-Morawitz, Elizabeth, and Dana Mastro. 2009. "The Effects of the Sexualization of Female Video Game Characters on Gender Stereotyping and Female Self-Concept." *Sex Roles* 61(11) 808–825.

Bennerstedt, Ulrika. 2008. "Welcome to the Digital Puppet Show: Positioning Work and Make-Believe Methods in Role Play." In *Proceedings from The [Player] Conference*, edited by Saro Mosberg and Olli Leino. Copenhagen: IT University of Copenhagen.

Berger, John. 1972. *Ways of Seeing*. London: Penguin Books.

Berlant, Lauren. 2004. *Compassion: The Culture and Politics of an Emotion*. New York: Routledge.

———. 2010. "Sex in the Event of Happiness." Keynote address at *Affective Tendencies: Bodies, Sexualities, Pleasures* at Women's and Gender Studies, Rutgers University, October 7–9.

Berlant, Lauren, and Michael Warner. 2000. "Sex in Public." In *Intimacy*, edited by Lauren Berlant, 311–330. Chicago IL: Chicago University Press.

Boellstorff, Tom. 2006. "A Ludicrous Discipline? Ethnography and Game Studies." *Games and Culture* 1(1): 29–35.

———. 2007a. "Queer Studies in the House of Anthropology." *Annual Review of Anthropology* 36: 17–35.

———. 2007b. *A Coincidence of Desire: Anthropology, Queer Studies, Indonesia*. Durham, NC: Duke University Press.

———. 2008. *Coming of Age in Second Life: An Anthropologist Explores the Virtually Human*. Princeton: Princeton University Press.

———. 2010. "Queer techne: Two theses on Methodology and Queer studies." In *Queer Methods and Methodologies: Intersecting Queer Theories and Social Science Research*, edited by Kath Browne and Catherine J. Nash, 215–230. Farnham: Ashgate.

Bogost, Ian. 2008. "The Phenomenology of Videogames." Keynote address at Philosophy of Computer Games Conference, Potsdam Germany, May 8, 2008.

Braidotti, Rosi. 1994. *Nomadic Subjects: Embodiment and Sexual Difference in Contemporary Feminist Theory*. New York: Columbia University Press.

Bromseth, Janne, and Jenny Sundén. 2011. "Queering Internet Studies: Intersections of Gender and Sexuality." In *The Blackwell Handbook of Internet Studies*, edited by Mia Consalvo and Charles Ess, 270–302. Oxford: Blackwell Publishing.

Brookey, Robert Alan, and Kristopher L. Cannon. 2009. "Sex Lives in Second Life." *Critical Studies in Media Communication* 26(2): 145–164.

Browne, Kath, and Catherine J Nash. 2010. *Queer Methods and Methodologies: Intersecting Queer Theories and Social Science Research.* Farnham: Ashgate.

Bruckman, Amy. 1993. "Gender Swapping on the Internet." *Proceedings of INET '93.* Reston, VA: The Internet Society. http://www.cc.gatech.edu/~asb/papers/conference/gender-swapping.ps. Date accessed: June 11, 2011.

Brushwood Rose, Chloe and Anna Camilleri, eds. 2002. *Brazen Femme: Queering Femininity.* Vancouver, BC: Arsenal Pulp.

Bryce, Jo, and Jason Rutter. 2002. "Killing Like a Girl: Gendered Gaming and Girl Gamers' Visibility." In *CGDC Conference Proceedings*, edited by F. Mayra. Tampere: Tampere University Press.

———. 2003a. "Gender Dynamics and the Social and Spatial Organization of Computer Gaming." *Leisure Studies* (22): 1–15.

———. 2003b. "The Gendering of Computer Gaming: Experience and Space." In *Leisure Cultures: Investigations in Sport, Media and Technology*, edited by S. Fleming and I. Jones, 3–22. Eastbourne: Leisure Studies Association.

———. 2007. "Not Much Fun: The Constraining of Female Video Gamers." *ADOZ Journal of Leisure Studies* 31: 97–108.

Buchanan, Elizabeth A. 2009. "Response Paper." In *Internet Inquiry. Conversations about Method*, edited by Annette Markham, N. and Nancy K. Baym, 88–93. Thousand Oaks, CA: Sage.

Burn, Andrew. 2006. "Playing Roles." In *Computer Games: Text, Narrative and Play*, edited by Diane Carr, David Buckingham, Andrew Burn and Gareth Schott, 72–87. Cambridge: Polity Press.

Burrill, Derek A. 2008. *Die Tryin': Video Games, Masculinity, Culture.* New York: Peter Lang.

Bury, Rhiannon 2011. "She's Geeky: The Performance of Identity among Women Working in IT." *International Journal of Gender, Science and Technology* 3(1): 34–53.

Butler, Judith. 1990. *Gender Trouble: Feminism and the Subversion of Identity.* New York and London: Routledge.

Bäckman, Maria. 2003. *Kön och känsla. Samlevnadsundervisning och ungdomars tankar om sexualitet.* Göteborg: Makadam.

Caillois, Roger. 1961/2001. *Man, Play and Games.* Urbana, IL: University of Illinois Press.

Campbell, John Edward. 2009. "Response to Lori Kendall." In *Internet Inquiry: Conversations about Method*, edited by Annette N. Markham and Nancy K. Baym, 124–130. Thousand Oaks, CA: Sage.

Carr, Diane. 2002. "Playing with Lara." In *Screenplay: Cinema/Videogames/Interfaces*, edited by G. King and T. Kryzwinska, 171–180. London: Wallflower Press.

———. 2005. "Contexts, Gaming Pleasures, and Gendered Preferences." *Simulation & Gaming*, 36(4): 464–482.

———. 2006a. "Games and Gender." In *Computer Games: Text, Narrative and Play*, edited by Diane Carr, David Buckingham, Andrew Burn and Gareth Scott, 162–178. Cambridge: Polity Press.

———. 2006b. "Play and Pleasure." In *Computer Games. Text, Narrative and Play*, edited by Diane Carr, David Buckingham, Andrew Burn, and Gareth Schott, 45–58. Cambridge: Polity Press.

———. 2006c. "Space, Navigation and Affect." In *Computer Games: Text, Narrative and Play*, edited by Diane Carr, David Buckingham, Andrew Burn, and Gareth Scott, 59–71. Cambridge: Polity Press.

———. 2010. "Constructing Disability in Online Worlds; Conceptualising Disability in Online Research." *London Review of Education: Special Issue 'Being Online: A Critical View of Identity and Subjectivity in New Virtual Learning Spaces'* 8(1): 51–61.

Cassell, Justine. 1998. "Storytelling as a Nexus of Change in the Relationship between Gender and Technology: A Feminist Approach to Software Design." In *From Barbie to Mortal Kombat: Gender and Computer Games*, edited by Justine Cassell and Henry Jenkins, 298–326. Cambridge, MA: MIT Press.

Castronova, Edward. 2005. *Synthetic Worlds: The Business and Culture of Online Games*. Chicago, IL: University of Chicago Press.

Cesara, Manda. 1982. *Reflections of a Woman Anthropologist: No Hiding Place*. London and New York: Academic Press.

Clifford, James, and George Marcus. 1986. *Writing Culture: The Poetics and Politics of Ethnography*. Berkeley, CA: University of California Press.

Clough, Patricia Ticineto, and Jean Halley. 2007. *The Affective Turn: Theorizing the Social*. Durham, NC: Duke University Press.

Cockburn, Cynthia. 1985. *Machinery of Dominance: Women, Men and Technical Know-how*. London: Pluto Press.

Colman, Felicity. 2008. "Affective Game Topologies: Any-Space-Whatevers." *Refractory: A Journal of Entertainment Media* 13. http://refractory.unimelb.edu.au/2008/05/21/affective-game-topologies-any-space-whatevers-felicity-j-colman/. Date accessed: June 11, 2011.

Conboy, Katie, Nadia Medina, and Sarah Stanbury. 1997. *Writing on the Body: Female Embodiment and Feminist Theory*. New York: Columbia University Press.

Connell, Robert W. 1995. *Masculinites*. Berkeley, CA: University of California Press.

Connell, Robert W, and James W. Messerschmidt. 2005. "Hegemonic Masculinity: Rethinking the Concept." *Gender & Society* 19(6):829–859.

Consalvo, Mia. 2003a. "Hot Dates and Fairy-tale Romances: Studying Sexuality in Video Games." In *The Video Game Reader*, edited by Mark J.P. Wolf and Bernard Perron, 171–194. New York: Routledge.

———. 2003b. It's A Queer World After All: Studying the Sims and Sexuality. *GLAAD Centre for the Study of Media and Society*. http://archive.glaad.org/documents/csms/The_Sims.pdf. Date accessed: June 11, 2011.

———. 2007. *Cheating: Gaining Advantage in Videogames*. Cambridge, MA: MIT Press.

Cornelius, Michael B. 2000. "Bear Culture." In *Reader's Guide to Lesbian and Gay Studies*, edited by Timothy F. Murphy. Chicago, IL: Fitzroy Dearborn.

Corneliussen, Hilde. 2008. "*World of Warcraft* as Playground for Feminism." In *Digital Culture, Play and Identity: A* World of Warcraft® *Reader*, edited by Hilde Corneliussen and Jill Walker Rettberg, 63–86. Cambridge, MA: MIT Press.

Corneliussen, Hilde G., and Jill Walker Rettberg. 2008a. "Introduction: 'Orc Professor LFG,' or Researching in Azeroth." In *Digital Culture, Play and Identity. A World of Warcraft Reader*, edited by Hilde G. Corneliussen and Jill Walker Rettberg, 1–18. Cambridge, MA: The MIT Press.

———. 2008b. *Digital Culture, Play, and Identity: A World of Warcraft Reader*. Cambridge, MA: MIT Press.

Correll, Shelley. 1995. "The Ethnography of an Electronic Bar: The Lesbian Café." *Journal of Contemporary Ethnography* 24(3): 270–290.

Crick, Timothy Paul. 2011. "The Game Body: Toward a Phenomenology of Contemporary Video Gaming." *Games and Culture* 6: 259–269.

Crogan, Patrick, and Helen W. Kennedy. 2009. "Special Section on Technologies Between Games and Culture." *Games and Culture* 4(2): 107–169.

Dahl, Ulrika. 2008. In *Femmes of Power: Exploding Queer Femininities*, by Del Lagrace Volcano and Ulrika Dahl. London: Serpent's Tail.

———. 2010. "Femme on Femme: Reflections on Collaborative Methods and Queer Femme-inist Ethnography." In *Queer Methods and Methodologies: Intersecting Queer Theories and Social Science Research*, edited by Kath Browne and Catherine J Nash, 143–166. Farnham: Ashgate.

Daneback, Kristian. 2006. *Love and Sexuality on the Internet*, Institution for Social Work, Gothenburg University, Gothenburg.
Danet, Brenda. 1998. "Text as Mask: Gender, Play and Performance on the Internet." In *Cybersociety 2.0: Revisiting Computer-mediated Communication and Community*, edited by Steven Jones, 129–158. Thousand Oaks, CA: Sage.
———. 2001. *Cyberplay: Communicating Online*. Oxford: Berg.
Danet, Brenda, Lucia Ruedenberg, and Yehudit Rosenbaum-Tamari. 1998. "Hmmm . . . Where is that Smoke Coming From? Writing Play and Performance on Internet Relay Chat." In *Network and Netplay. Virtual Groups on the Internet*, edited by Fay Sudweeks, Margaret McLaughlin and Sheizaf Rafaeli, 41–76. Menlo Park: AAAI Press/The MIT Press.
de Castell, Suzanne, and Mary Bryson. 1998a. "Retooling Play: Dystopia, Dysphoria, and Difference." In *From Barbie to Mortal Kombat: Gender and Computer Games*, edited by Justine Cassell and Henry Jenkins, 232–261. Cambridge, MA: MIT Press.
———. 1998b. "Queer Ethnography: Identity, Authority, Narrativity, and a Geopolitics of Text." In *Inside the Academy and Out: Lesbian/Gay/Queer Studies and Social Action*, edited by Janice L. Ristock and Catherine Taylor, 97–110. Toronto: University of Toronto Press.
Delamere, Fern M. , and Susan M. Shaw. 2008. "'They see it as a guy's game': The Politics of Gender in Digital Games." *Leisure/Loisir, Special Issue, The Politics of Popular Leisure* 32(2): 279–302.
Deleuze, Gilles and Félix Guattari. 1987. *A Thousand Plateaus: Capitalism and Schizophrenia*. Translation and foreword by Brian Massumi. Minneapolis, MN: University of Minnesota Press.
Denzin, Norman K. 2003. *Performance Ethnography: Critical Pedagogy and the Politics of Culture*. Thousand Oaks, CA: Sage.
Dibble, Julian. 1993. "A Rape in Cyberspace. How an Evil Clown, a Haitian Trickster Spirit, Two Wizards, and a Cast of Dozens Turned a Database Into a Society." *The Village Voice* (December 23).
Dickey, Michele.D. 2006. Girl gamers: The controversy of girl gamers and the relevanceof female-oriented game design for instructional design. *British Journal of Educational Technology*, 37(5): 785–793.
Djerf-Pierre, Monika. 2005. "Lonely at the Top: Gendered Media Elites in Sweden." *Journalism* 6(3): 265–290.
———. 2007. "The Gender of Journalism. The Structure and Logic of the Field in the Twentieth Century." *Nordicom Review* (Jubilee Issue):81–104.
Donath, Judith S. 1999. "Identity and Deception in the Virtual Community." In *Communities in Cyberspace*, edited by Marc A. Smith and Peter Kollock, 29–59. London: Routledge.
Dovey, Jon, and Helen W. Kennedy. 2006. *Game Cultures; Computer Games as New Media* Berkshire: Open University Press
Doyle, Jennifer. 2007. "Between Friends." In *A Companion to Lesbian, Gay, Bisexual, Transgender, and Queer Studies*, edited by George E Haggerty and Molly McGarry, 325–340. Malden, MA: Blackwell.
Dubrovsky, Vitaly J., Sara Kiesler, and Beheruz N Sethna. 1991. "The Equalization Phenomenon: Status Effects in Computer-Mediated and Face-to-Face Decision-Making Groups." *Human-Computer Interaction* (6): 119–146.
Ducheneaut, Nicolas, Nick Yee, Eric Nickell, and Robert J. Moor. 2006. "Building an MMO with Mass Appeal: A Look at Gameplay in World of Warcraft." *Games and Culture* 1(1):281–317.
Duggan, Lisa and Kathleen McHugh. 2002. "A Fem(me)inist Manifesto." In *Brazen Femme: Queering Femininity*, edited by Chloe Brushwood Rose and Anna Camilleri, 165–170. Vancouver, BC: Arsenal Pulp.

Dunkels, Elsa. 2005. "Nätkulturer—vad gör barn och unga på Internet?" *Tidskrift för lärarutbildning och forskning* (1–2): 41–49.

Ehn, Billy. 1996. "Närhet och avstånd." In *Vardagslivets etnologi. Reflektioner kring en kulturvetenskap*, edited by Billy Ehn and Orvar Löfgren, 89–176. Stockholm: Natur och Kultur.

Elliston, Deborah. 2002. "Anthropology's Queer Future: Feminist Lessons from Tahiti and Its Islands." In *Out in Theory: The Emergence of Lesbian and Gay Anthropology*, edited by Ellen Lewin and William Leap, 287–315. Urbana, IL: University of Illinois Press.

Emerson, Robert M, Rachel Fretz, I, and Linda L. Shaw. 1995. *Writing Ethnographic Fieldnotes*. Chicago IL: The University of Chicago Press.

Enevold, Jessica, and Charlotte Hagström. 2008. "My Momma Shoots Better Than You: Who is the Female Gamer?" In *Proceedings from The [Player] Conference*, edited by Sara Mosberg and Olli Leino. Copenhagen: IT University of Copenhagen.

———. 2009. "Mothers, Play and Everyday Life: Ethnology Meets Game Studies." *Ethnologia Scandinavica: A Journal for Nordic Ethnology* 39: 27–41.

———. 2005. "Ett annat sätt att umgås: yngre tonåringar i virtuella gemenskaper." *Tidskrift för lärarutbildning och forskning* (1–2): 81–99.

Enochson, AnnBritt. 2007. "Differences and Similarities in Girls' and Boys' Internet Use." In *Cyberfeminism in Northern Lights: Gender and Digital Media in a Nordic Context*, edited by Malin Sveningsson Elm and Jenny Sundén, 182–195. Cambridge: Cambridge Scholars Publishing.

ESA, The. 2010. 2010 Essential Facts about the Computer and Video Game Industry. http://www.theesa.com/facts/pdfs/ESA_Essential_Facts_2010.pdf. Date accessed: June 11, 2011.

Faulkner, Wendy. 2000. "Dualisms, Hierarchies and Gender in Engineering." *Social Studies of Science* 30: 759–792.

Ferrell, J, and M.S Hamm. 1998. *Ethnography at the Edge: Crime, Deviance and Field Research*. Boston: Northeastern University Press.

Fine, Gary Alan. 1993. "Ten Lies of Ethnography: Moral Dilemmas in Field Research." *Journal of Contemporary Ethnography* 22(3): 267–294.

Fiske, J. 1989. *Understanding Popular Culture*. London: Routledge.

Flanagan, Mary. 2005. Troubling 'Games for Girls': Notes from the Edge of Game Design. Paper read at DiGRA 2005 Conference: Changing Views—Worlds in Play, October 27, 2008.

———. 2009. *Critical Play: Radical Game Design*. Cambridge, MA: MIT Press.

Foucault, Michel. 1969/1979. "What is an Author?" In *Textual Strategies: Perspectives in Post-Structuralist Criticism*, edited by Josue V. Harari, 141–160. Ithaca, NY: Cornell University Press.

———. 1979. *Discipline and Punish: The Birth of the Prison*. New York: Vintage Books.

Frasca, Gonzalo. 2001. *Videogames of the Oppressed: Videogames as a Means for Critical Thinking and Debate*. Master Thesis, Georgia Institute of Technology. http://www.ludology.org/articles/thesis/FrascaThesisVideogames.pdf. Date accessed: June 11, 2011.

Freeman, Elizabeth. 2007. "Queer Belongings: Kinship Theory and Queer Theory." In *A Companion to Lesbian, Gay, Bisexual, Transgender, and Queer Studies*, edited by George E. Haggerty and Molly McGarry, 295–314. Malden, MA: Blackwell.

Fron, Janine, Tracy Fullerton, Jacquelyn Ford Morie, and Celia Pearce. 2007. "The Hegemony of Play." *Situated Play, Proceedings of DiGRA 2007 Conference*: September 24th–28th Tokyo, Japan, 309–318.

Frosh, Stephen, Ann Phoenix, and Rob Pattman. 2002. *Young Masculinities*. Houndmills: Palgrave.

Fullerton, Tracy , Jacquelyn Ford Morie, and Celia Pearce. 2008. A Game of One's Own: Towards a New Gendered Poetics of Digital Space. *The Fibreculture Journal* (11). http://journal.fibreculture.org/issue11/issue11_fullerton_morie_pearce.html. Date accessed: June 11, 2011.

Ganetz, Hillevi. 1997. *Hennes röster. Rocktexter av Turid Lundqvist, Eva Dahlgren och Kajsa Grytt*. Eslöv: Symposion.

———. 2008. *Talangfabriken. Iscensättningar av genus och sexualitet i svensk talang-reality*. Uppsala: Centrum för Genusvetenskap.

Gavanas, Anna. 2009. "'You Better be Listening to My Fucking Musik You Bastard!' Teknologi, genusifiering och andlighet bland DJs på elektroniska dansmusikscener i Berlin, London och Stockholm." In *Rundgång: genus och populärmusik*, edited by Hillevi Ganetz, Anna Gavanas, Hasse Huss and Ann Werner. Stockholm: Makadam.

Geertz, Clifford. 1988. *Works and Lives: The Anthropologist as Author*. Cambridge, MA: Polity Press.

Gemzöe, Lena. 2004. *Feminism*. Stockholm: Bilda Förlag.

Glas, René. 2007. "Playing another Game: Twinking in World of Warcraft." *Proceedings of DiGRA 2007 Conference: Situated Play*. http://www.digra.org/dl/db/07311.13119.pdf. Date accessed: June 11, 2011.

Gorton, Kristyn. 2008. "Desire, Duras, and Melancholia: Theorizing Desire After the Affective Turn." *Feminist Review* 89: 16–33.

Greenberg, Bradley S., John Sherry, Kenneth Lachlan, Kristen Lucas, and Amanda Holmstrom. 2010 "Orientations to Video Games Among Gender and Age Groups." *Simulation & Gaming* 41(2): 238–259.

Grimes, Sara M. 2003. "You Shoot Like a Girl!" The Female Protagonist in Action-Adventure Video Games. Paper read at Level Up. Digital Games Research Conference 2003, November 4–6, 2003 University of Utrecht, The Netherlands.

Grosz, Elizabeth. 1995. *Space, Time, and Perversion: Essays on the Politics of Bodies*. New York and London: Routledge.

Halberstam, Judith. 1998. *Female Masculinity*. Durham, NC: Duke University Press.

———. 2005. *In a Queer Time and Place: Transgender Bodies, Subcultural Lives*. New York: New York University Press.

Hammersley, Martyn, and Paul Atkinson. 1995. *Ethnography: Principles in Practice*. 2nd ed. London: Routledge.

Haraway, Donna. 1991. *Simians, Cyborgs, and Women: The Reinvention of Nature*. New York: Routledge.

———. 1997. *Modest Witness@Second Millennium. FemaleMan© Meets OncoMouse™: Feminism and Technoscience*. New York: Routledge.

Harré, Rom, and Luk van Langenhove. 1999. *Positioning Theory*. Oxford: Blackwell.

Harris, Laura and Elizabeth Crocker, eds. 1997. *Femme: Feminists, Lesbians, and Bad Girls*. New York: Routledge.

Hartmann, Tilo, and Cristoph Klimmt. 2006. "Gender and Computer Games: Exploring Females' Dislikes." *Journal of Computer-Mediated Communication* 11(4). http://jcmc.indiana.edu/vol11/issue4/hartmann.html. Date accessed: June 11, 2011.

Hayles, Katherine N. 1999. *How We became Posthuman: Virtual Bodies in Cybernetics, Literature, and Informatics*. Chicago, IL: The University of Chicago Press.

Hearn, Jeff. 1996. "Is Masculinity Dead? A Critique of the Concept of Masculinity/Masculinities." In *Understanding Masculinities: Social Representations and Cultural Arenas.*, edited by Màirtin Macan Ghaill, 202–217. Buckingham, Philadelphia: Open University Press.

Hennen, Peter. 2005. "Bear Bodies, Bear Masculinities: Recuperation, Resistance, or Retreat?" *Gender & Society*, 19(1): 25–43.

———. 2008. *Faeries, Bears, and Leathermen: Men in Community Queering the Masculine.* Chicago, IL: University of Chicago Press.

Hermes, Joke. 1995. *Reading Women's Magazines: An Analysis of Everyday Media Use.* Cambridge: Polity Press.

Hill, Simon. 2010. Finding Love and Relationships in MMOs. *Bright Hub—The Hub for Bright Minds*, http://www.brighthub.com/video-games/mmo/articles/29575.aspx. Date accessed: June 11, 2011.

Hillis, Ken. 2009. *Online a Lot of the Time: Ritual, Fetish, Sign.* Durham, NC: Duke University Press.

Hine, Christine. 2000. *Virtual Ethnography.* London: Sage.

Holmberg, Carin. 1993. *Det kallas kärlek.* Stockholm: Alfabeta.

Iser, Wolfgang. 1974. *The Implied Reader: Patterns of Communication in Prose Fiction from Bunyan to Beckett.* Baltimore and London: Johns Hopkins University Press.

Ito, Mizuko. 2008. "Gender Dynamics of the Japanese Media Mix." In *Beyond Barbie & Mortal Kombat: New Perspectives on Gender and Gaming*, edited by Yasmin B. Kafai, Carrie Heeter, Jill Denner, and Jennifer Y. Sun, 97–110. Cambridge, MA: MIT Press.

Ivory, James D. 2006. Still a man's game: Gender representation in online reviews of video games. *Mass Communication and Society*, 9(1), 103-114.

Jackman, Michael Connors. 2010. "The Trouble with Fieldwork: Queering Methodologies." In *Queer Methods and Methodologies: Intersecting Queer Theories and Social Science Research*, edited by Kath Browne and Catherine J Nash, 113–128. Farnham: Ashgate.

Jansz, Jeroen., & Martis, Raynel. 2003. *The representation of gender and ethnicity in digital interactive games.* Paper presented at the Level up: Digital games research conference 2003, 4-6 November, Utrecht University, The Netherlands.

Järvinen, Aki. 2008. *Games Without Frontiers: Methods for Game Studies and Design.* Tampere: Tampere University Press.

Jenkins, Henry. 1998. "Complete Freedom of Movement." In *From Barbie to Mortal Kombat: Gender and Computer Games*, edited by Justine Cassell and Henry Jenkins, 262–297. Cambridge, MA: MIT Press.

Jennings, Brian. 2008. "WTFpwned by Chinese Gold Farmers: Translating 'Otherness' into Synthetic Worlds through Culture and Language Hierarchies." In *Extending Experiences: Structure, Analysis and Design of Computer Game Player Experience*, edited by Olli Leino, Hanna Wirman and Amyris Fernandez, 93–109. Rovaniemi: Lapland University Press.

Jenson, Jennifer, and Suzanne de Castell. 2005. Her Own boss: Gender and the Pursuit of Incompetent Play. In *Proceedings of DiGRA 2005 Conference: Changing Views—Worlds in Play.* http://www.digra.org/dl/db/06278.27455.pdf. Date accessed: June 11, 2011.

———. 2007. "Girls and Gaming: Gender Research, 'Progress' and the Death of Interpretation." In *Situated Play, Proceedings of DiGRA 2007 Conference*, 769–771. http://www.digra.org/dl/db/07311.36536.pdf. Date accessed: June 11, 2011.

———. 2008. "Theorizing Gender and Digital Gameplay: Oversights, Accidents and Surprises." *Eludamos: Journal for Computer Game Culture* 2(1), 15–25.

———. 2010. "Gender, Simulation, and Gaming: Research Review and Redirections." *Simulation & Gaming* 41(1): 51–71.

———. 2011. "Girls@Play: An Ethnographic Study of Gender and Digital Gameplay." *Feminist Media Studies* 11(2): 167–179.

Jenson, Jennifer, Suzanne de Castell, and Stephanie Fisher. 2007. "Girls Playing Games: Rethinking Stereotypes." In *Proceedings of the 2007 Conference on Future Play, Toronto, Canada,* 9–16.

Jenson, Jennifer, Stephanie Fisher, and Suzanne de Castell. 2011. "Disrupting the Gender Order: Leveling Up and Claiming Space in an After-School Video Game Club." *International Journal of Gender, Science and Technology* 3(1): 149–169.

Jørgensen, Kristine. 2009. *A Comprehensive Study of Sound in Computer Games: How Audio Affects Player Action.* New York: Mellem Press.

Juul, Jesper. 2001. Games Telling Stories? A Brief Note on Games and Narratives. *Game Studies* 1(1). http://www.gamestudies.org/0101/juul-gts/. Date accessed: June 11, 2011.

———. 2009. "Fear of Failing? The Many Meanings of Difficulty in Video Games." In *The Video Game Theory Reader* 2, edited by Mark J.P. Wolf and Bernard Perron, 237–252. New York: Routledge.

Kafai, Yasmin B, Carrie Heeter, Jill Denner, and Jennifer Y Sun. 2008. "Preface: Pink, Purple, Casual or Mainstream Games: Moving beyond the Gender Divide." In *Beyond Barbie & Mortal Kombat: New Perspectives on Gender and Gaming,* edited by Yasmin B. Kafai, Carrie Heeter, Jill Denner, and Jennifer Y. Sun, xi–xxv. Cambridge, MA: MIT Press.

Kaufman, Margo. 1996. "They Call it Cyberlove." In *Computerization Controversy: Value Conflicts and Social Choices,* edited by Rob Kling. San Diego: Academic Press.

Kendall, Lori. 1998. "'Are You Male or Female?' Gender Performances on Muds." In *Everyday Inequalities: Critical Inquiries,* edited by Jodi O'Brien and Judith Howard, 131–153. Malden, MA: Blackwell.

———. 2002. *Hanging Out in the Virtual Pub: Masculinities and Relationships Online.* Berkeley, CA: University of California Press.

———. 2009a. "How Do Issues of Gender and Sexuality Influence the Structures and Processes of Qualitative Internet Research?" In *Internet Inquiry. Conversations about Method* edited by Annette N. Markham and Nancy K. Baym, 99–118. Los Angeles: Sage.

———. 2009b. "Response to Christine Hine." In *Internet Inquiry: Conversations about Method,* edited by Annette N. Markham, 21–25. Thousand Oaks, CA: Sage.

Kennedy, Helen W. 2002. Lara Croft: Feminist Icon or Cyberbimbo? On the Limits of Textual Analysis. *Game Studies* 2(2). http://www.gamestudies.org/0202/kennedy/. Date accessed: June 11, 2011.

———. 2006. "Illegitimate, Monstrous and Out There: Female 'Quake' Players and Inappropriate Pleasures." In *Feminism in Popular Culture,* edited by J Hollows and R Moseley. 183–202. Oxford: Berg.

Kerr, Aphra. 2003. Women Just Want to Have Fun: A Study of Adult Female Players of Digital Games. *Level Up Conference Proceedings.* University of Utrecht, Utrecht , pp. 270–285.

Kisliuk, Michelle. 1997. "(Un)doing Fieldwork: Sharing Songs, Sharing Lives." In *Shadows in the Field: New Perspectives for Fieldwork in Ethnomusicology,* edited by Gregory F. Barz and Timothy J. Cooley, 23–44. New York: Oxford University Press.

Klastrup, Lisbeth. 2008. "What Makes WoW a World? A Note on Death and Dying." In *Digital Culture, Play, and Identity: A World of Warcraft Reader,* edited by Jill Walker and Hilde Corneliussen, 143–166. Cambridge, MA: MIT Press.

Kroløkke, Charlotte. 2007. "Performing and Positioning PowerBabes." In *Cyberfeminism in Northern Lights: Digital Media and Gender in a Nordic context,* edited by Malin Sveningsson Elm and Jenny Sundén. Cambridge: Cambridge Scholars Publishing.

Krotoski, Aleks. 2006. "How Queer: WoW and their Unfortunate LGB Policy." http://www.guardian.co.uk/technology/gamesblog/2006/jan/30/howqueer-wowa. Date accessed: June 11, 2011.

Krueger, Katherine, and Kerry Chamberlain. 2005. Identity Management and the Role of Partial Anonymity in a Computer-mediated Context. Paper read at Internet Research 6.0: Internet Generations. International and Interdisciplinary Conference of the Association of Internet, October 5–9, 2005, Chicago.

Krzywinska, Tanya. 2006. "The Pleasures and Dangers of the Game: Up Close and Personal." *Games and Culture,* 1: 119–122.

Kücklich, Julian. 2008. "Forbidden Pleasures: Cheating in Computer Games." In *The Pleasures of Computer Gaming: Essays on Cultural History, Theory and Aesthetics*, edited by Melanie Swalwell and Jason Wilson, 52–71. Jefferson, NC: McFarland & Co.

Kulick, Don. 1995. "Introduction. The Sexual Life of Anthropologists: Erotic Subjectivity and Ethnographic Work." In *Taboo: Sex, Identity and Erotic Subjectivity in Anthropological Fieldwork*, edited by Don Kulick and Margaret Willson, 1–28. London: Routledge.

———. (1998) *Travesti: Sex, Gender, and Culture Among Brazilian Transgendered Prostitutes.* Chicago, IL: University of Chicago Press.

Kulick, Don and Margaret Willson, ed. 1995. *Taboo: Sex, Identity and Erotic Subjectivity in Anthropological Fieldwork.* London: Routledge.

Lahti, Martti. 2003. "As We Become Machines: Corporealized Pleasures in Video Games." In *The Video Game Theory Reader*, edited by Mark J.P. Wolf and B. Perron, 157–170. London: Routledge.

Lammes, Sybille. 2007. "Approaching Game-Studies: Towards a Reflexive Methodology of Games as Situated Cultures." *Proceedings of DiGRA 2007 Conference: Situated Play.* http://www.digra.org/dl/db/07311.28016.pdf. Date accessed: June 11, 2011.

Langenhove, Luk van, and Rom Harré. 1999. "Introducing Positioning Theory." In *Positioning Theory*, edited by Rom Harré and Luk van Langenhove, 14-–1. Oxford: Blackwell.

Langer, Jessica. 2008. "The Familiar and the Foreign: Playing (Post)Colonialism in World of Warcraft." In *Digital Culture, Play and Identity: A World of Warcraft® Reader*, edited by Hilde Corneliussen and Jill Walker Rettberg, 87–108. Cambridge, MA.: MIT Press.

Lanier, Jaron and Frank Biocca. 1992. "An Insider's View of the Future of Virtual Reality." *Journal of Communication* 42(4): 150–172.

Laurel, Brenda. 2008. "Notes from the Utopian Entrepreneur." In *Beyond Barbie & Mortal Kombat: New Perspectives on Gender and Gaming*, edited by Yasmin B Kafai, Carrie Heeter, Jill Denner and Jennifer Y Sun, 21–32. Cambridge, MA: MIT Press.

Lazzaro, Nicole. 2008. "Are Boy Games Even Necessary?" In *Beyond Barbie & Mortal Kombat: New Perspectives on Gender and Gaming*, edited by Yasmin B. Kafai, Carrie Heeter, Jill Denner, and Jennifer Y. Sun. Cambridge, MA: MIT Press.

Lea, Martin, and Russell Spears. 1995. "Love at First Byte? Building Personal Relationships over Computer Networks." In *Understudied Relationships: Off the Beaten Track*, edited by J.T Wood and S Duck. Thousand Oaks, CA: Sage.

Leap, William L., ed. 1995. *Beyond the Lavender Lexicon: Authenticity, Imagination, and Appropriation in Lesbian and Gay Languages.* Amsterdam: Gordon & Breach.

Leigh McGregor, Georgia. 2006. "Architecture, Space and Gameplay in *World of Warcraft* and *Battle for Middle Earth 2.*" Paper presented at *The Joint International Conference on CyberGames and Interactive Entertainment*

2006 (CGIE2006), December 4–6, Perth Australia. http://www.users.on.net/~georgia88/files/Architecture,%20Space%20and%20Gameplay%20-%20Georgia%20Leigh%20McGregor.pdf. Date accessed: June 11, 2011.

Lewin, Ellen. 2002. "Another Unhappy Marriage? Feminist Anthropology and Lesbian/Gay Studies". In *Out in Theory: The Emergence of Lesbian and Gay Anthropology*, edited by Ellen Lewin and William Leap, 110–127. Urbana, IL: University of Illinois Press.

Lewin, Ellen and William Leep, eds. 1996. *Out in the Field: Reflections of Lesbian and Gay Anthropologists*. Urbana, IL: University of Illinois Press.

Lewis, Lisa A. 1993. "Being Discovered: The Emergence of Female Address on MTV." In *Sound and Vision: The Music Video Reader*, edited by Lawrence Grossberg, Andrew Goodwin and Simon Frith, 129–152. London: Routledge.

Light, Ben 2009. More Than Just a Combo of Slaps? Representations and Experiences of LGBT Gamers On and Beyond the Screen In *DIGRA 2009: Breaking New Ground: Innovation in Games, Play, Practice and Theory*. London: Brunel University.

Liljeström, Marianne, and Susanna Paasonen. 2010. *Working with Affect in Feminist Readings: Disturbing Differences*. London: Routledge.

Lin, Holin. 2005. "Gendered Gaming Experience in Social Space: From Home to Internet Café." *Proceedings of DiGRA 2005 Conference: Changing Views—Worlds in Play*. http://www.digra.org/dl/db/06278.26054.pdf. Date accessed: June 11, 2011.

———. 2008. "Body, Space, and Gendered Gaming Experiences: A Cultural Geography of Homes, Cybercafés, and Dormitories." In *Beyond Barbie and Mortal Kombat: New Perspectives on Gender and Gaming*, edited by Yasmin B Kafai, Carrie Heeter, Jill Denner and Jennifer Y Sun, 67–82. Cambridge, MA: MIT Press.

Linderoth, Jonas. 2008. "Datorspelens fängslande kraft." In *Den kompetenta gamern: En konferens om ny mediekompetens: Rapport från nordiskt kulturforum 23 november 2007*, 15–19. Göteborg: Nordicom.

Linderoth, Jonas, and Camilla Olsson. 2010. Världen som spelplan—gränsöverskridande i onlinespelkulturen. Stockholm: Medierådet.

Lipton, Mark. 1996. "Forgetting the Body: Cybersex and Identity." In *Communication and Cyberspace. Social Interaction in an Electronic Environment*, edited by Lance Strate, Ron Jacobson and Stephanie B Gibson. Cresskill, NJ: Hampton Press.

Lowood, Henry. 2006. "High-Performance Play: The Making of Machinima." *Journal of Media Practice* 7(1): 25–42.

Lugones, María. 1987. "Playfulness, 'World'-Travelling, and Loving Perception." *Hypatia*, 2(2): 3–19.

Ma, Ringo. 1996. "Computer-Mediated Conversations as a New Dimension of Intercultural Communication between East Asian and North American College Students." In *Computer-Mediated Communication. Linguistic, Social and Cross-Cultural Perspectives*, edited by Susan Herring, 173–185. Amsterdam: John Benjamins Publishing Company.

MacCallum-Stewart, Esther. 2008. "Real Boys Carry Girly Epics: Normalising Gender Bending in Online Games." *Eludamos: Journal for Computer Game Culture* 2(1):27–40.

MacCallum-Stewart, Esther, and Justin Parsler. 2008. "Role-play vs. Gameplay: The Difficulties of Playing a Role in World of Warcraft." In *Digital Culture, Play, and Identity: A World of Warcraft Reader*, edited by HIlde Corneliussen and Jill Walker Rettberg, 225–246. Cambridge, MA: MIT Press.

Malinowski, Bronislaw. 1967. *A Diary in the Strict Sense of the Term*. London: Routledge.

Manalansan, Martin. 2003. *Global Divas: Filipino Gay Men in the Diaspora.* Durham, NC: Duke University Press.

Marcus, George, and Michael Fischer. 1986. *Anthropology as Cultural Critique: An Experimental Moment in the Human Sciences.* Chicago, IL: University of Chicago Press.

Markowitz, Fran and Michael Ashkenazi, eds. 1999. *Sex, Sexuality and the Anthropologist.* Urbana, IL: University of Illinois Press.

Massumi, Brian. 2002. Parables for the Virtual: Movement, Affect, Sensation. Durham, NC: Duke University Press.

Mäyrä, Frans. 2008. *An Introduction to Game Studies: Games in Culture.* Los Angeles, CA: Sage.

McGregor, Georgia Leigh 2006. Architecture, Space and Gameplay in World of Warcraft and Battle for Middle Earth 2. Paper read at The Joint International Conference on CyberGames and Interactive Entertainment 2006 (CGIE2006, December 4–6, Perth, Australia.

McKee, Heidi A, and James E Porter. 2009. *The Ethics of Internet Research. A Rhetorical, Case-Based Process.* New York: Peter Lang.

McRobbie, Angela, and Jenny Garber. 1976. "Girls and Subcultures: An Exploration." In *Resistance through Rituals: Youth Subcultures in Post-war Britain,* edited by Stuart Hall and Tony Jefferson, 209–222. Oxon: Routledge.

Melin, Margareta. 2008. *Gendered Journalism Cultures: Strategies and Tactics in the Fields of Journalism in Britain and Sweden.* Gothenburg: University of Gothenburg.

Miller, Daniel and Don Slater. 2000. *The Internet: An Ethnographic Approach.* Oxford: Berg.

Miller, Monica K. & Summers, Alicia. 2001. Gender differences in video game characters: Notes, Appearances, and attire as portrayed in video game magazines. *Sex Roles* (97): 733–742

MMOData.net. *MMORPG Subscriptions with a Peak between 1.000.000 and 12.000.000* 2011. Available from http://www.mmodata.net/. Date accessed: June 11, 2011.

Monaghan, Lee. 2005. "Big Handsome Men, Bears and Others: Virtual Constructions of 'Fat Male Embodiment'". *Body & Society* 11(2): 81–111.

Mortensen, Torill Elvira. 2004. "Flow, Seduction and Mutual Pleasure." In *Other Players Conference Proceedings*, edited by Miguel Sicart and Jonas H. Smith. Center for Computer Game Research, IT University of Copenhagen, Denmark, December 6–8, 2004.

———. 2007. "Me, the Other." In *SecondPperson: Role-Playing and Story in Games and Playable Media*, edited by Pat Harrigan and Noah Wardrip-Fruin, 297–305. Cambridge, MA: MIT Press.

———. 2008. "Humans Playing World of Warcraft: or Deviant strategies." In *Digital Culture, Play and Identity. A World of Warcraft Reader*, edited by Hilde Corneliussen and Jill Walker Rettberg, 203–224. Cambridge, MA: MIT Press.

Munster, Anna. 2006. *Materializing New Media: Embodiment in Information Aesthetics.* Hanover, NH: Dartmouth College Press.

Murray, Janet H. 1997. Hamlet on the Holodeck: The Future of Narrative in Cyberspace. . New York: The Free Press.

Myers, David. 1987. "Anonymity is Part of the Magic: Individual Manipulation of Computer-Mediated Communication Contexts." *Qualitative Sociology* 19(3): 251–266.

Nakamura, Lisa. 2008. *Digitizing Race: Visual Cultures of the Internet.* Minneapolis, MN: University of Minnesota Press.

———. 2009. "Don't Hate the Player, Hate the Game: The Racialization of Labor in World of Warcraft." *Critical Studies in Media and Communication* 26: 128–144.

Nardi, Bonnie. 2010. *My Life As a Night Elf Priest. An Anthropological Account of World of Warcraft.* Ann Arbor, MI: University of Michigan Press.

Nardi, Bonnie and Justin Harris. 2006. "Strangers and Friends: Collaborative Play in *World of Warcraft*." In *Proceedings of the Conference on Computer-Supported Cooperative Work*, 149–158. New York: ACM Press.

Nash, Catherine J. 2010. "Queer Conversations: Old-time Lesbians, Transmen and the Politics of Queer Research." In *Queer Methods and Methodologies: Intersecting Queer Theories and Social Science Research*, edited by Kath Browne and Catherine J Nash, 129–142. Farnham: Ashgate.

Newton, Esther. 1993. "My Best Informant's Dress: The Erotic Equation of Fieldwork." *Cultural Anthropology* 8(1): 3–23.

Ngai, Sianne 2005. Ugly Feelings. Cambridge, MA: Harvard University Press.

Nielsen. 2008. The State of the Video Gamer. PC Game and Video Game Console Usage Fourth Quarter 2008. http://blog.nielsen.com/nielsenwire/wp-content/uploads/2009/04/stateofvgamer_040609_fnl1.pdf. Date accessed: June 11, 2011.

Nielsen, Henrik Smed. 2010. "The Computer Game as a Somatic Experience." *Eludamos: Journal for Computer Game Culture* 4(1):25–40.

O'Brien, Jodi. 1999. "Writing in the Body." In Communities in Cyberspace, edited by Marc A. Smith and Peter Kollock, 76–104. London: Routledge.

O'Riordan, Kate, and David J. Phillips. 2007. *Queer Online: Media Technology and Sexuality*. New York: Peter Lang.

Paasonen, Susanna. 2007. "Strange Bedfellows: Pornography, Affect and Feminist Reading." *Feminist Theory* 8(1): 43–57.

Pace, Tyler, Shaowen Bardzell and Jeffrey S. Bardzell. 2010. "The Rogue in the Lovely Black Dress: Intimacy in World of Warcraft." *Proceedings of the 28th International Conference on Human Factors in Computing Systems*. Atlanta, GA, April 10–15.

Parks, Malcolm R., and Kory Floyd. 1996. "Making Friends in Cyberspace." *Journal of Communication* 46(1): 80–97.

Pascoe, Cheri Jo. 2007. *Dude, You're a Fag: Masculinity and Sexuality in High School*. Berkeley, CA: University of California Press.

Patton, Michael. 1987. *How to Use Qualitative Methods in Evaluation*. Newbury Park: Sage.

Patton, Michael Quinn. 1990. *Qualitative Evaluation and Research Methods*. Newbury Park: Sage.

Pearce, Lynne. 1997. *Feminism and the Politics of Reading*. London: Arnold.

Pearce, Celia, and Artemesia. 2009. *Communities of Play: Emergent Cultures in Multiplayer Games and Virtual Worlds*. Cambridge, MA: MIT Press.

Pelletier, Caroline. 2008. "Gaming in Context: How Young People Construct Their Gendered Identities in Playing and Making Games." In *Beyond Barbie & Mortal Kombat: New Perspectives on Gender and Gaming*, edited by Yasmin B. Kafai, Carrie Heeter, Jill Denner, and Jennifer Y. Sun, 145–160. Cambridge, MA: MIT Press.

Peterson, Holly. 2007. *The Game of (Family) Life: Intra-family Play in World of Warcraft*. Ph.D. diss., London School of Economics.

Peterson, Louise, and Anna Munters. 2007. "Man kan beställa ett hembiträde: Om pojkars interaktion i The Sims." In *Datorspelandets dynamik. lekar och roller i en digital kultur*, edited by Jonas Linderoth, 31–48. Lund: Studentlitteratur.

Pettersson, Lena, Alma Persson, and Anders W Berggren. 2008. "Changing Gender Relations: Women Officers' Experiences in the Swedish Armed Forces." *Economic and Industrial Democracy* 29(2): 192–216.

Pettman, Dominic. 2006. *Love and Other Technologies: Retrofitting Eros for the Information Age*. Bronx, New York: Fordham University Press.

Pratt, Mary Louise. 1986. "Fieldwork in Common Places." In *Writing Culture: The Poetics and Politics of Ethnography*, edited by James Clifford and George Marcus, 27–50. Berkeley, CA: University of California Press.

———. 1992. *Imperial Eyes: Travel Writing and Transculturation.* London: Routledge.

Price, Janet, and Margrit Shildrick. 1999. "Feminist Theory and the Body: A Reader." In. Edinburgh: Edinburgh University Press.

Probyn, Elspeth. 1993. *Sexing the Self: Gendered Positions in Cultural Studies.* London: Routledge.

———. 2005. *Blush: Faces of Shame.* Minneapolis: University of Minnesota Press.

Rabinow, Paul. 1977. *Reflections on Fieldwork in Morocco.* Berkeley, CA: University of California Press.

Radway, Janice. 1984. *Reading the Romance: Women, Patriarchy, and Popular Literature.* Chapel Hill: University of North Carolina Press.

Reichelt, Leisa. 2007. Ambient Intimacy. Blog entry on March 1, 2007. http://www.disambiguity.com/ambient-intimacy/. Date accessed: June 11, 2011.

Reid, Elizabeth M. 1995. "Virtual Worlds: Culture and Imagination." In *Cybersociety. Computer-Mediated Communication and Community*, edited by Steven G. Jones, 164–183. Thousand Oaks. CA: Sage.

Rettberg, Scott. 2008. "Corporate Ideology in *World of Warcraft.*" In *Digital Culture, Play and Identity: A* World of Warcraft® *Reader*, edited by Hilde Corneliussen and Jill Walker Rettberg, 19–38. Cambridge, MA: MIT Press.

Rice, John. 2009. *Latest Nielsen Report on Video Gamers Shows Surprising Statistics.* http://www.associatedcontent.com/article/1635176/latest_nielsen_report_on_video_gamers.html. Date accessed: June 11, 2011.

Rich, Adrienne. 1980. "Compulsory Heterosexuality and Lesbian Existence." *Signs* 5(4): 631–660.

Rofel, Lisa. 2007. *Desiring China: Experiments in Neoliberalism, Sexuality, and Public Culture.* Durham, NC: Duke University Press.

Rooke, Alison. 2009. "Queer in the Field: On Emotions, Temporality, and Performativity in Ethnography." *Journal of Lesbian Studies* 13: 149–160.

———. 2010. "Queer in the Field: On Emotions, Temporality, and Performativity in Ethnography." In *Queer Methods and Methodologies: Intersecting Queer Theories and Social Science Research*, edited by Kath Brown and Catherine J Nash, 25–40. Farnham: Ashgate.

Rosenberg, Tiina. 2002. *Queerfeministisk agenda.* Stockholm: Atlas.

Roseneil, Sasha and Shelley Budgeon. 2004. "Cultures of Intimacy and Care Beyond 'the Family': Personal Life and Social Change in the Early 21st Century." *Current Sociology* 52: 135–159.

Royse, Pam, Joon Lee, Baasanjav Undrahbuyan, Mark Hopson, and Mia Consalvo. 2007. "Women and Games: Technologies of the Gendered Self." *New Media and Society* 9(4): 555–576.

Rubin, Gayle S. 1993. "Thinking Sex: Notes for a Radical Theory of the Politics of Sexuality." In *The Lesbian and Gay Studies Reader*, edited by Henry Abelove, Michèle Aina Barale and David M. Halperin, 3–44. New York: Routledge. Originally published in Carole Vance, ed., *Pleasure and Danger,* (Routledge & Kegan, Paul, 1984).

Russ, Joanna. 1975. *The Female Man.* Boston: Beacon Press.

Rutter, Jason, and Jo Bryce. 2006. *Understanding Digital Games.* London: Sage.

Ryan, Marie Laure. 2001. *Narrative as Virtual Reality: Immersion and Interactivity in Literature and Electronic Media.* Baltimore, MD: John Hopkins University Press.

———. 2004. *Narrative Across Media: The Languages of Storytelling.* Lincoln: University of Nebraska Press.

Salen, Katie and Eric Zimmerman. 2004. *Rules of Play: Game Design Fundamentals.* Cambridge, MA: MIT Press.

Schaap, Frank. 2002. *The Words that Took Us There: Ethnography in Virtual Reality.* Amsterdam: Aksant.

Schleiner, Anne-Marie. 2001. Does Lara Croft wear fake polygons? Gender and gender-role subversions in computer adventure games. *Leonardo*, 34(3), 221-22.

Schmieder, Christian. 2009. "World of Maskcraft vs. World of Queercraft? Communication, Sex and Gender in the Online Role-playing Game World of Warcraft." *Journal of Gaming & Virtual Worlds* 1(1): 5–21.

Schofield Clark, Lynn. 1998. "Dating on the Net: Teens and the Rise of 'Pure' Relationships." In *Cybersociety 2.0: Revisiting Computer-mediated Communication and Community*, edited by Steven G Jones. Thousand Oaks, CA: Sage.

Schott, Gareth R, and Kirsty R Horrell. 2000. "Girl Gamers and Their Relationship with the Gaming Culture." *Convergence* 6(4): 36–53.

Sedgwick, Eve Kosofsky. 1985. *Between Men: English Literature and Male Homosocial Desire*. New York: Columbia University Press.

———. 1990. *Epistemology of the Closet*. Berkeley, CA: University of California Press.

———. 2003. "Touching Feeling: Affect, Pedagogy, Performativity." In. Durham, NC: Duke University Press. Sedgwick, Eve Kosofsky and Adam Frank, eds. 1995. *Shame and Its Sister: A Silvan Tomkins Reader*. Durham, NC: Duke University Press.

Shapiro, Judith. 2005. "Transsexualism: Reflections on the Persistence of Gender and the Mutability of Sex." In *Same-Sex Cultures and Sexualities: An Anthropological Reader*, edited by Jennifer Robertson, 138–161. Malden, MA: Blackwell Publishing.

Shaw, Adrienne. 2009. "Putting the Gay in Game: Cultural Production and GLBT Content in Video Games." *Games and Culture* 4(3): 228–253.

Shibutani, Tamotsu. 1986. *Social Processes. An Introduction to Sociology*. Berkeley, CA: University of California Press.

Shinkle, Eugénie. 2005. "Corporealis Ergo Sum: Affect in Digital Games." In *Digital Gameplay: Essays of the Nexus of Game and Gamer*, edited by Nathan C. Garrelts, 21–35. Jefferson, NC: McFarland Press.

Sihvonen, Tanja. 2009. *Players Unleashed! Modding the Sims and the Culture of Gaming*. Amsterdam: Amsterdam University Press.

Silvén, Eva. 1999. "Det materiella." In *Etnologiskt fältarbete*, edited by Lars Kaijser and Magnus Öhlander, 89–108. Lund: Studentlitteratur.

Sinnot, Megan. 2004. *Toms and Dees: Transgender Identity and Female Same-Sex Relationships in Thailand*. Honolulu: University of Hawaii Press.

Skeggs, Beverley. 1997. *Formations of Class and Gender: Becoming Respectable*. London: Sage.

Smelik, Anne, & Lykke, Nina. (Eds.) 2008. *Bits of life: feminism at the intersection of media, bioscience and technology*. Seattle: University of Washington Press.

Sobchack, Vivian. 2004. "Carnal Thoughts: Embodiment and Moving Image Culture." Berkeley, CA: University of California Press.

Sotamaa, Olli. 2007. "On Modder Labour, Commodification of Play, and Mod Competitions." *First Monday* 12(9–3) September. http://firstmonday.org/htbin/cgiwrap/bin/ojs/index.php/fm/rt/printerFriendly/2006/1881. Date accessed: June 11, 2011.

———. 2010. "When the Game Is Not Enough: Motivations and Practices Among Computer Game Modding Culture." *Games and Culture* 5(3): 239–255.

Sproull, Lee, and Sara Kiesler. 1991. *Connections. New Ways of Working in the Networked Organization*. Cambridge, MA: MIT Press.

Stone, Alluquère Rosanne. 1991. "Will the Real Body Please Stand Up? Boundary Stories about Virtual Cultures." In *Cyberspace: First Steps*, edited by Michael Benedikt, 81–118. Cambridge, MA: MIT Press.

———. 1995. *The War of Desire and Technology at the Close of the Mechanical Age*. Cambridge, MA: MIT Press.

Storey, John. 1993. *An Introductory Guide to Cultural Theory and Popular Culture.* New York: Harvester Wheatsheaf.

Suchman, Lucy. 2007. *Human-machine reconfiguration plans and situated actions.* Cambridge: Cambridge University Press.

Sundén, Jenny. 2003. *Material Virtualities: Approaching Online Textual Embodiment.* New York: Peter Lang.

———. 2007. "On Cyberfeminist Intersectionality." In *Cyberfeminism in Northern Lights: Gender and Digital Media in a Nordic Context*, edited by Malin Sveningsson Elm and Jenny Sundén, 30–50. Cambridge: Cambridge Scholars Publishing

———. 2008. "What if Frankenstein('s Monster) was a Girl? Reproduction and Subjectivity in the Digital Age." In *Bits of Life: Feminism and the New Cultures of Media and Technoscience*, edited by Anneke Smelik and Nina Lykke, 147–162. Seattle, WA: Washington University Press.

———. 2009a. "Response to Lori Kendall." In *Internetlinquiry: Conversations about <ethod*, edited by Annette Markham, N. and Nancy K. Baym, 119–123. Thousand Oaks, CA: Sage.

———. 2009b. "Play as Transgression: An Ethnographic Approach to Queer Game Cultures." *Proceedings of DiGRA 2009 Breaking New Ground: Innovation in Games, Play, Practice and Theory*, London, UK, September 1–4. http://www.digra.org/dl/db/09287.40551.pdf. Date accessed: June 11, 2011.

———. 2010a. "A Sense of Play: Affect, Emotion, and Embodiment in World of Warcraft." In *Working with Affect in Feminist Readings: Disturbing Differences*, edited by Marianne Liljeström and Susanna Paasonen, 45–57. London: Routledge.

———. . 2010b. "Blonde Birth Machines: Medical Simulation, Techno-Corporeality and Posthuman Feminism." In *Technology and Medical Practices: Blood, Guts and Machines,* edited by Ericka Johnson and Boel Berner, 97–118. Farnham: Ashgate.

Sundén, Jenny, and Malin Sveningsson Elm. 2007. "Cyberfeminism in Northern Lights. Introduction." In *Cyberfeminism in Northern Lights: Gender and Digital Media in a Nordic Context*, edited by Malin Sveningsson Elm and Jenny Sundén, 1–29. Cambridge: Cambridge Scholars Publishing.

Sutton-Smith, Brian. 1997. *The Ambiguity of Play.* Cambridge, MA: Harvard University Press.

Svahn, Margareta. 1999. *Den liderliga kvinnan och den omanlige mannen. Skällsord, stereotyper och könskonstruktioner.* Stockholm: Carlsson.

Sveningsson Elm, Malin. 2009. "Exploring and Negotiating Femininity: Young Women's Production of Style in a Swedish Internet Community." *YOUNG* 17(3): 241–264.

———. Forthcoming. "Pity there's so few girls!" Attitudes to Female Participation in a Swedish Gaming Context. In *International Handbook of Digital Game Studies: Computer Games /Players / Game Cultures,* edited by Johannes Fromme and Alexander Unger. Springer Verlag.

Sveningsson, Malin. 2001. *Creating a Sense of Community. Experiences from a Swedish Web Chat.* Linköping: Linköping Studies in Art and Science.

———. 2002. "Cyberlove. Creating Romantic Relationships on the Net." In *Digital Borderlands: Cultural Studies of Identity and Interactivity on the Internet*, edited by Johan Fornäs, Kajsa Klein, Martina Ladendorf, Jenny Sundén and Malin Sveningsson, 79–111. Amherst: Peter Lang.

———. 2003. "Ethics in Internet Ethnography." In *Virtual Research Ethics: Issues and Controversies*, edited by Elizabeth A. Buchanan, 45–61. Hershey: Idea Group Publishing.

———. 2006. "Anonymitet och identitet i gemenskaper på Nätet." In *Att skapa lärgemenskaper på Nätet.*, edited by Ove Jobring, 117–132. Lund: Studentlitteratur.

Sveningsson, Malin, Mia Lövheim, and Magnus Bergquist. 2003. *Att fånga Nätet: Kvalitativa Metoder för Internetforskning.* Lund: Studentlitteratur.

Taylor, Nicholas, Jen Jenson and Suzanne de Castell. 2009. "Cheerleader/Booth Babes/ Halo Hoes: Pro-gaming, Gender and Jobs for the Boys." *Digital Creativity* 20(4): 239–252.

Taylor, Nicholas T. 2011. "Play Globally, Act Locally: The Standardization of Pro Halo 3 Gaming." *International Journal of Gender, Science and Technology* 3(1): 229–242.

Taylor, Nick. 2008a. Periscopic Play: Re-positioning "the field" in MMO Studies. *Loading . . .* 1(3). http://journals.sfu.ca/loading/index.php/loading/article/view/43/40. Date accessed: June 11, 2011.

Taylor, T.L. 2003a. "Multiple Pleasures: Women and Online Gaming." *Convergence* 9: 21–46.

———. 2003b. "Intentional Bodies: Virtual Environments and the Designers Who Shape Them." *International Journal of Engineering Education* 19(1): 25–34.

———. 2003c. "Power Gamers Just Want To Have Fun? Instrumental Play In A MMOG." In *Level Up Conference Proceedings*, edited by Marinka Copier and Joost Raessens, 300–311. Utrecht: Utrecht University.

———. 2006a. "Does WoW Change Everything? How a PvP Server, Multinational Player Base, and Surveillance Mod Scene Caused Me Pause." *Games and Culture* 1(4): 318–337.

———. 2006b. *Play between Worlds: Exploring Online Game Culture.* Cambridge, MA: MIT Press.

———. 2006c. "Beyond Management: Considering Participatory Design and Governance in Player Culture." *First Monday*, Special Issue 7: *Command Lines: The Emergence of Governance in Global Cyberspace.* http://firstmonday.org/htbin/cgiwrap/bin/ojs/index.php/fm/article/view/1611/1526. Date accessed: June 11, 2011.

———. 2008b. "Becoming a Player: Networks, Structure, and Imagined Futures." In *Beyond Barbie and Mortal Kombat: New Perspectives on Gender and Gaming,*, edited by Yasmin B. Kafai, Carrie Heeter, Jill Denner and Jennifer Y. Sun, 51–66. Cambridge, MA: MIT Press.

———. 2008c. "Does World of Warcraft Change Everything? How a pvp Server, Multinational Playerbase, and Surveillance Mod Scene Caused Me Pause." In *Digital Culture, Play and Identity*, edited by Hilde G. Corneliussen and Jill Walker Rettberg, 187–202. Cambridge, MA: MIT press.

———. 2010. Roundtable: The Internet of Affect. In *Internet Research 11.0—Sustainability, Participation, Action.* Gothenburg, Sweden.

Thiel, Shayla Marie. 2005. "IM me." In *Girl Wide Web. Girls, the Internet, and the Negotiating of Identity*, edited by Sharon. R Mazzarella, 179–202. New York: Peter Lang.

Tronstad, Ragnhild. 2008. "Character Identification in World of Warcraft: The Relationship between Capacity and Appearance." In *Digital Culture, Play and Identity*, edited by Hilde G. Corneliussen and Jill Walker Rettberg, 249–264. Cambridge, MA: MIT Press.

Turkle, Sherry. 1995. *Life on the Screen: Identity in the Age of the Internet.* New York: Simon & Schuster.

Tynes, John. 2007. "Prismatic Play: Games as Windows on the Real World." In *Second Person. Role-playing and Story in Games and Playable Media*, edited by Pat Harrigan and Noah Wardrip-Fruin, 221–228. Cambridge, MA: MIT Press.

Unnithan-Kumar, Maya. 2006. "Sensing the Field: Kinship, Gender and Emotion in an Anthropologist's Way of Knowing." In *Critical Journeys: The Making of Anthropologists*, edited by Geert De Neve and Maya Unnithan-Kumar, 129–148. London: Ashgate.

Valentine, David. 2002. "We're 'Not About Gender': The Uses of 'Transgender.'" In *Out in Theory: The Emergence of Lesbian and Gay Anthropology*, edited by Ellen Lewin and William Leap, 222–245. Urbana, IL: University of Illinois Press.

———. 2007. *Imagining Transgender: An Ethnography of a Category*. Durham, NC: Duke University Press.

Valkyrie, Zek Cypress. 2011. "Cybersexuality in MMORPGs: Virtual Sexual Revolution Untapped." *Men and Masculinities* 14(1): 76–96.

Van Gelder, Lindsy. 1991. "The Strange Case of the Electronic Lover." In *Computerization and Controversy. Value Conflicts and Social Choices*, edited by Charles Dunlop and Rob Kling, 364–375. Boston: Academic Press.

Van Maanen, John. 1988. *Tales of the Field: On Writing Ethnography*. Chicago, IL: University of Chicago Press.

———. 1995. "An End to Innocence. The Ethnography of Etnography." In *Representation in Ethnography*, edited by J. Van Maanen. Thousand Oaks, CA: Sage.

van Zoonen, Lizbeth 1994. *Feminist Media Studies*. Los Angeles: Sage.

Wajcman, Judy. 1991. *Feminism Confronts Technology*. Cambridge: Polity Press.

———. 2004. *Technofeminism*. Cambridge: Polity Press.

Walkerdine, Valerie. 1990. *School Girl Fictions*. London: Verso.

Weathers, Sanya. 2008. Horde vs. Alliance Data Smackdown! *GamerDNA The Blog* (Friday Oct 24, 2008), http://blog.gamerdna.com/blog/2008/10/24/horde-vs-alliance-data-smackdown/#comment-5224. Date accessed: June 11, 2011.

Weeks, Jeffrey, Brian Heaphy, and Catherine Donovan. 2001. *Same Sex Intimacies: Families of Choice and Other Life Experiments*. London: Routledge.

Weiss, Gail, and Honi Fern Haber. 1999. *Perspectives on Embodiment: The Intersections of Nature and Culture*. New York: Routledge.

Wekker, Gloria. 2006. *The Politics of Passion: Women's Sexual Culture in the Afro-Surinamese Diaspora*. New York: Columbia University Press.

Weston, Kath. 1991. *Families We Choose: Lesbians, Gays, Kinship*. New York: Columbia University Press.

———. 1993. "Lesbian/Gay Studies in the House of Anthropology." *Annual Review of Anthropology* 22: 339–367.

Williams, Dmitri , Nicolas Ducheneaut, Li Xiong, Yuanyuan Zhang, Nick Yee, and Eric Nickell. 2006. "From Tree House to Barracks: The Social Life of Guilds in World of Warcraft." *Games and Culture* 1(4):338–361.

Williams, Dmitri, Mia Consalvo, Scott Caplan, and Nick Yee. 2009. "Looking for Gender: Gender Roles and Behaviors among Online Gamers." *Journal of Communication* 59: 700–725.

Williams, Dmitri, Nicole Martins, Mia Consalvo, and James D. Ivory. 2009. "The Virtual Census: Representations of Gender, Race and Age in Video Games." *New Media and Society* 11(5): 815–834.

Williams, Linda. 1991. "Film Bodies. Gender, Genre, and Excess." *Film Quarterly* 44(4): 2–13.

Williams, Patrick J, and Jonas Heide Smith. 2007. "Introduction: From Moral Panics to Mature Games Research in Action." In *The Players' Realm: Studies on the Culture of Video Games and Gaming*, edited by Patrick J. Williams and Jonas Heide Smith, 1–16. Jefferson, NC: McFarland & Co.

Wilson, Elizabeth. 1993. "Is Transgression Transgressive?." In *Activating Theory: Lesbian, Gay, Bisexual Politics*, edited by Joseph Bristow and Angela R. Wilson, 107–117. London: Lawrence & Wishart.

Wirman, Hanna. 2008. "Virtual Threads of a Skin: Women Weavers and the Practice of Skinning in The Sims." *Proceedings of [The Player] Conference*, Copenhagen, Denmark, August 26–29.

Wittig, Monique. 1969. *Les guérillères*. Paris: Minuit.

Wright, Les. 1997. "Introduction: Theoretical Bears." In *The Bearbook*, edited by Les Wright, 1–17. NewYork: Harrington Park Press.

Wu, Weiha, Steve Fore, Xiying Wang, and Petula Sik Ying Ho. 2007. "Beyond Virtual Carnival and Masquerade: In-game Marriage on the Chinese Internet." *Games and Culture* 2(1): 59–89.

Yao, Mike Z., Chad Mahood, and Daniel Linz. 2010. "Sexual Priming, Gender Stereotyping, and Likelihood to Sexually Harass: Examining the Cognitive Effects of Playing a Sexually-Explicit Video Game." *Sex Roles* 62(1–2): 77–88.

Yee, Nick. 2003. "Gaming with Romantic Partners and Family Members." The Daedalus Project: The Psychology of MMORPGs. http://www.nickyee.com/daedalus/archives/000430.php. Date accessed: June 11, 2011.

———. 2005a. "WoW Gender Bending." The Daedalus Project: The Psychology of MMORPGs. http://www.nickyee.com/daedalus/archives/001369.php. Date accessed: June 11, 2011.

———. 2005b. "Server Type Preference." The Daedalus Project: The Psychology of MMORPGs, http://www.nickyee.com/daedalus/archives/001466.php. Date accessed: June 11, 2011.

———. 2006a. "The Demographics, Motivations and Derived Experiences of Users of Massively-Multiuser Online Graphical Environments." *PRESENCE: Teleoperators and Virtual Environments,* 15(3): 309–329.

———. 2006b. "The 'Impossible' Romance." The Daedalus Project: The Psychology of MMORPGs, http://www.nickyee.com/daedalus/archives/pdf/4–4.pdf. Date accessed: June 11, 2011.

———. 2006c. "The Labor of Fun. How Video Games Blur the Boundaries of Work and Play." *Games and Culture* 1(1): 68–71.

———. 2006d. *Love Is in the Air. The Daedalus Project: The Psychology of MMORPGs*, Available from http://www.nickyee.com/daedalus/archives/001528.php?page=2. Date accessed: June 11, 2011.

———. 2006e. "Playing with Someone, Part 2." The Daedalus Project: The Psychology of MMORPGs, http://www.nickyee.com/daedalus/archives/001495.php?page=1. Date accessed: June 11, 2011.

———. 2007a. "Status Reversal." The Daedalus Project: The Psychology of MMORPGs, http://www.nickyee.com/daedalus/archives/001585.php?page=2. Date accessed: June 11, 2011.

———. 2008. "Maps of Digital Desires: Exploring the Topography of Gender and Play in Online Games." In *Beyond Barbie & Mortal Kombat: New Perspectives on Gender and Gaming*, edited by Yasmin B. Kafai, Carrie Heeter, Jill Denner, and Jennifer Y. Sun, 83–96. Cambridge, MA: MIT Press.

———. 2009. "The Demographics of Guild Membership." The Daedalus Project: The Psychology of MMORPGs, http://www.nickyee.com/daedalus/archives/000552.php. Date accessed: June 11, 2011.

———. 2007b. "Motivations of Play in Online Games." *Journal of CyberPsychology and Behavior* 9: 772–775.

Zimmerman, Bonnie. 1990. *The Safe Sea of Women: Lesbian Fiction, 1969–1989.* Boston: Beacon Press.

Zwicky, Arnold M. 1997. "Two Lavender Issues for Linguists." In *Queerly Phrased: Language, Gender, and Sexuality*, edited by Anna Livia and Kira Hall, 21–34. New York: Oxford University Press.

# Web Sites


Blizzard Support, World of Warcraft, Harassment Overview. http://us.blizzard.com/support/article.xml?locale=en_US&articleId=20455. Date accessed: June 11, 2011.

Blizzard Support, World of Warcraft, Harassment Policy. http://us.blizzard.com/support/article.xml?locale=en_US&articleId=20226. Date accessed: June 11, 2011.

Border House Blog. October 1, 2010. "A guide to gay characters in World of Warcraft." http://borderhouseblog.com/?p=2896. Date accessed: June 11, 2011.

gaygamer.net. February 13, 2007. "World of LoveCraft?" http://gaygamer.net/2007/02/world_of_lovecraft.html#comment-30324. Date accessed: June 11, 2011.

Fuska.nu. http://www.fuska.nu/. Date accessed: June 11, 2011.

Gameplayer.se. http://gameplayer.se. Date accessed: June 11, 2011.

Goodgame.se. http://www.goodgame.se. Date accessed: January 01, 2008

Kotaku, the Gamer's Guide. February 6, 2006. "WoW: Blizzard Gets Gay Rights Warning." http://kotaku.com/153075/wow-blizzard-gets-gay-rights-warning. Date accessed: June 11, 2011.

Kotaku, the Gamer's Guide. March 9, 2006. "Blizzard's Reaction to Gay Guilds an 'Unfortunate Mistake.'" http://kotaku.com/159536/blizzards-reaction-to-gay-guilds-an-unfortunate-mistake. Date accessed: June 11, 2011.

Multe Music: A blog and weekly audio show/podcast exploring the roots, shoots and fruits of Scandinavian and Nordic traditions. Swedish nyckelharpa on World of Warcraft. http://multemusic.com/2008/12/16/swedish-nyckelharpa-world-warcraft/. Date accessed: June 11, 2011.

PMS Clan. http://www.pmsclan.com. Date accessed: June 11, 2011.

The Pink Pigtail Inn: Larisa's Corner. Tickled Pink: Music from the Hearts of Warcraft. http://www.pinkpigtailinn.com/2010/01/tickled-pink-music-from-hearts-of.html. Date accessed: June 11, 2011.

The Skinny Blood Elf Preservation Society at Livejournal: http://community.livejournal.com/bringingbesback/. Date accessed: June 11, 2011.

World of Warcraft—English (NA) Forums—General discussion forum http://forums.worldofwarcraft.com/thread.html?topicId=37185748&pageNo=12&sid=1. Date accessed: November 22, 2010.

World of Warcraft—English (NA) Forums—General discussion forum http://forums.worldofwarcraft.com/thread.html?topicId=13275279006&sid=1. Date accessed: November 22, 2010.

World of Warcraft Quest Help. WoW: Wrath of the Lich King—Grizzly Hills Soundtrack. http://www.worldofwarcraftquesthelp.net/uncategorized/wow-wrath-of-the-lich-king-grizzly-hills-soundtrack. Date accessed: June 11, 2011.

Wowwiki: Emote. http://www.wowwiki.com/Emote
Wowwiki: Flirt. http://www.wowwiki.com/Flirt
Wowwiki: List of emotes. http://www.wowwiki.com/List_of_emotes. Date accessed: June 11, 2011.

# Index

www.ingramcontent.com/pod-product-compliance
Ingram Content Group UK Ltd.
Pitfield, Milton Keynes, MK11 3LW, UK
UKHW022000180926
475701UK00003B/123
* 9 7 8 0 4 1 5 7 1 9 7 0 4 *